Prime Chaos

OTHER TITLES FROM NEW FALCON PUBLICATIONS

Prime Chaos

Adventures in Chaos Magic

by

Phil Hine

Foreword by Grant Morrison

NEW FALCON PUBLICATIONS
TEMPE, ARIZONA, U.S.A.

International Standard Book Number: 1-56184-137-4
Library of Congress Catalog Card Number: 98-86243

First Edition 1993 (Chaos International Publications)
Second Revised Edition 1999 (New Falcon)
Second Falcon Printing 2002

Cover art by William S. Burroughs
(from the painting "Creation of the Homunculus IV")

The paper used in this publication meets the minimum requirements of the American National Standard for Permanence of Paper for Printed Library Materials Z39.48-1984

Address all inquiries to:
NEW FALCON PUBLICATIONS
1739 East Broadway Road #1-277
Tempe, AZ 85282 U.S.A.
(or)
320 East Charleston Blvd. #204-286
Las Vegas, NV 89104 U.S.A.

website: http://www.newfalcon.com
email: info@newfalcon.com

ACKNOWLEDGEMENTS & DEDICATION

Thanks to the individuals and groups without whose inspiration, insights and shared experiences this book would not have phenomenized, including:

Kathy Arden, Sheila Broun, William Burroughs Communications, Hannibal The Cannibal, Peter J. Carroll, Janet Cliff, John Eden, Fireclown, Gyrus, Dave Lee, Thessalonius Loyola, Rex Monday, Grant Morrison, Paul 777, Gordon the Toad, R.B.B., Ian Read, Stephen Sennitt, Estelle Seymour, Maria Strutz, Nicholas Tharcher, Don Webb and Vishvanath. Particular thanks go to my agent, Doug Grant without whose continual support and insight, this book would not have come about.

Also: The Mad Shamans, the Ganna Chakra, the Z-Cluster, and the Illuminates Of Thanateros.

Dedicated to the memory of William S. Burroughs and Robert "Bob" Williams—two wild-eyed avatars of Baphomet.

AUTHOR'S NOTE

A little knowledge is a dangerous thing (in the right hands).
— Thessalonius Loyola

Prime Chaos is a companion volume to my earlier book, *Condensed Chaos* (New Falcon Publications, 1995), which introduced the basic principles of Chaos Magic and contained enough practical material for the reader to get the ball rolling. Prime Chaos explores further the possibilities offered by the Chaos perspective on modern magic, focusing in particular on ritual magic, working with other people (either in magical groups or society at large) and how Chaos Magic relates to modern magical trends such as Discordianism or the Cthulhu Mythos.

Phil Hine can be contacted at:
a5e@ndirect.co.uk

or

BM Coyote
London
WC1N 3XX, UK

(Please enclose a Self Addressed, Stamped Envelope or a Self Addressed Envelope and an International Reply Coupon.)

See also Phil Hine's Web Site at www.phhine.ndirect.co.uk

TABLE OF CONTENTS

FOREWORD

by Grant Morrison

The initiate in the Tibetan *Chöd* ritual is required to undergo a visionary experience in which the physical body is dismembered and devoured by demons while the 'higher self' watches, unmoved by the gruesome destruction of its flesh. This type of experience, common to the shamanic tradition, demonstrates the sometimes violent and uncompromising nature of 'spiritual' or 'paradigm' change.

Emerging from the eerie lunar zones between the polar fires of punk rock and the Thatcher rave years, Chaos Magic has grown and multiplied and diversified, evolving out through the minds of its practitioners; it has no shape, it breeds like a fractal and mutates as it goes. 'It' currently embraces aspects of the Crowley cult, shamanism, NLP, Reichian bodywork, Eastern thought, voodoo, Situationist theory, H.P. Lovecraft, Clive Barker, Walt Disney and anything else you might care to add to that list. Shattering and binding simultaneously, always up for a laugh, Chaos provides one useful model for the next stage in the collective upgrading of human consciousness.

Early signs may indicate that human society is entering a time in which the creative synthesis of apparently contradictory positions will become fundamental to our thinking. In the current magical subculture, no one sythesizes with the encyclopaedic range and creativity of Phil Hine.

Phil is, in my opinion, the foremost interpreter of the chaos paradigm. His researches, in territories fraught with confusion and glamour, are not only innovative and imaginative, not only free from self-aggrandizement and dogma, but are also immensely lucid and readable. Phil offers practical, detailed information on how magic operates and suggests experiments which can (and should) be duplicated and verified. He never obscures or over-elaborates but still manages to astound with the depth of his experience and the scope of his speculations. *Prime Chaos* pulls back the moth-eaten curtains to expose and dismiss much of the pseudo-goth theatricality which still hampers the understanding of magic, but at the same time, never loses sight of the wonder, the terror and the awe of true *gnosis*.

Phil brings humanity, sanity, insanity and wit to a subject which will, I believe, penetrate more deeply into the fabric of our lives, as science adapts its boundaries to accommodate some of the conclusions magicians have already reached, and as magic lets go of the 'occult' aspects which once protected its practitioners from the power of a totalitarian church but which serve now only to obscure.

Direct confrontation with Chaos is unmistakable and available to anyone who is prepared to simply do the work and open the doors. This book represents the cutting edge of magic theory and practice; it will provide as many keys as you need but, as ever, the theory may fire the imagination but cannot in the end substitute for personal experience. Read then DO.

The penis of the President of the USA is the subject of media debate; a British football star announces to newspapers that five separate demons are occupying his body; a fairytale princess is killed by cameras. If ever the time was ripe for the wider emergence of the Chaos current, that time is surely now.

Charles Fort made the gnomic observation that it steam engines when it's steam engine time.

Well...it's steam engine time and the *chöd* ritual has already begun for global culture. The world that was, is now in the process of watching its own disintegration with horror and exhilaration. What possible transformations lie ahead when, finally, we let the old corpse go?

Nothing is true, everything is permitted.

As the roller-coaster ride into the future gathers speed, *Prime Chaos* is a survival manual for the 21st century.

Grant Morrison
July 1998

PART I

CHAOS IS EVERYWHERE

ADVENTURES IN MAGIC

I strayed onto the path direct.

— Austin Osman Spare

A friend said to me recently, "I'm just not doing enough magical work at the moment." I nodded, thinking, "Yeah, I've been there." There is a kind of creeping Protestant Work Ethic implicit in modern magic, a view that you have to work at magic before you get anywhere, doing your regular practice—visualisation, meditation, daily banishing, muttering your chosen mantra on the train, controlling your dreams etc.—until it becomes 'hard work' accompanied by a guilt trip if you slacken off or take a break. Some time ago I was reading a basic magical training programme in some book or other and I thought, "Yeah, I bet this guy went to a public school"—the kind of place where you get up at dawn for a cold bath, run round the playing fields and get beaten senseless at every opportunity. The way the guy was going on, I wouldn't have been surprised if some Archangel had appeared, thundering, "HINE! You didn't do your daily banishing this morning! Stand in the corner boy until you can recite all the god-names in Assiah!" That sort of thing.

I hate doing other people's magical training courses, as my natural inclination is to jump around from one area of interest to another. In the middle of a Tantric phase of magical work, I might suddenly get a 'flash' insight into some aspect of western Qabalah, and go off at a tangent. Most magical training programmes don't account for this sort of thing. So I have found that for me, the best way to stick to a programme is to run away to foreign parts. Nowadays, there are lifestyles package holidays where you can jet out to South America, tour the local sacred sites in the company of some New Age 'shamanic' teacher, visit a Bruja and have some kind of psychedelic concoction poured down your throat. Or you can book onto 'magical' tours of Egypt, and discover your past life as a High Priest of Isis at Giza. This is simply paying to have your fantasies confirmed, and it leads to situations where New Agers and reformed druids come over to the UK and start burying crystals at sacred sites to 'correct' their alignments. If you really want to have a magical time in foreign parts, avoid this sort of thing like the plague. Go somewhere that isn't heavily media-saturated. Detached from the cushion of friends, language, and television, it's much easier to get into magical practice in a big way, partially 'cos it's much easier to find the time. And the whole thing becomes more interesting as you're not merely doing pranayama three times a day, you're having an adventure! And magicians are larger-than-life characters. Having adventures is almost mandatory! I mean, which sounds better, boasting that you've invoked the great god Pan from a bedsit in Basingstoke, or coolly mentioning that you did three hours of no-mind meditation stuck in a bunker whilst the PLO launched rockets at the Kibbutz you were staying on?

If you can't just drop everything and run off to Ibiza, then make doing magic an adventure at home. And again, this for me is something near to the core of what magic is about—learning to experience your world in different ways, if only so that you can start tweaking it gently at the edges. Doing magic is about being *responsive* to the challenges of your environment—often a response borne out of necessity. When you find yourself dumped in Cairo at 4 a.m. with your luggage at the other end of the city you can begin to appreciate the strengths of a freestyle approach to practical magic which enables you to shape ideas and approaches and pulling together an *ad hoc* enchantment to sort out the situation. The mistake that newcomers to practical magic often make is that, having identified a problem, they go looking for a 'ritual' or spell which they believe will remove it. Now I've never seen a spell to 'discover where the hell your luggage has got to' and it's impossible to come up with a spell/ritual for everything which life might throw at you. So it's more effective, in my view, to be able to pull 'something' together out of a hat.

Some years ago I was approached by a friend who evinced an interest in practising magic. But, she said, she didn't want to bother with the (quote) "boring" preliminary exercises in the books. Now the generally-accepted received wisdom regarding magical training is that before you can get to the exciting stuff—chatting up gods or summoning things with tentacles—you have to have gained some proficiency with the basic magical skills of concentration, visualization, mantra, breath control, etc. Indeed, it's often implied that those foolhardy souls who *do* leap in, wands blazing, come to grief later on. So I asked this friend what she particularly enjoyed doing—which for her was going to raves and grabbing the occasional toy-boy, watching Star Trek and playing Role-Playing Games. Together we discussed a way of doing magical exercises which she could use whilst having fun. So she could develop magical skills for getting served quickly at the bar, finding an empty seat in a crowded room, or sussing out whether someone was offering her an E or a Vitamin C capsule. Okay, not very spiritual, but she wasn't looking for spirituality as mysticism but some way of relating magic to her everyday life.

Sidling Towards Magical Practice

Books

Books are often the *bête noire* of the magician. There's a common misconception that before you can practise magic properly, you have to have read loads of books. Whilst there's nothing wrong with reading widely about magic, it can lead to problems. One is that you spend so much time reading that you never actually get around to trying anything out for yourself. Another is that you can unconsciously acquire all kinds of opinions—limitations about what you can or can't do, for example—from them. Timothy Leary once remarked that "dangerous, habit-forming books" should be locked away. Books are no substitute for practical experience or conversations with other people. So treat them with respect, but don't worship them. When I was first getting into magic, I would often read a book, then make notes on what I considered were the key points and practical bits. I then worked from my notes and not the book. This, I found, was an excellent way of building up a 'personal grimoire' of techniques and observations. And don't restrict yourself to books on the occult, either. Most of the key ideas which have influenced *my* views about magic haven't come from books on magic.

Keeping a Magical Diary

It's generally accepted that keeping a strict magical diary is a prerequisite for successful practice. But let's not be too strict about this. There's no point in keeping a strict diary if not keeping up your entries is going to become a guilt trip for you. Personally, I go through phases when I keep a record of activities and insights, and at other times, I can't be bothered. It can be useful to train yourself to remember things—creating association chains using pictures, photos, scents, objects—whatever you like.

Explore!

It's very easy for magicians to lock themselves into a limited space, retreating from the world at large into the world of words (be it in books or the internet) and the safety of their own headspace. If you feel you're slipping into this state, put aside your books and go out and explore! Go for a stroll in the park, or a walk on your local 'wild side.' Magic is (in my opinion) a process of engagement with the world at large, not a retreat from it. Seek wonder in what is around you, rather than in dusty tomes or the astral world—which tends to lack those little things like ants in your sandwiches or dog-turds on the pavement. Go places where you wouldn't ordinarily go. Crowley said something to the effect that if a dog disturbs your meditation—shoot it. Why not go and make friends with it instead?

Daily Practice

Again, there are many books on magic which recommend that the student works through a daily practice routine of meditations, banishing rituals, visualization exercises, etc. The general view seems to be that doing daily exercises at fixed times builds character and self-discipline. This is fine if you have a lifestyle which can be easily structured in this way, but many people (particularly those with children, families or unsympathetic partners) often don't. Fit magic into your lifestyle. For example, you can easily meditate whilst doing a household chore. I occasionally do quick spells in the middle of washing up, and they seem to be no more or less effective than when I do the full-on ritual stuff. I also feel it's important to take time off occasionally and just do nothing. In fact, doing nothing can be as difficult for some of us as trying to perform some complex mental exercise.

A further issue related to practice routines is that it's too easy to let them regiment your life. Yes, I could spend years using techniques of dream control until I have complete mastery over my dream-life. But is this necessarily a good thing? I rather like the unpredictability and weirdness of my dreams, and don't want to impose too much control over them. I could do a daily tarot spread before going out every morning, but is it really going to help me in the long run?

Having made these points, practice is undeniably an important part of magical work. Whilst I admitted earlier that I don't like doing magical training courses I should also point out that over the last two decades I have deliberately put myself through several training programmes devised by others. Magic requires the development and integration of a wide variety of skills which requires that you practise them, both as individual disciplines and as integrated techniques.

Beginner's Mind

Approaching magical practice with an open mind is possibly one of the most important requisites to success. Keeping a Beginner's Mind is more difficult. There are no experts in magic, it's just that some people have been doing it for longer than others. When we run into people who are speaking (or writing) authoritatively about some aspect of magic, it's easier to nod wisely rather than saying, "What the hell are you on about?" Or, "Could you explain this in more detail?" Ask people questions, be naïve, seek clarification and don't hesitate to put your own point of view across. This sounds rather obvious, but fear of asking questions and voicing one's own opinions due to the idea that "Well I'm a beginner, so I don't have anything to contribute," does tend to hold people back. In my experience, beginners often come up with the most novel and interesting ideas for magical techniques or their application precisely because they have not yet assimilated other people's fixed notions of what you can and cannot do magically.

Another issue which is related to "Beginner's Mind" is that we are often reluctant to acknowledge what we do know, and the value of our own experience, particularly in respect to what is written in some book or other, or when we encounter those who've been doing magic for much longer. We all have things we can offer each other. Sharing experiences may well be something of a cliché, but its nonetheless a true one.

THE DYNAMICS OF SORCERY

Magic, like sexual intercourse, needs to be experienced to be fully understood. Similarly, the first few times that one tries it, it might not live up to preconceived expectations. It might even be a dismal failure, but that shouldn't put you off forever, right? However, the suspicion that it is all nonsense lurks in a corner of the psyche, armed with justifications, rationalisations, excuses: all the embedded cultural programming which says that magic is superstition, fantasy, and something that can't 'really' happen. The fact that much of what passes for Consensus Reality is based on superstition, fantasy and things which defy rational explanation, is neither here nor there.

To overcome this suspicion, the would-be magician has to prove to himself that MAGIC WORKS, and the only way to do this is by trying it out. Proving that Magic works, even in a small way, begins the process of pushing back the boundaries of Achievable Reality. Suddenly, nothing is as clear-cut as it formerly seemed. Keep 'doing' magic for long enough and it becomes an embedded part of personal reality—as familiar as the sky, earth, and buildings seen every day. At this point one ceases to believe in magic as something 'separate' to the rest of one's familiar world. Rather, the world is becoming magical. Practical Sorcery, as the application of magical methods to the needs of everyday life, is a good starting point.

Orthodox magical systems make a distinction between 'Low' Magic (Sorcery) which is concerned with bringing about change in one's immediate circumstances, and 'High' Magic which is concerned with Spiritual Evolution. The Chaos perspective generally rejects this distinction, as it implies a philosophy which rejects the physical world as being somehow inferior to a spirituality which is above the everyday world. Also, this distinction is not an accurate reflection of magical experience.

Being able to see the results of Sorcery workings (even in small ways) shifts the boundary of what we accept can be done with magic and successfully embeds the fact that *Magic Works*.

It also raises one's confidence in both personal abilities and the techniques themselves, and leads to a more expansive outlook.

Also, success with Sorcery techniques requires that one develop the ability to assess self-performance, and critically examine desires, which in itself leads to change. Bringing about direct changes in the world necessitates that the magician pay close attention to what he is about. Sorcery, with its emphasis on pragmatic techniques and observable results, directs attention to the world as it is experienced, rather than some simplistic idea that has hitherto been accepted as 'real.' Reality is more complex than many people generally like to think.

The dynamics of sorcery are fairly simple, and there is a wide variety of techniques available. Also, it's not difficult to devise personal techniques which are unique to oneself. The application of Sorcery too is very wide. The following is a simple overview of Sorcery procedures. I will look into the dynamics of ritual magic more closely in Part Two, and more information on sorcery in general can be found in *Condensed Chaos* (New Falcon Publications, 1995).

Core Elements of Sorcery

1. Intention

Most acts of Sorcery begin with the *Statement of Intent*. This is a simple declaration of what one is about to do, and for what final purpose. Since vague intentions tend to give rise to, at best, vague results, the magician should formulate a Statement of Intent which is as precise as possible, without becoming overly verbose. Two techniques which may be of assistance here are:

a) Divination Systems

The surface desire for change may well not be the best point from which to work. This is where Divination Systems such as Tarot, I Ching, Runes, Astrology, or self-created systems can be brought in. For example, a Sorcerer is desirous of obtaining employment—getting a job is his surface desire. However, using a divination system to examine the components of the situation, he finds that a key element which blocks his desire is lack of confidence. So he performs a working where improving self-confidence is the main focus of the Enchantment.

Divination systems can also be used when examining a situation which involves other people. It may occasionally be useful to examine one's motives for intervening in a situation involving other people, and also looking for hidden factors which may not be immediately apparent.

b) Cognitive Restructuring

There is often a good deal of difference between what we think we ought to be doing, and what can realistically be achieved. This difference is often a contributing factor to work and life stresses. Magicians often have high ideals, but may sometimes find that it is difficult to bring those ideals down to earth. It can be useful, in this regard, to take an overall intention and break it down into smaller stages, each of which is more readily realised than the overall objective. Rather than trying for a sudden push of the Achievable Reality threshold, it may be more realistic to attempt this in stages.

Sorcery Event Series

A Sorcery Event Series (S.E.S) is a series of linked Sorcery operations. A long-term goal is broken down into smaller, related steps. As one result manifests, the momentum of success carries the magician into the next working in the series. This sets up a condition where each single event concluded in the series increases the probability of the overall intent manifesting. The S.E.S is a particularly useful tactic for working with establishing long-term projects. The effect can be likened to setting up a line of dominoes, and then pushing the first domino into its neighbour.

2. Probability Pathways

Contrary to popular opinion, magical results do not pop up out of thin air, and it does help enormously, with Sorcery workings, if there is a pathway along which the desired result can manifest. This can also be examined in terms of probabilities. A Sorcerer who performs a ritual to ensure that he passes an exam, but does no revision or cramming, is not creating a situation where there is a reasonable probability that he will pass with flying colours. If, however, he does study, the probability of success is likely to be higher. Sorcery does seem to achieve the best results when the probability factor is at least fractionally higher than zero. To take another example, when planning workings for financial gain, it is useful to have a number of projects on the go, any of which may result in increased funds—hence the sorcery working is more likely to yield some kind of positive result.

3. Timing

Timing is an important yet often underrated factor in practical magic. A good example of how timing can critically affect the outcome of a working is that of Healing. If a client has a long-term, progressive disease, then sorcery workings to impede its progress may be more successful at an early, rather than a late stage, in the course of the illness. Complex life situations can be examined for the purposes of Sorcery as unfolding event series. In the early stages of a developing situation, there may be more fluidity and flexibility than at a later stage where it is less easy to influence probable outcomes. Events which can be perceived are macroscopic changes which have been brought about by the unseen interaction of microscopic fluctuations. In other words, an avalanche can be seen, but not the very small factors which brought it about. Developing strategies that allow the identification of small changes, and then influencing them so that they lead to a change which fulfills the conditions of one's statement of intent, can therefore be useful for Sorcery working. In other words, learn to 'nudge' a situation at the right moment. Paying close attention to what is happening in a given situation is useful, and using Divination systems can also help here.

Sorcery Operations — Basic Procedure

Once a Statement of Intent has been formulated, and any other relevant factors taken into account, the next general step in any Sorcery operation is to move into a *Free Area*.

In orthodox magical systems, this tends to involve ritual procedures for setting up a magical Circle, making any psychological adjustments for magical work, or assuming particular postures. From a Chaos perspective, a *Free Area* is any space which has been redefined as a zone where normal Consensus Reality is suspended, and Magical Reality is operant. Thus a Free Area may refer to a previously-prepared Temple, a space in which ritual is to be performed, or a state of Consciousness.

Within the Free Area, the magician uses any proffered technique/trick deemed appropriate to clear his awareness of anything but the impending magical act. This can range from full ritual procedures (performing a Banishing ritual, setting up an altar, etc.,} to merely closing one's eyes and concentrating. The techniques used to define a Free Area often depend upon:

  i) Circumstances
  ii) Available Time
  iii) Necessity
  iv) Individual Preference

Following the definition of, and entry into the Free Area, the next stage is to move towards a state of consciousness known in the Chaos approach as *Gnosis*. Gnosis is a condition of one-pointed consciousness wherein awareness is emptied of all save the object of concentration; where will is given both intentionality and vector. The main routes to Gnosis are threefold: Excitatory—anything which stimulates the BodyMind, such as dancing, drumming, hyperventilation or sexual arousal; Inhibitory—anything which stills the BodyMind, such as passive meditation, slow chanting, hypnotic agents, or slow breathing; and Indifferent Vacuity—a state of no-mind, or Non-Disinterest, where the object of desire flickers briefly in a mind emptied of all content—no emotional attachment to the desire.

Upon entering the peak of Gnosis, the desire in its chosen representative form (a sigil, for example) is projected forth, towards its target or into the void of the multiverse. It is then banished from awareness, that is to say, forgotten.

Following projection of the desire, the Free Area is closed using any preferred method, such as manic laughter, a Banishing Ritual, or a hand gesture. The Magician then moves onward, having set up the conditions whereby his desire will manifest accordingly.

It should be noted that a key to Sorcery is that, on completion of a working, it should be considered—at least on a magical level—to be finished with, and nothing more in the way of magical work needs to be done. The deep certainty that one's Sorcery *will* yield the desired result will only come through continued practice, effort, and refinement of technique, but it is not unusual for advanced practitioners to claim a success rate with this kind of magic of around 80-90%.

The above description of General Sorcery Procedure could be used to describe any sorcery working, from a three-hour group ritual involving prolonged dancing, drumming and chanting, to an act of 'Empty-Handed' magic which can be performed anywhere, and need only last a few seconds. In general, magicians tend to proceed from the former to the latter type of working. As one continually progresses, the definitions of what constitutes a magical action tend to become fairly fluid. At the beginning of magical practice, it is usual to perceive magical operations as being separate from everyday experience. Later, however, acts of magic become a part of everyday experience, as one makes the transition between inhabiting a Consensus Reality which is gradually widening to admit the possibilities of magic, to creating a personal Magical Reality—a *Psychocosm*.

Evolving a Psychocosm

In becoming familiar with magical ideas, reading books, learning symbol systems and correspondences, one comes to learn the 'game rules' of magic. Like any other game, the rules define the framework of the activity. For a game to be worthwhile, its rules must be flexible, open to different interpretations, and allow for different needs and situations.

Involvement with magical practice shows that the game rules of Consensus Reality are more flexible, and have more loopholes than one may have originally thought.

Developing a magical Psychocosm is a slow process, as one gathers momentum in magical practice, shifting from the tentative position of having read a few books and probably having thereby set up preconceptions as to what magic is about, to beginning to practise magical techniques in earnest. One of the strengths of the Chaos approach is that *experience* is stressed over pre-experiential beliefs. Do it first, then consider which beliefs and concepts seem to be most appropriate, in the light of personal experience.

In modern culture, there are hundreds of magical systems available, with more being discovered, recovered and invented every year. Beginners in magic often adopt a system which reflects their core self-beliefs and ideas, or, as is sometimes the case, the first system that is encountered or made accessible. Since few people get anything from an approach they are not even remotely interested in, it is usually best to choose a magical system that is attractive, for whatever reasons. It is important to note, however, that our beliefs relating to magic, be they general or particular, do not necessarily remain constant. They are likely to change according to our experience and changes in personal perspective.

Our primary sources of information which help us in forming a psychocosm tend to be books and other people. A rather amusing example of this is how I formed my early beliefs concerning the inviolability of the magical circle. In the first magical group I worked in, I was taught that once a magical circle had been set up, that it was dangerous to cross its boundary without ceremonially opening a gateway in it first. Lacking any other opinions on the subject, and lacking the confidence to make my own judgements on the matter, this became an article of faith for me. Imagine then, my amazement when, working with a different group, I saw people blithely nipping out of the magical circle to fetch forgotten implements or texts, or to visit the bathroom. My first conclusion was that these people were obviously so advanced that they could cross the psychic barrier of the circle with impunity. Later on though, I came to revise my opinions as to the nature of the barrier created by the circle. In retrospect, I would say that it was useful for me to hold that first, strong belief in the power of the circle—that nothing could cross it unless invited—and that this applied to me as much as any denizens of the astral realm. This belief also led me to develop a tendency for self-organization—making sure I had everything required before beginning a ritual, and that I had visited the toilet beforehand.

This example illustrates the expansion, or loosening of belief through reality-testing. This is not always easy to do, particularly if one has limited opportunities for doing so. When magicians lack opportunities for reality-testing, beliefs about the nature of magic can quickly become dogmas to be defended at all costs. In part, this is due to the ways in which magical theory is generally perceived.

Theory and Glamour

I have met, over the years, a good many people who have professed to have studied magic—meaning that they have read a large number of books which claimed to explain how magic worked. Largely, these folk had not got down to actually trying out something practical, and many ascribed to the erroneous belief that, before raising a finger to trace a pentagram in the air, or closing one's eyes in meditation, one needed to assimilate a great deal of abstract theory. However, magic is, in this respect, dissimilar to the classical sciences. Whilst a student of physics needs to be familiar with certain theories before performing an advanced experiment, a magician does not need to have absorbed a huge chunk of abstract theory in order to cast a spell.

Much of what passes for magical theory is, at root, a matter of belief. As such, it is more relevant to the successful outcome of the magician's spell, that he has some degree of *belief* in what he is doing. Moreover, whereas scientific theories are based (at least so we are told by scientists) on mathematical proofs, magical theories are rooted in the personal beliefs of whoever is expounding them. Whereas scientific theories at least have the *appearance* of being unified and consistent, magical theories do not, nor is it a requirement, from the position of practical magic, that they do.

Henceforth, whilst there are a great many theories and models proposed as to how, or why, magic works (based on subtle energies, animal magnetism, psychological concepts, quantum theory, mathematics or the so called anthropomorphic principle} it is not a case that one of them is more 'true' than others, but a case of which theory or model *you* choose to believe in, or which theory you find the most attractive. Indeed, from a Chaos Magic perspective, you can selectively believe that a particular theory or model of magical action is true only for the duration of a particular ritual or phase of work.

As has been stated, magical theory is unlike scientific theory. You can learn a good deal about science by reading other peoples' experiments and theories. Whilst you can read a lot about how other people have practised magic, the chances are that it won't make much sense until you have a go yourself.

There is a tendency for people to treat occult theories in the same way as general scientific descriptions of the world. That is, they are presumed to be 'true' independently of human experience. These are known as *Theories-of-Action* They tend to be written and discussed in an abstract, divorced-from-human-experience fashion, as though they are immutable laws. Indeed, for some magical authors, these *are* immutable laws or principles, which have been delivered by some kind of higher intelligence, and are not, therefore, open to scrutiny or debate. Those who *do* question, may be met with the brush-off that they are not 'initiated enough' to appreciate the higher truth of the situation, or they would instantly recognise "that I am the living representative of god, and what I say is holy law." This is all very well, if you wish to accept, on face value, what you are being told, but magic, at least from the viewpoint of the Chaos Magic perspective, benefits from you having an open and curious mind.

However, there is a second type of theory, *Theory-in-Use,* which relates to the guidelines and patterns that a practitioner learns, through practice and individual experience, which enable him to be effective.

Theories-in-use cannot be taught: they are personal and tend to operate at the level of unconscious assumptions. They can only be learned by the individual by a process of practice in 'live' experience. In the same way, magical theories-in-use cannot be taught. A fledgling magician can be given general magical theories-of-action and taught basic techniques and the application of them, but he will, of necessity, develop his own theories-of-use as part of the process of becoming proficient and practised at magical activities.

Mistaking Metaphors

Despite various efforts to set the language of magic on a 'scientific' footing, much of one's magical experience can only be adequately communicated in the language of myth, poetry, or metaphor. This is very useful, particularly when we desire to inspire or illumine others through the eloquent description of our own inner experience. Unfortunately, there is a common tendency (believed by many to be a side-effect of western education) to fall into the belief that all metaphorical speech has some basis in fact. In short, westerners tend to take everything *too* literally.

A good example of this tendency is the Hindu system of chakras. Now most people who have done some reading of magical texts will have come across the chakras, as they have become a fairly basic element of what is known as the Western Esoteric Tradition. So much so in fact, that it is more or less taken for granted that the chakras have some factual basis for existence. The original tantric texts which describe the varying systems of chakras (some describe six, others, seven, nine, eleven or even twenty-four!) use a great deal of symbolic language and metaphor, much of which western authors have mistakenly taken literally. Sir John Woodroffe, in his book *The Serpent Power,* gives an example of this when he presents a critique of C.W Leadbeater's book *The Inner Life.* Leadbeater claims to have counted the number of petals of the Sahasrara Chakra (clairvoyantly) and says that the number is not 1,000, as is often given in tantric texts, but exactly 960.

Woodroffe points out that the Indian use of 'thousand' is a metaphor for a great magnitude, and not a literal count. Leadbeater has mistaken a metaphorical statement for a literal one, which makes nonsense of his assertion.

This situation is not helped by the fact that a good deal of occult theories appear to pass, as Pete Carroll once said, from book to book, without any intervening thought. Whilst it is understandable that authors should try and attempt to place magic on a similar footing to the classical sciences, it is all too easy to create dogmas in this fashion. Indeed, I was once privileged to overhear, during a discussion about the validity of modern models of the chakras, that the Indian sages who developed the system, were wrong in their writings about them! Similarly, it is common for occultists to base a particular theory on some popular scientific model and, when the model is discredited or modified by further research, to loudly defend their belief and decry the scientists for not understanding the 'true' significance. Such uncritical thinking can easily lead to dogmatism—the enemy of magic.

Models and Maps

Most approaches to magical development use some kind of general map or model for structuring experience, such as the Kabbalistic Tree of Life, or the aforementioned chakras. However, it is important to bear in mind Robert Anton Wilson's advice that *the Map is not the Territory*.

Magical maps and models are useful in that they can provide a consistent framework for us to make sense of our experiences with. But they are not static entities in themselves—like any other model, they change over the course of time as new ideas are suggested, expounded by authors and esoteric schools, and become an accepted part of the overall model. Moreover, models have their restrictions. Some are good at explaining or understanding particular aspects of magical work, but poor at explaining others. Just as scientists have spent a great deal of time and energy chasing a 'grand theory' which, ultimately, will explain everything, so many occultists spend a great deal of time constructing esoteric models that can explain and interpret any magical event. In my opinion, at least, such attempts are doomed to failure. For example, the influx of psychology in magical models has been both beneficial and not-so beneficial to magic in general. On the one hand, the understanding of applied psychology has helped develop our understanding of magic as an agent of self-development. On the other, however, it is a mistake to try and reduce all magical phenomena to psychological processes. For example, psychological explanations of magic explain curses in terms of auto-suggestion. This is all very well until one brings up cases whereby the recipient of a curse is unaware of what has taken place, yet still falls ill.

Once again, which theory or model you subscribe to is basically a matter of personal choice: the only yardstick being—does it *work* for you?

Results and Magical Advancement

There is a story about a student of the Zen master Dogen who came to the master and reported that, deep in his meditation, he had seen a great white light, in the centre of which was the Buddha. Expecting praise at his spiritual advancement, he was somewhat crestfallen when Dogen replied "That's nice. If you concentrate on your breathing, it will go away." During one's magical development, one is quite likely to experience intense states of awareness, visions, unusual perceptions, precognitive phenomena or the joyful amazement that, against all odds and rationality, one's simple piece of candle magic actually brought forth the result that was desired. Some of these experiences will be potentially life-changing, unpleasant and even threatening. That is all part of the course, too. The problem comes when one begins to attribute such experiences to being signs of great magical illumination or spiritual realisation. Sometimes, you might not even be the direct source of the tendency. Whilst I was writing this piece, a friend rang me to say that she'd been getting some intense visions of my explaining various esoteric matters to her. Now I could have said, "Well done, you're picking up on my astral wavelength" or something which, whilst sounding impressive, would have been a lie on my part (if I'd been deliberately attempting to project my presence to her, it would have been a slightly different matter), and we mutually discussed the phenomena and came up with an explanation which I felt was more reasonable.

Metaprogramming & Magical Belief

A key to magic is what we choose to believe about magic and ourselves. In certain respects, the universe conforms to our beliefs. Again, the chakras form a useful example of this process. The popular view of chakras is that we have seven. Meditate on the chakras, hammer the symbolism into your head and, eventually, you'll start having 7-Chakra experiences—from body sensation to dreams about them. There are basically two ways of looking at this result—one is that the chakras are 'real' and have been waiting for you to come along and 'awaken' them; the other that you've imposed a map over your perception of your bodymind, which has structured itself accordingly. You can test this by switching to a different subtle body map such as the Middle Pillar of the Tree of Life, and doing the same, until you obtain the result of experiences and sensations concordant with the symbolism of the Middle Pillar.

Any belief system can be used as a basis for magic, so long as you can invest commitment and emotional attachment into it. Looking back at my earlier magical experiments, I guess that what used to be important for me was the strong belief that the system I was using was ancient wisdom, based on traditional formulae, passed down from initiate to initiate. As it was, much of this turned out to be glamour or hype, but it helped me a lot as I struggled to gain confidence in my own magical ability.

A belief system can be seen as a matrix of information into which we can pour emotional energy—we do as much, when we become so engrossed in watching a play, film, or TV programme that for a moment, it becomes real for us, and invokes appropriate emotions. Much of what we see served up on the silver screen is powerful mythic images and situations, repackaged for modern tastes.

The Power Of Discrimination

In approaching all world-views, models, and theories, it is useful to develop one's faculty for *discrimination*. In a religious, or absolutist sense, this would require the differentiation of Truth from Non-Truth. However, from a magical perspective, discrimination acts in the following way:

> *It is the process of moving beyond merely accepting*
> *other people's models and theories, by doing your own*
> *research/magical work.*

A simple example of this process is that, when reading a book about runes, you might well find yourself following that author's interpretation of the runes. This is fine for a while, but if you never try and find out anything more, then you have accepted the restriction of this one viewpoint. If you read a different author on the subject, you are likely to find differences of attribution. Which author is right? You can accept one opinion over the other, but until you begin to find out why a particular rune is given one or another attribution, then you are merely accepting other people's opinions with no other knowledge on which to base your own ideas. Until you try and find out why something has been given a particular attribute, it will be difficult to discriminate between one opinion and another.

Magical learning is not just about taking in 'facts' which someone else provides, in the form of a book, for example. One needs to actively experiment and work with magical information, in order for it to become personally meaningful.

This implies that magical models and theories are open to question, and they are also open to change. In particular, they are open to question as one begins to ask questions, and seek answers. And they are open to change as one might change one's mind about a model and elaborate it, recognise it's limited application, or even discard it altogether.

Discrimination is also the process of finding out what is appropriate for yourself—based on your own feelings, rather than what other people might say, or what you read in books. This does not require any special powers of intuition, but it does require the willingness to pay attention to the way in which you take on board magical ideas and concepts.

Magical Glamour

In addition to particular magical theories, there is also a further complicating factor which influences belief, which for purposes of discussion I have chosen to refer to as the 'glamour' which surrounds a particular belief system or approach. This relates both to how adherents of a particular magical system describe themselves in relation to others, and how that system of belief is broadly perceived in a variety of wider contexts. This includes the memes which circulate both in mainstream culture and the various layers of alternative milieus. For example, early on in its development, Chaos Magic acquired the glamour of being somehow 'sinister' or 'satanic' which, while inaccurate, has doubtless drawn quite a few people to become interested in it. Some magical systems have strong quasi-religious overtones, and for practitioners of these systems, the glamours can become faiths. Elements of glamour include not only beliefs and concepts, but styles of writing, narrative content, images, overall presentation, buzz-words, and occasionally the participation of charismatic figureheads.

Often, the attractiveness of a glamour for an individual reflects personal tastes in literature, music, or other fashions. For Chaos Magicians, the power of glamour becomes yet another technique to be understood and utilised. For example, successfully weaving the glamour of being a shaman will significantly alter other people's reactions to the magician, as would successfully weaving the glamour of being a satanist. Indeed, it is possible for a magician who is adept in the projection of glamours to be perceived as both (by different sets of people), when in fact, neither glamour is particularly 'true.'

One of the most persistent and attractive glamours is that of the magician as an 'outsider' figure. Many people who are attracted to magic want to think of themselves as outsiders—individuals who stand beyond the boundaries of everyday society, separated from everyone else by dint of their 'knowledge of the mysteries.' Unfortunately, thinking of oneself as an 'outsider' can become an excuse for not getting one's act together. The 'outsider stance' can often be equated with no direction, low quality of life, no social skills, unrealistic self-expectations and a huge chip on one's shoulder. Addiction to those virulent memes, Being Right and Getting Even is also common amongst wannabe Outsiders. The other main problem with being an Outsider is that one needs something to be outside of. Again this pulls the individual back into dualistic opposition-oriented thinking habits. Having to have an enemy against which to define yourself, be it society, an imaginary black lodge that is psychically attacking you; mehums; the masses; robotniks; proles or whatever term used, hides, I think, a nagging insecurity. If you see yourself in opposition to that other, then it's all too easy to think of yourself as being superior to them, and the more you have to be superior, the less able you are to admit to having personal faults and weaknesses, or even that other people may be as complex and interesting as you are. This kind of arrogance is all too common, and not therefore, as élite as its exponents fondly imagine themselves to be.

INITIATION

To initiate something is to begin, or embark upon a particular course of action. To be *initiated*, in the magical sense of the word is to recognize that you are moving through a threshold of change—that you are in a period of transition. The key to understanding initiation is recognizing consciously what is happening, rather than simply wondering what the hell's going on. For many magicians and pagans, the recognition of moving into a period of initiation is marked by a ritual or magical retirement. Thus in this context, an *Initiate* is someone who is intensely aware of his or her condition, and is surfing the crest of the wave, rather than struggling to hold it back. Initiation is a time of letting go. It is a time of 'loosening up'—when habits, beliefs, attitudes and self-identifications suddenly (or gradually) seem to be less concrete than they were previously. One's grip on 'normality' may be temporarily lost, only to be eventually (one hopes) regained, but not quite the same as it what before. Dealing with this loss of certainty, and the necessary confrontation with self, can be difficult at times. Some never manage to go the distance, and instead opt for fantasies wherein they are mighty adepts rather than simply accepting their own humanity, which necessitates a degree of humility, to say the least. Re-acquaintance with self then, is one of the core by-products of initiation. Another is confidence—the confidence which springs from the ability to let go—to be able to loose control of something when you realise that control is no longer a valid option. The confidence to make mistakes freely and to be able to admit "I don't know..." rather than fearing loss of face. The confidence of meeting an uncertain world head-on, smiling. Further, having gone through the painful process of shaking loose one's web of beliefs, values and identifications, then other people's truths no longer seem as threatening to one's own. These factors and others contribute to one's own sense of poise—the easy, self-assured manner which is one of the hallmarks of the effective magician.

What kind of time-period are we talking here? That's difficult to say. As I noted in *Condensed Chaos*, initiation is a process. It has its peaks, troughs and plateaus. It highs, lows, and periods of nothing much happening. One thing I am sure about is that once is not enough. Initiatory trials come up time and time again as changes in our lives impact upon us. Change, the only constant in magic, is something that is mostly resisted, but occasionally is as stimulating as a shot of coke. One period of initiation doesn't mean you're now sorted, for the rest of your life, but is more likely to leave you understanding how little you understand. Initiatory cycles can take years to work themselves through. When you think it's all over, it usually isn't.

Related to initiation is the idea of magical progress. It is often difficult for non-magicians to understand why those of us so afflicted are so passionate about what we do and what we get out of it, much less why we bother with it in the first place. One of the things that keeps us going is a sense of going somewhere or making progress in magic—to be "on the path" to use an occult colloquialism. This sense of progress does not come automatically to us; it is more that it sneaks up unawares until one begins to think of oneself as going somewhere definite as opposed to simply experimenting or messing around. Where one is going, of course, is up to each alone, depending on what they conceive progress to be—something which of itself, is likely to change as one progresses, and according to the company one keeps.

Ideas of progress may also be shaped by any particular belief system or magical theory that one has chosen to give shape to experiences. Magical Psychocosms, ways of structuring the universe and our place in it using symbolic structures, are often used as the basis of systems of initiation—that is to say they are means by which magical progress is cut-up into discrete steps, often known as *Magical Grades*. Each Grade deals with a specific set of experiences and magical methods, allowing the individual to concentrate on one thing at a time, rather than floundering about. One of the arguments for systems of initiation then, is that they give individual magicians a structure with which to approach their magical development, and interpret and then assimilate their experiences according to a framework of theory and belief. That's the theory, anyway. How far one goes with any one system of initiation is again a matter of preference and changing needs. There are arguments that favour following systems set up by particular occult orders, teachers or esoteric systems of belief, and those that say that creating one's own system gives the best results. Having done both, I will say that each approach has its pros and cons. Probably the best-known magical grades are those associated with the Hermetic Order of the Golden Dawn: Neophyte, Zelator, Practicus, etc. Each grade had particular magical aims and objectives associated with it, as well as characteristic mystical experiences. The problem which has become identified with this kind of grading system is the way in which it lends itself to the creation of abusive hierarchical authority in a group, or ego-inflation for solo magicians. Anyone can claim to have attained a particular magical grade—but in the long run this counts for very little unless other people recognise such an assertion and support it. It's pointless saying you're a Magus if everyone else thinks you're a prat!

So what, then, are *Initiation Rituals* about? Basically, there are two types of initiation ritual: Self-Initiation, and Initiation into, or via a Group. I will deal with the latter first.

Initiation by a Group

Initiation by a Group has many shades. When individuals belonging to a particular magical tradition or system talk about rituals of initiation, it is usually in the context that the ritual serves to identify the candidate as a full member of that particular group, organization or tradition, rather than a supplicant or novice. Thus the ritual marks the end of that person's apprenticeship with the group in question—he is now fully accepted and recognized as equal to the others. This may be the primary consideration of the group, whereas stimulating or intensifying any intrapsychic change on the part of the candidate may be of secondary importance. This is not to say however, that group initiation rituals cannot trigger periods of the personal initiatory cycle in people who undergo them—they can do so effectively, although a great deal depends on how the candidate is treated prior to the ritual event, during it, and afterwards.

A rather extreme example of an initiation by a group was my own initiation into a Wiccan coven some 17 years or so ago. As is not unusual for Wiccan covens, I had to wait 'a year and a day' before becoming initiated. This kind of trial period is often used in magical groups and orders as a time of the group getting to know the candidate, and vice versa. During this period a candidate may be required to undertake a basic magical training programme or otherwise fulfill any entry requirements the group has. Most of all though, it is a period where both group and individual strive to suss each other out, to find out whether or not the other is suitable in terms of personality, common beliefs and values, etc. I was asked to keep a magical diary and to follow a regimen of meditation, yoga, banishing rituals, practice at divination and to try and visit some natural setting—be it park, woodland, or seashore once a week. As I moved gradually towards the time of being ready for initiation into the coven proper, the leaders of the coven dropped quite a few hints about how my magical work would change after initiation. The ritual itself I recall with a mixture of awe and amusement. Amusing, as the coven had based it on a Golden Dawn initiation ritual which called for more ritual officers than they then had members, and the temple space was also rather cramped for the activities that the ritual called for. The feeling that I will never forget however, is the moment of fear and uncertainty which rushed through my head as I was led, naked and blindfolded, into a room and the first thing I came up against was a sharp magical dagger against my breast. And I thought, "Ohmigod what if I've misjudged these people and they are loonies after all." The realisation that I had to abandon myself to trusting the people I'd given myself up to was an indescribable rush. The initiation ritual consisted of various symbolic recognition's that I was committing myself to the coven, the magico-religious tradition of goddess veneration, and to my own magical development. As part of this process I was given a magical name by which I would be known during ritual and sacred events, and after the ritual had closed, was welcomed by the coven members with a party.

However, the initiation wasn't over yet. A few days later I was asked to visit the coven, to discuss 'something.' On arrival, the first thing I noticed was that the people there were distinctly cool towards me—not exhibiting the friendly warmth I had come to value so much from the coven. I listened with growing horror as the High Priestess of the coven explained to me that they'd made a mistake—that I wasn't suited for magical pursuits and that if I continued I would probably go mad. The initiation ritual they said was invalid, I couldn't be in the coven and moreover, I should not do any more magical work! I was devastated by this revelation. I left Britain to travel around Israel and Egypt, and on my eventual return, became interested in Zen meditation. I corresponded occasionally with some others who I'd met through the coven, but gave little thought to the occult practices and beliefs which previously, had rather dominated my life. Nearly two years after my 'failed' initiation, I received a letter out of the blue from the High Priestess of the coven saying that she was "pleased with my progress" and I would like to visit the coven again. I did so, and shortly after was reinstated as an initiated member of the coven.

On my return to the coven, I discovered that the 'rejection' had been deliberate—that the trial of the initiation had not been the rite itself or being made to wait a year and a day for it, but to go through all that and then told that being a magician which I'd decided I was going to devote my life to becoming (as you do) back then, was not possible, by someone I'd accepted as a trustworthy authority figure. Yes, I could have argued, blustered or put up a fight. I couldn't have gone to another group as I didn't then know any other groups and had met a sum total of five other practising magicians in my entire life. In retrospect, what the coven did was exactly what I needed at the time and when I eventually came back to them I had gained a good deal of perspective about magic and myself. I can only admire the way in which the coven's act plunged me into an initiatory crisis and left me largely alone until I'd come through it.

The element of the trial is a key feature of initiation rituals. In some tribal cultures for example, the candidate is expected to endure pain without crying out—pain itself being of course a route into gnosis. In the Eleusinean Mysteries' initiation, a celebrant, prepared by fasting and hallucinogenics might be lowered into a cave complex where beast-masked priests enacted the parts of gods and spirits. In modern magical groups, a candidate's initiation trial might consist of being led and misdirected across a wilderness until he stumbles across the appointed spot for the climax of the rite; being asked to defend a place or not to move from it despite all temptations or fear; alternatively the trial might involve the candidate's direct confrontation of a personal taboo or having to give up a major attachment (being asked to shave one's hair being a simple example). In Aleister Crowley's novel *Moonchild*, one of the protagonists undergoes an initiation ceremony, wherein she surrenders her personal freedom, in the belief she is helping another woman escape the Order, who are made out to be cruel torturers. The test here is of selfless sacrifice. Another kind of trial is a ritual wherein the candidate is told to demonstrate his commitment to the group by choosing one of several courses of action—all of which involve varying degrees of subjugation to authority or unpleasantness. In this instance, the candidate's refusal to follow any of the choices laid before him—despite pressure—can be seen as a test of the candidate's individual spirit.

Related to the element of the trial is the element of surprise in initiation rituals. There are different schools of thought here. One argument is that by using the same initiatory ritual structure for each candidate, the group builds up a layer of shared, common experience which helps build up the sense of 'we-ness.' A counter-argument however, is that initiation rituals require an element of risk. If the candidate has only a few cues about what will happen during his initiatory ritual, he or she is much more likely to be in a state of heightened awareness and it is therefore more likely that the ritual will impact upon the candidate at a deep level. For much the same reason, it is held by advocates of this approach that initiatory rites should be carefully tailored to reflect the groups' observation of each particular candidate. For example, it would be pointless using quasi-S&M trappings in an initiation ritual if the individual it is aimed at is into S&M anyway.

The sense of apprehension in a candidate for initiation can be gradually fostered through the pre-ritual behaviour of the rest of the group. This can be heightened during the ritual itself by the use of blindfolds, earplugs or other props designed to obscure sensory input, and again by the ritual officers distancing themselves from the candidate—addressing him in the third person, for example.

Group initiation rituals may also involve elements whereby the candidate demonstrates personal commitment to the group and vice versa. Rituals are often closed with the other celebrants greeting the new initiate with a warmth and friendliness that previously may have been held back. Polite distance may be changed for joking, insults, arguments and the implication that the individual will no longer be expected to behave like a polite visitor in front of everyone else but can expect the joys of the full rough-and-tumble of group life.

If a group initiation ritual is going to be successful in triggering a personal initiatory crisis for the candidate, there has to be, I feel, a bond of trust between the candidate and the group member responsible for orchestrating that person's initiation. The initiator needs to have formed some baseline ideas about how the candidate will perform under stress, and also to have observed the candidate long enough to have some ideas as to what for him will constitute a suitable ritual event. Also, the mere fact that for the candidate during the ritual, the initiator's change in demeanour from his or her normal behaviour towards the candidate to one of ritual formality can act to increase apprehension and expectation. This bond of trust is particularly important after the ritual, especially if the ritual is aimed at triggering an initiatory crisis. Such personal initiation cycles are often marked by periods of depression, uncertainty and varying degrees of neurosis. Getting through this period successfully is all the more likely if the individual concerned has a trustworthy person he or she can discuss feelings and perceptions with. Preferably someone who has gone through the initiation crisis-cycle often enough to help the *initiate* find his own way out of it.

Self-Initiation

The process of self-initiation is central to magical development in that the aspiring magician must, at some point, voluntarily open himself to initiatory crisis and indeed, be prepared to engage in such initiatory trials time and time again. Several misunderstandings are circulating concerning Self-Initiation. One such is the idea that all Self-Initiation requires is undergoing a simple ritual of dedication to a particular tradition or belief-system. Such rituals of dedication can act as Statements of Intent, as

Recognitions of one's entry into the initiatory cycle, or rites of closure once one feels that things have calmed down somewhat. Self-Initiation, however, being a process of intense self-discovery and reappraisal, requires a great deal of hard work on the part of the individual and is unlikely (in my opinion) to be sorted out after a half-hour ritual. Another misconception is that once one has passed through a particular initiatory trial, any changes of perception or insight that one may gain are fixed for eternity. During an initiatory crisis, one may experience both the lows which are termed "the dark night of the soul" and the highs of oneness with the Universe, God, the Tao, the bliss of ego-loss and the intense feeling that one's accrued habits and limitations have fallen away. This is normal. It is also transitory. In my own experience at any rate, I have found that a lot depends on what you do about any insights or new understandings that arise out of initiatory highs and lows—in other words, insights must be acted upon, and understood gradually. Making small changes in thought, word and deed is usually more effective than making big sweeping declarations.

A further misconception around the issue of Self-Initiation is the idea, popular amongst some occultists, that Self-Initiation is somehow second-rate compared to Initiation by a particular group. Related to this is the idea that one is not a proper magician, witch or whatever, unless one is a member of a coven, magical order, or group. Of course one can take this still further until it can be asserted that is not a 'proper' magician unless one is a member of 'X' group. Some modern Wiccans for example, seem particularly obsessed with proving lines of initiation back to a particular authority-figure. Whilst this might well give rise to a certain sense of historical continuance, it's by no means essential. There seems to be some implication that by virtue of having a historical sense of continuance through being able to trace one's line of initiation gives credence and some kind of authentication to one's current magical practices and beliefs. But why should it? And why should this be necessary? I will admit that it's nice to be able to say "Well, I was initiated by x, and x by z, and z by y, and y by w." But it doesn't make what I do now somehow 'more valid' than someone else who has merely initiated themselves, working alone from books. All a group or teacher can do is perhaps no more than point in a particular direction or provide a helping hand along the way. In fact, I would argue that membership of a group can be the perfect setting for those who are unwilling to initiate themselves, preferring fantasies of being powerful magicians to the hard work of self-appraisal and self-acceptance.

Steps Towards Self-Initiation

How then does one proceed towards initiation? This again, is somewhat amorphous. Many spend a lifetime seeking 'enlightenment' but get not so much as a glimpse. Many expend a great deal of energy being spiritually correct only to find that the dull person next door is gifted with a remarkable vision of the All, in the midst of watching "I Love Lucy" or something seemingly equally banal. There is. I feel, an element of such elusiveness to the process of initiation, particularly one's first experience of personal crisis as a result of magical work. It is sometimes characterized by feelings that your occult studies or practices are not taken you anywhere, that the initial success that one is sometimes granted after a few months of occult working, has suddenly dried up. There comes a desire to give up on everything, to abandon exercises and meditation, as nothing seems to be working. It may also be experienced as an existential crisis of belief and self-doubt. Fears of going mad are not uncommon either. It is not, on the whole, a very enjoyable time to go through.

It is impossible to predict how and when initiatory crises will explode upon us—other than in retrospect. Its impossible to generalize, other than tentatively. Gradually, in my experience, one develops a sense of their onset, amplified through dream, intuition and omen—but one has to be able to read one's personal signs correctly, which takes some experience. It is believed by some magicians that initiatory crises arise as a by-product of intense periods of magical workings and practices. Any kind of magical work it is held, can lead to initiation and by the same token, any particular magical project can be used (i.e., dedicated) to contribute to furthering one's initiation. Some magicians do construct magical retirements for themselves which are aimed at uncovering some particular aspect of self through intense application of magical techniques. Examples of such retirements

include the creation of a personal Alphabet of Desire, or identifying and binding one's own demon-horde. Others may choose
to pursue themselves through some form of psychotherapy or
one of the myriad systems of self-discovery available. Indeed,
Israel Regardie recommended that serious magical practice be
prefaced by undergoing psychoanalysis, and this for a time, was
a requirement for a Golden Dawn-style order that he was assisting (see *Rebels & Devils*, New Falcon Publications for a further
discussion of this). The various techniques and approaches which
come under the broad umbrella of Ego Magic are also apposite
for self-initiation. Certainly, intensely challenging one's own
self-identifications, beliefs, values and habits of thinking and
action can provoke an intrapsychic crisis. But this has to be
approached authentically—which is to say not merely as an
intellectual exercise. The initial aim (that of initiation) must be
subsumed into the details of the practice itself, else one is forever
on the lookout for one's 'initiation coming,' whereas it is not apt
to sneak up and bash you on the head until you've forgotten
about it. Individuals who seek spiritual progress are often driven
by a desire to achieve enlightenment (Buddha-hood, magus-
hood, whatever) now and there is a dash to find the most powerful techniques or methods which will guarantee success. Similarly, there is no one technique or practice that will guarantee a
successful initiation.

It is this amorphous nature of initiation which causes some
magicians to argue that one needs a guide of some sorts, be it a
teacher, group, or merely friends with open minds, in order to
successfully get through periods of initiation. Certainly, having
someone you can discuss all your hopes, fears, suspicions and
occasional mad thoughts with is very helpful. Of course, those
with various mandates and agendas of their own, may see one
person's vulnerability as an opportunity to sow their own brand
of truth on fertile soil. Religious cults do this very well, hanging
around colleges where they can draw in new students, away from
home and unsure of their new-found freedoms. When the world
we have taken for granted suddenly fragments around us, truths
can act as anchors against uncertainty. In such moments, the realization that "Nothing is True" can be horrific, or vastly amusing.

EXPERIMENTS IN BELIEF

One of the central assertions of Chaos Magic is that *belief structures reality*. If you believe in faeries it's much more likely that you're going to be able to see them. If you believe that the only way to do something is what you've learned so far, then you're less likely to consider alternative approaches. Related to this is the idea that beliefs are tools or *conceptual weapons*, rather than fixed perspectives, which can be drawn upon in any given situation. A good practical example of this in practice is healing. We would not, for example, except an allopathic healer to accept the possibility of spirits influencing the course of an illness. A magician however, might well do so, and at the same time, be able to accept the relevance of the allopathic perspective.

The beliefs we hold about ourselves, things in particular and in general, and how the world works, are both personal and social, particularly when we begin to express them or seek out other people in order to gain confirmation or verification of them. So experimenting with our own beliefs, by necessity, involves other people. And this of course, invites the complexity that always appears when one moves out of one's own 'it-seems-obvious-to-me' headspace, towards other people. It has been said that other people provide the backdrop against which we display our personal differences and thus maintain our sense of being an individual. There is an element of truth in this, in that we often tend not to expect other people to be as complex as *we know we are* to ourselves.

The sense of being a unique individual—the Ego is maintained by a pattern which basically makes a divide between what it 'is' and what is 'not.' An individual's attitudes, beliefs, and allegiance to various ideologies and social groups reinforce the sense of selfhood, against the projected 'other.' These structures are responsible for maintaining one's perception of the way things 'are'—the embedded perception of that which is perceived as; (to use Berger & Luckmann's term) 'Paramount Reality'; echoed back through all aspects of one's life, so that there is little sense of reality being fragile or unstable (except at

45

times of stress). One's world-view literally becomes the World—
embedded and reinforced so that its limitations and parameters
are experienced unreflectively, as self-evident 'truths.' This is
everyday life as it is experienced on a day-to-day basis. It is, to a
great extent, constructed from routines and our sense of comfort
that nothing much will hopefully occur to interrupt the flow of
events between one moment and the next. Of course interrup-
tions occur all the time, but there is a tendency to treat them as if
they were aberrations that cause us to side-step for a moment
before swinging back on course.

Habits & Routines

Although we are creatures of habit and routine, we tend to have a
paradoxical relationship with those very habits and routines (of
behaviour, thought, etc.) which maintain our sense of everyday
reality. We mostly allow them to pass unnoticed—after all, what
is there to ponder about the way we dress in the morning, put on
our shoes or wash up after dinner? Occasionally though, we feel
oppressed by our own routines, and feel the need to break out.
Habit becomes restriction. When this mood sweeps in, it is a
good time to try out the various habit-breaking exercises—write
with your non-dominant hand; speak backwards; attempt to
delete one habit from your behavioural repertoire replacing it
with another. Part of the point of such exercises is that you are
introducing conscious reflection into an event which, prior to the
exercise, you did more-or-less automatically. So instead of
eating while you watch TV, you just eat—concentrating on the
sensations, actions and flavours. Instead of listening with only
half an ear to another person while you think of a witty rejoinder—you just listen, keeping your mind blank and giving the
other full attention. There are hundreds of such little gambits and
they can be fun to try out periodically. Just don't get into the
habit of viewing them as having to be done and feeling guilty
when you forget. "My god, I ate that sandwich without even
tasting it!" Habits have their uses. Indeed, one can argue that the
more we assign the low-priority aspects of our lives to unreflec-
tive behaviour, the more attention we can pay to being free in
those arenas which *do* matter to us.

As we can experiment with personal habits and routines, we can so do with social routines of behaviour. In the 1970s, an American sociologist asked his students to go home and behave as though they were guests in their own homes. He was inundated with complaints from angry parents who had wondered why their offspring were politely asking them if they could use the bathroom or retire to their rooms. Even minor changes in social behaviour can have far-reaching effects.

Individuals with a rigid ego-complex tend to react to any perceived threat to their world-view by suppressing, denying, or attacking the source of dissonance. The more loose one's ego-complex, the more adaptive and tolerant the individual is to new ideas, change, understanding another person's viewpoint, and, perhaps most important—the ability to interact with others across a wide social range, without requiring a complete consensus of attitude and belief.

The Paradigm Shift

The term "Paradigm Shift" was coined by the scientific philosopher Thomas Kuhn in his book, *The Structure of Scientific Revolutions*. According to Kuhn, a paradigm is an archetypal example, a norm which sets the standards for further activity in that field. It is, if you like, a particular illustration which expresses a wider general theory. So the infamous Schroedinger's Cat experiment would be a paradigm of Quantum Physics. A paradigm, therefore, is a concrete example of a wider world-view. A Paradigm Shift occurs when a new paradigm arises which addresses the important problems of the day more effectively than the old one did. Again, a scientific example of a Paradigm Shift would be the replacement of Aristotle's dynamics of motion with those of Newton's *Principia*, and, in turn, Einstein's Theory of Relativity.

Chaos Magicians have borrowed the term Paradigm Shift and given it their own spin. In chaos-speak, the term paradigm has become equated with a particular world-view, and so the chaote version of paradigm shift (as I understand it) is to make deliberate shifts of belief (and behaviour) aimed at embracing a particular world-view. Typically, this is a world-view associated with a particular lifestyle or belief-system.

The aim here is to loosen one's personal web of beliefs and attitudes: to become more adaptive to new situations and attitudes. Shifting into a new world-view is instructive, not only in terms of empathy (understanding another persons' outlook on life} but also, by bringing about a deliberate change which occurs across different strata of one's life, the magician undergoes a process of ego-fracturing and remoulding.

It should be understood that making a belief shift is not easy. It is not merely a matter of deciding one day to be a hedonist, and the next, a medieval ascetic. Merely playing around with beliefs and attitudes in the safety of one's own head-space is little more than mental masturbation.

Belief shifts are rarely effective unless they are enacted fully within the consensus reality of a social space. Shifting from Hippie to Yuppie necessitates a change of clothes, speech, self-affirmations, time-sense, everyday habits, the social circles in which one moves; and the most difficult part of the process may be coping with the reactions of friends and peers. There's an element of being a 'secret agent' here—of going under cover, playing a role. You may find however, that there will be moments when you're not merely playing the role, but that you've become emotionally engaged in it.

Entering any particular world-view as an ego-deconstructive exercises implies a stance of total involvement and the embracing of any associated beliefs, attitudes, and behaviours. This process takes time. It takes time to establish oneself comfortably within a particular world-view; time to experience consensus reality totally within that world-view, and time to withdraw from it and evaluate the experience.

Some world-views are easier to enter and leave than others. It is relatively easy, for example, to shift from being a fanatical follower of a religion to a fanatical exponent of a magical system. All that a person has changed, in this example, is the surface content of the beliefs. The embedded patterns of behaviour and attitude have remained intact, and it is these 'embedded' beliefs and behaviours which are at the root of the more conscious responses to situations and life-changes.

The first stage of moving into a Belief Shift is made when one begins to question the validity of these self-evident truths—to begin to experience consensus Reality as fragile, where one's own individual beliefs are seen as much a prop as those held by others. A great many people do this as a matter of course and, as this process leads to anxiety and alienation, seek to resolve the inner conflict by embracing an ideology which gives them the illusion of solid ground—meaning, participation and a secure place to be. Many religious and quasi-magical cults recruit their members by deliberately targeting individuals who have begun to question their participation in consensus Reality.

Ego Mapping

In deliberately setting out to enter into a Belief Shift, the magician is preparing to assault the fortress of his own identity. A ground plan of the area is therefore useful. Ego Mapping requires the articulation and unraveling of one's own beliefs and attitudes: ideologies that the magician is attracted to or equally, is repelled by; perceived strengths and weaknesses, fears, ego-propping fantasies, desires, dreams, nightmares. The magician writes an account of himself, as he is, how he would like to be, and how he thinks others see him; he trawls back through his personal history, attempting to identify major turning-points, successes, incidents of failure, embarrassment, blunders, traumas and ecstasies. An account of himself in the third person may be useful, as might be an obituary, written in the present, or ten years in the future.

As the process gains momentum, there comes the understanding that one's own world-view, which may well have been tacitly accepted as 'true' so far, is merely one of many, in a bewilderingly complex, expanding culture. An initial choice of Belief Shift may be the movement into a world-view which is diametrically opposed to a belief-system which one has invested a good deal of time, energy, and self-esteem into. A change of political ideology is a good example, as it requires a radical transition towards embracing and experiencing a world-view which has been, for years, the 'opposition.' Here, the magician may have spent years viewing a particular ideology through stereotyped 'others.' By deliberately becoming one of those 'others,' he challenges the 'truth' of his previous world-view. Of course, this is risky, especially as it will affect every aspect of one's lifestyle, particularly interactions with family, friends, peer group, etc.

Sub-Belief Shifts

The kind of Belief Shift examined so far is broad in its scope. It can also be instructive, from time to time, to make occasional sub-Belief shifts within a specific context. The symbolic and ontological models that make up occult belief systems come within this category. So, for Chaos Magicians, modern witchcraft can be considered a particular subset of an overall magical belief-system: as could Theosophy or Voudoun. Shifting between magical belief-systems is relatively easy. Magicians do tend to move between magical perspectives in the course of their development, as one is attracted to belief systems which offer different degrees of explanatory strength, freedom of expression, personal meaning and participation. Entering a specific magical perspective, and working within its parameters until they are experienced as 'true,' and then moving to another belief-system, is instructive.

Such experiences tend to lead to the conclusion that magical belief systems are not necessarily 'true' descriptions of the territory, but merely structures for organising, assimilating, and integrating experience. To do this successfully requires that the magician works with any chosen system over time. Thus magical models become themselves tools, rather than rigid parameters. Some tools are likely to be better for some types of exploration than others, and Chaos Magicians tend to the view that it is more efficient to have a wide range of *conceptual weapons* to choose from, rather than be limited to one paradigm that cannot possibly account for everything. Tools, however, can be subtle traps. A magical model which at first appears liberating, yielding new insights, information and experiences can, become eventually, restrictive.

The inability to move beyond the limits of one's chosen dominant belief-system seriously hampers one's ability to be adaptive to life-changes, and the exploration of new possibilities. A strength of the Chaos approach to magic is the *freedom* to draw inspiration, creativity, and structure from *any* area of human endeavour, and not be restricted to what is usually perceived as 'magic.' Hence a rising interest in cybernetics, science-fiction, biology, communications, non-linear dynamics, and other diverse contributions to contemporary culture. Rather than attempting to accommodate ideas within existing belief-systems, Chaos Magicians create new perspectives based on current ideas and possible futures, rather than continually attempting to rewrite and recycle the past.

The cumulative effects of Belief Shifting, practised on all possible levels are: the deep understanding that all beliefs are relative, that one can consciously adopt a particular stance and successfully weave a projective glamour (both for self and others) from it; that one is able to accept new information and ideas without perceiving them as a threat; and that one can live comfortably within many different roles and selves. All individuals are free to make contradictory statements, be wrong occasionally, and admit to errors in judgement, without suffering a serious blow to their ego. This transition is known as the shift from Ego-centric behaviour, to Exo-centric behaviour. That is, the process of movement from a position where a stable sense of self has to be maintained at all costs, to a position where a multitude of possibilities is acknowledged, with a continual sense of engagement towards those selves which are, as yet, unknown. Further, it requires the identification and acceptance of that which the magician has previously found fearful, distasteful and unacceptable—the demon-selves which, having been faced and bound, become routes into power.

This practice is not easy, as it requires the ability to move freely within one's Social World, and the continual reassessment of one's Personal World.

Useful Gambits

Going Away

Travelling not only broadens the mind, it also provides a useful opportunity to adopt Belief Shifts in a social space where few others are likely to be familiar with one's 'normal' identity.

Self-Observation

Here, the magician develops the ability to observe himself dispassionately, so that he becomes aware of how he creates, projects, and maintains a distinct identity. Awareness of the dynamics of Identity maintenance is essential when attempting to alter that projection at will. It is also important to be able to observe how other people react to willed identity projection. Self-Observation becomes a continual meditation. It is also instructive to pay attention to how others maintain and project different identities.

Shock Tactics

Individuals have a natural tendency to attribute their own behaviour to situational factors, yet at the same time, attribute the behaviour of others to their personality. The process of labelling others on the basis of their dress, peers, and given opinions can become a subtle trap. Knowledge of this tendency can be turned to the magician's advantage. If, for example, he knows that another personal has tagged him as holding generally liberal views on various issues, then choosing the appropriate moment to make a comment which implies the opposite view, is likely to give the other person a considerable shock. Such tactics may be used to enhance personal power, or, to appear to collude with another, whilst maintaining a hidden agenda.

The above might prompt the question "do Chaos Magicians ever remain in one belief-system or sub-belief for any length of time?" Of course. The practice of making Belief Shifts allows the magician to move between perspectives, so that he develops, over time, a web of personally significant beliefs, based on developing personal and ethical stances, embedded beliefs, a mobile sense of identity, and whatever magical models are being used at any one time. This sounds complex, but is experienced as simple or self-evident. The Chaos Magician is more likely to accept that his belief-web is likely to change, and that he is quite likely to find himself doing things which were previously outside of his known repertoire of experiences. It is also important to remember that Chaos Magic is not an overall belief-system in quite the same way that other magical belief-systems are often perceived. Chaos Magicians are quite likely to identify themselves with other magical belief-systems at the same time as identifying themselves as 'Chaos Magicians.' For example, at the time of writing, my own major magical interests are free-form shamanic practice and Tantric Magic. For me there is no conflict between these two areas of interest and Chaos Magic.

Similarly, a colleague who played a key role in the formation of the Illuminates of Thanateros (the first organisation of Chaos Magicians) is by his own admission, primarily a Runemaster.

Identity & Self

What is the sense of self? The idea of the self as a fixed, unambiguous point of reference is a much sought-for prize, promised by the varying therapies and manuals for alternative living. When we come to recognise our existence as being made up of various life-worlds (none of which we are fully committed to} the sense of the real me is something which is presented, to varying degrees, in all of them, but fully realised in none. The relationship between the sense of self and the myriad social worlds we participate in is paradoxical. In that, without a sense of belonging to something, there is no sense of stability, yet total commitment to any one social world implies a selflessness which is highly suspect in modern culture. To paraphrase Erving Goffmann; our sense of status is derived from the solid constructions of (social) reality, yet our sense of personal identity derives from the ways in which we resist total participation in them. So whilst we place ourselves within society, we simultaneously resist it, so that we might declare that we are something more than what we do within it, or how we are perceived by others. In modern culture, individuality is wrested from our struggles against both social institutions and our peers.

This very idea that identity is a construction, rather than a fixed absolute, has allowed alternative theories of self to arise. A notion popular with some Chaos Magicians is that there is no single self, but a multiplicity of selves. This argument is, that although we experience ourselves as cohesive personalities, we are each composed of a cluster of selves. Bandler & Grinder, the chief exponents of Neuro-Linguistic Programming, take this idea further, by stating that we are all "multiple personalities." This apparently schizoid view of the self reflects the increasingly fragmented experience of self through the pluralisation of the life-worlds in which we participate. The key difference though, seems to be that, instead of attempting to firmly establish what Lacan called the 'fiction' of the true self, one strives to give free reign to the multiple selves.

How useful is such theorising at ground-zero? If we accept that the sense of selfhood is an emergent property of continual movement through zones of social dynamics—that there is no core behind the masks we wear as we move through our social worlds; then if nothing else this frees us from the impetus to assert ourselves as individuals against each other. The search for an overall pattern of coherence by which we can discern self, meaning and a sense of progress crumbles. In this is possibly the most radical aspects of the Chaos Magic perspective: stop looking for truth and have fun with your beliefs; stop trying to pull together a single identity and enjoy many identities—much as Aleister Crowley did. In contrast to other magical perspectives, Chaos Magic is not concerned with the evasion or transcendence of everyday life, but its *transformation*, through the re-injection of the marvellous into everyday life. The statement "Nothing is True, Everything is Permitted" can be a slogan of supreme pessimism and cynicism. It can also be a clarion call to life as William S. Burroughs put it, as art, play, or make-believe. Aleister Crowley is himself, a paradigmatic example of the extremes implied by such a stance.

"I don't want realism, I want magic," says Blanche Dubois, in *A Streetcar Named Desire.* Aleister Crowley deserves our accolade because of the way he made his entire *life* magical; the way he gave himself the grandest of roles, played against the backdrop of normality which could not but pale in comparison. There is a grandeur and passion which is unequalled in Crowley's life, in the way he laid claim to the events of his time. He played Prospero on the world's stage. This is for me, the essence of Crowley's magic, and his bequest to this latter half of the 20th century. True, he left more than enough to satisfy those who seek consolation in numbers or in shadowed emulation of only a few of his parts. Scottish nobleman, oriental prince, poet, high priest of the mysteries, Great Beast, gargantuan seducer. Whatever he did, Crowley did in *style.* The great conflicts of that era were simply emanations of his will; the turbulent social change of the twenties and thirties no more than the response of the world to the fact of his existence. Understanding the need for spectacle all too well, he ensured that every act of will he made became Spectacular. He fulfilled all the popular scripts for the rebel, from starting his own commune, to living down-and-out in a Parisian garret.

Words imprison. Crowley placed himself beyond all attempts at definition, by turns outraging both his followers, friends, and detractors alike. Critics often point to the contradictions he displayed. He declared himself a holy guru and shat on carpets. He worshipped goddesses and kicked his scarlet women downstairs. He placed himself beyond the pale, and everything paled into insignificance beside him. A great man casts a long shadow, as is evident by those who seek to emulate him. Sad Crowley-wannabes. How he would have laughed. Those who've mastered the heroin habit and the arts of deceiving the weak. But the mountain-climbing and getting extradited from countries will take a little more time. Lacking the strength to discover themselves, they settle for living in the shadow of the Beast.

Crowley was impelled by his sense of destiny. In this modern age, the complete and selfless surrender to the destiny of one's life is something that provokes both admiration and unease. The pursuit of individuality makes total adherence to any one perspective seem suspect. Crowley offered no apologies, no protection, and no comfort for those who sought him out or fell at his feet to learn. In the same way that he surrendered himself to his destiny, he demanded the total surrender of would-be followers—wives, wallets and arseholes were all fair game. Madness and suicide trailed in his wake. Scandal dogged his footsteps, yet he was not dragged down by the failures of his fellows. His modern-day admirers seek to explain his contradictions and justify his acts of moral outrage. Yet Crowley was neither interested in explanations or justifications. The fact of his existence was enough. With the absorption of a child playing his own game, the rules known only to himself, he wandered across the world, immune to disaster and oblivious to the possibility of failure.

It has been said that Crowley would have fitted well into the 1990's. Indeed, Les Miller's play *Raising Hell*, allowed him such a comeback. I am sure that he would have been delighted by modern 'political correctness' and turned it into another magical weapon to bite at the world. He had no time for political causes. He would find laughable the obsession of contemporary pagans with seeking respectability and acceptance. Compromise was not his forté. Indeed, his very unwillingness to compromise is part of

his attraction. We are attracted to him due to the total engagement with his subject which he projects, whether it is charting
the course of his heroin habit or the number of magical blow-
jobs he gives to passing strangers. At no point does he seem to
be saying "this isn't the real me." He does not argue his position
or distance himself from his life, he presents himself with a
matter-of-factness which both attracts and repels.

The myth of Crowley has retained its power and, if anything,
gathered momentum. His face scowls out of the Sergeant
Pepper's Lonely Hearts Club Band cover. His symbols have
crept from his leather-bound editions onto skin, T-shirts and CD-
covers. His advertising copy for his own books has spawned an
entire style. His followers squabble over legal charters and who
has the 'right' to continue his sacred lineage. Though Leaming-
ton Spa's councillors turned down a request to blue-plaque his
birthplace, he has had a tremendous influence upon modern
culture. Crowley deserves our applause if only because he per-
sisted in choosing the life he wanted to live to the end and, in so
doing, achieved a kind of immortality.

The notion of multiple selves also provides a sharp contrast to
the Neoplatonic view of the self—that there is a part of us which
partakes of the Absolute, around which much of magical theory
is based. If there is no 'True Self', then the validity of magical
ideas such as the True Will or Holy Guardian Angel are called
into question. Indeed, both Peter J. Carroll and Dave Lee have
(in different ways) pointed out that from the Chaos perspective at
least, the notion of the Holy Guardian Angel—for so long considered the lynch-pin of a magicians' magical aspiration is fast
approaching obsolescence.

The HGA — Mask of the Void

Personally, I have never found the idea of the Holy Guardian
Angel as a distinct 'being' to be particularly appealing. However
I have found it useful to relate the idea of the HGA to Crowley's
remarks in *Moonchild* concerning the workings of the inner
genius. This is something along the lines that man reduces himself to a negative and allows his genius to come through him as it
will. Rather than interacting with a HGA as a particular entity
with a distinct name, persona and appearance, I have tended to

view the HGA as a temporary 'Mask of the Void'—as a gateway to inspiration and illuminations. Thus, for a while, my 'HGA' was characterised as a shadowy woman with the name 'Azoora' but this has changed as the perspective of my magical interests has changed. Having observed how quickly contacts with 'higher entities' can quickly devolve into pathological obsession—correspondingly degrading the quality of information received from such a contact—I have accordingly kept my conceptualisation of my HGA as deliberately ephemeral. I find Crowley's portrait of the entity LAM—described as "the voice of the silence" to be an apposite example—for that voice can take many forms and speak with many tongues.

The Magical Self:
An Exercise in Empowerment

Creating a Magical Self is a process of deciding what qualities, abilities and skills the magician wishes to acquire, and creating a role which is the encapsulation of these projections. The Magical Self is a persona-mask which the magician 'wears' each time he performs any act of magic. It may be associated with a particular symbol, item of adornment, or clothing. Each act of magic reinforces the role. A related practice is that of adopting magical names. Some magicians choose a name or motto which reflects their magical aspirations. Such names are usually chosen due to association with particular magical concepts. The magician identifies himself with the name—thereby invoking his Magical Self. As the magician develops, so may his name change. An example of a magical name is PACHAD—a Hebrew word which can be translated as 'Fear.' It is also a title of the Cabbalistic Sephiroth GEBURAH, which corresponds to the planet Mars. This name might thus be adopted by a magician who wishes to identify his magician self with a martial current.

There is little point however, in designing a magical persona which merely reinforces qualities that the magician already possesses in abundance. The Magical Self is an invocation of future otherness—a self which one might sense the need of, but has not yet developed the requisite abilities and powers of.

In a sense, the Magical Self is merely a heuristic device. As we begin to practise and live magically, the Magician Self is a temporary identification whilst our magical practice is taken as a particular activity-enclave distinct from the rest of our lives. Indeed, classical magical theory expounds the view that the magician-persona should be kept apart from the rest of our life-experience—a 'secret life' if you will, which is only revealed to fellow initiates. If however, one comes to view magic as a thread which may reveal itself in all aspects of one's life, then the sense of having a distinct Magician Self may become blurred (though not necessarily weakened) as by exerting a magical perspective into 'everyday life,' then one is making one's whole life *magical*.

Working, living and acting within a magical psychocosm, one discovers that the sense of identity becomes inextricably inter-woven with one's magic. There is a graduated progression from magic being something that one is 'interested' in, to something that one is 'engrossed' by, to being a magician more or less full time. In terms of the Chaos approach, this implies continual change, modification of identity, entering different paradigms of belief and behaviour, learning new skills, and shedding life-patterns which have outworn their usefulness. There is thus a shift from a core Ego which is based on differences, the self-other divide, to Exo, the self in a continual process of *engagement*. As one continues to expand and develop the personal psy-chocosm, the size of the social group which reinforces that sense of identity grows smaller.

Self Love

The aim of this process is to reach the point where identity is continually being deconstructed—when a measure of fluidity of expression is attained and one is released from the necessity of seeking self-validation from others. This is what Austin Osman Spare referred to with his doctrine of 'Self Love.' This is no narcissistic basking in the glamours of the ego, rather, it is the discovery of the void at the core of an identity which is freely able to move into any desired set of social relations, without feeling trapped or constrained by them. As the core of the sense of self is 'Self-Love,' rather than any limited label, one attains a state of great freedom of movement and expression.

Self Love does not necessarily imply alienation or withdrawal from Consensus Reality. Modern culture is saturated with escape routes by which one is encouraged to resist the routines of reality. Drugs, sex, fantasy scripts, social enclaves, ideologies, therapies, mindscapes, the past, utopia—all clearly sign-posted escape routes that ultimately, reveal themselves to be dead-ends. This is especially true of so-called revolutionary escape routes—political, alternative lifestyles, magical endeavour. They support, rather than threaten, consensus reality, whilst feeding the illusion of escape. Many of these escape routes require a change in social scripts and masks and do little more than create fragile enclaves within consensus reality, which inevitably are recaptured and recuperated into fashions and trends. While the majority of magical paradigms seek to reject consensus reality in favour of 'higher' states of being, the Chaos approach makes consensus reality into a playground for the phenomenizing of will and desire. By experiencing consensus reality from the basis of Self Love, the magician may begin the long and fascinating process of bringing to earth whatever shards of the Pandaemonaeon— and whatever may lie beyond it—that engage attention.

MICROAEONICS

It is a popular pastime of occultists to search backwards through the tracks of history, selectively editing, and sometimes fabricating evidence to support particular models and propositions. The results of such musings, while incomplete and biased, can sometimes provide useful pointers to understanding present and possible future trends. The following example is a brief tour through the Aeons, examining how social change brings about a change in the relationship between individual and society, and how this change is reflected by magical paradigms.

As societies develop, so too the dominant magical paradigms reflect and reinforce the complexities of consensus reality. Early tribal societies evolved an Otherworld which had many points of contact with their day-to-day experience of reality. The prototypic shamanic otherworld relates to the basic patterns of tribal living: hunting, gathering, ancestor worship, spirits of local flora and fauna, systems of taboo. Often, the otherworld interpenetrates the local landscape. The state of 'participation mystique' in which these cultures are thought to have lived, implies a total fusion of Personal, Social and Mythic Worlds.

Fast-forward into the Pagan Aeon: the growth of settled agriculture, cities, trading—the development of more complex social dynamics. Here, mediation of the Otherworld becomes the function of a specialised priesthood. Eventually there arises a division between state-approved myths and the survival of earlier lore. New pantheons arise, assimilating those of earlier epochs, so that they become subservient to the new order, or are demonized. An example of such a transition can be seen in Ancient Greece, where the Olympian pantheon supplanted the elder, Titanic deities. However, there is still a high degree of overlay between the worlds of experience—the mythic patterns which function to maintain social cohesion become a function of the state, and the sacred topologies of earlier conditions become the sites for formalised ritual and the ceremonial reflection of history.

The transition from polytheism towards monotheism pushes the three worlds of experience apart, as the priesthood seek to maintain social control through the strict regulation of mythic experience. Competing realities are assimilated, or eradicated. Another contributing factor is the rise in the power of the concept of a personal soul, and the idea that each individual engages in a personal relationship with the supreme deity. The growth of monotheist theocracy inevitably produces conflict, as the need to maintain social order requires that transgressions become heresies. Behaviours and beliefs which formerly, were tolerated or socially mediated in the Pagan era become potential disasters that must be contained. Yet at the same time, these problematic areas are promoted by the priesthood, throwing up, as seen in medieval Europe, numerous witch-hunts, and proclamations of the impending end of the world. For example, during the medieval era, the end of the world was variously predicted for 1186, 1229, 1290, 1300,1310, 1325, 1335, 1346, 1360, 1365, 1375, 1395, 1400, 1419, and 1429.

Shifts within a culture's growth are marked by 'seismic' changes during which accepted cultural values are challenged, and there is an explosion of new ideas, beliefs, and behaviours. Such periods are inevitably followed by periods where the threatened orthodoxy attempts to re-establish itself, or accommodate itself to the new situation. The forces that contribute to these seismic shifts are complex, involving demographic change (urbanization, industrialization) economic expansion, technological change, natural disasters, and invasion by a foreign culture which can all contribute to rapid cultural transitions.

As monotheist societies continue to develop, they set up resonances which eventually come to threaten their mythic control of reality. City-states grow into national monarchies, money economics replaces qualitative exchange, and commercial growth leads to the establishment of commercial law. Vendettas or blood-feuds are replaced by law courts. The official perception of the monotheist society is that of a community of the faithful wherein the individual is placed as an obedient servant of the one God, and his masters. In the early stages of monotheism in Europe, penance for transgressions is characterized by communal confessions and exclusion from the community. However, by the 12th Century, this communal experience was largely replaced by individual confession and personal negotiation with a priest. The individual's quest for salvation and the private relationship with the divine was superseding the communal participation of earlier phases. It is also significant that the *intention* to transgress became more significant than the actions alone. This growth in the concept of the individual also gives power to a new concept of citizenship, and hence, rights and duties, and the notion of individual conscience. As monotheist culture develops, there is an increasing shift from communally-determined social maintenance, towards personal involvement. This, together with the rise of logic and reason, inevitably brings the individual into conflict with the orthodoxy as heresies of behaviour and belief are identified. Threats to the stability of the Mythic control system are responded to via witch-hunts, scape-goating, and wars. Any magical paradigms which survive in these conditions tend to be theurgical, stress the personal union with the divine, be highly symbolic, and yet also reflect the relationship between the individual (microcosm) and the Whole (macrocosm). Thus magic, from this era, is redefined as a route to personal salvation, rather than an engagement with a Mythic World which paralleled social reality.

As monotheist society becomes increasingly complex, the rise of technology and economics, together with reason and logic, leads to a division between the temporal and the spiritual. The temporal becomes the domain of logic, reason, and law, whilst the spiritual remains in the hands of the priesthood. As individuals gain more freedom of belief and action, the importance of the spiritual realm of experience is eclipsed by the growth of materialist philosophy, which regards Mythic experience as unimportant. As monotheism becomes less influential, new forms of mythic experience arise, in response to social change and new ideas. Religion, as an agent of social control, becomes supplanted by law, social morality, and agencies created by government.

At this point, the individual experience of consensus reality is divorced from the social (communal) or Mythic (religious) worlds. Personal experience becomes paramount. In western society, religious concepts of the soul were displaced by the fragmentation of the self into divisions—higher and lower self, id, ego, superego. Science took over as the narrator of internal experience, and mythic experience was dismissed as escapism, fantasy, or mental aberration. The notion of a purely mechanistic universe gained force as Enlightenment thinkers attempted to develop an objective science which one day would discover universal laws, and develop rational forms of social organization which would free humanity from religion, myth, superstition and the randomness of nature. Doctrines of universal reason, liberty and equality became popular, together with optimism for the future and utopian thinking.

By the 19th century, the erosion of religion and the rise of scientific determinism, together with rapid social changes, the influx of new ideas and the proliferation of new movements in arts and literature, produced a condition where occult beliefs could come forth. Spiritualism, Psychic Research, and Theosophy became popular movements, to be followed, later, by the occult fraternities, such as the Hermetic Order of the Golden Dawn.

These later developments are particularly important, as they set up patterns of thinking which modern magic is only recently beginning to extricate itself from. By this time, the Mythic world of the magician had become almost entirely abstract and symbolized, using, for example, Jacob's Ladder as the basic map for Mythic experience. Here the only points of contact are the physical and mental worlds, which are on the lowest rungs of the ladder which climbs away from earth into abstract spaces—the planes of spirit. These systems placed great emphasis on transcendental experience; upon the union of the individual self with the divine totality. In many ways, these occult movements reflected the concerns of the Enlightenment—a scientific understanding of mythic experience, a concern with the structuring and codification of the universe. These systems were also attempts to create a meta-narrative; a model which, given time, would account for and explain everything. This can be seen as much in the vast tracts of doctrine produced by the Theosophists as in the carefully cross-referenced systems of the Golden Dawn. The faith in higher powers, the masters or inner-plane adepti, also reflects the Enlightenment vision of wise sages who, while existing outside society, would exercise extraordinary power over it.

The supreme optimism of the Enlightenment was shattered somewhat by the Great War and the chaos that followed it. Following the war, there was a rise in interest in Occultism, particularly Psychic Research and Spiritualism. The utopian idealism of the Enlightenment was cracking, beginning to show the darkness gathering behind the dream. For occultists, the forces that swept across the world in those tumultuous first decades of the 20th century, are encapsulated in that mythic magus of the apocalypse: Aleister Crowley. Crowley was the supreme Faustian avatar of the Modernist world; one who felt the necessity of challenging traditional values and religious myths; a destroyer of the old ways, in order to build a brave new universe from the rubble of the old. Crowley can be seen as a Dionysian messenger of the Modernist vision—a creative, heroic effort, prepared to sweep away everything which does not fit into the total vision. Like Faust, Crowley became a tragic figure, as much changed by the creative destruction which was his message, as the world through which he moved. Crowley was not, however, the sole prophet of this vision. Artists, writers, poets and philosophers resorted to shock tactics and dramatic gestures.

In the inter-war years, the tensions in the West multiplied. Modernist thought wavered between a fascination with machine-rationalism and reactionary mythologies. These themes can be seen within the Futurist and Surrealist movements. The search for an overall mythic vision which could cushion against the quake-shocks of social chaos. The marriage of machine-rationalism and a total, encompassing myth brought forth National Socialism in Germany. The Second World War was the last act in this phase of development, curtained by the blossoming of mushroom clouds as the Lord of Fire set his foot against the world.

If nothing else, the emergence of the demonic face of the Modernist vision may act as a warning to those who would construct a single overall vision and then seek to realise it at any cost. The vision of a utopian future remains as a powerful glamour for many, even in the closing act of this century. In the post-war years, the Modernist dream was recovered by, and developed for the advantage of corporate and national power-blocs. Movements within art and literature that had initially been revolutionary became part of the establishment; the province of a cultural elite. Meanwhile, the towers of the brave new world rose across the cities of the west, producing mass alienation as entire communities were displaced into high-rise flats. The trend towards uniformity in all aspects of life displaced the personal.

The 1960s have been identified as the second occult explosion of this century. The various counter-culture movements arose against the crushing conformity of state bureaucracy, rationalism, and growing institutionalized power. Resistance took the form of new styles which emphasized individuality and self-consciousness, together with the search for meaning and spiritual vision. Cults and sects proliferated, catering for the growing drive to seek meaningful vision and myth which challenged the Protestant ethic and the uniformity of social space. Thirty years on, it is too easy to judge this experiment a failure. The optimism for a new world can be seen as a lingering influence of the shards of Modernism, yet the melting-pot of beliefs, styles, and the individual quest for meaning brought forth the current phase of development: Postmodernism, and its emergent magical ethos— Chaos Magic.

Postmodernism can be characterized as a multi-cultural, multi-stylistic cauldron bubbling with competing experiences and attitudes, lacking any coherent overall narrative. Modern society is chaotic and fragmentary, coming increasingly to resemble a fractal structure; a bewilderingly complex organism, in contrast to the stark functionalism of the Modernist style. Diversity rules, in a display of increasingly fragmented subcultures and nested beliefs, all jostling for attention in the marketplace. Mass communication systems have shrunk the world, and it is possible to discern a wide variety of cultural styles and epochs melting together in music, art, fashion, literature, and food. The profusion of magical and mythological systems available to the modern occultist also demonstrates this trend. Magical subcultures multiply and coexist within a complexity of belief and orientation which outsiders to the scenes find difficult to grasp. At the same time, the distinction between magical enclaves becomes blurred as individuals are able to cross back and forth between them. Although modern magicians, like their forebears, tend to identify themselves as being apart from the rest of modern culture, magic, as with any other product, is swayed by trends and fashions.

As a cultural trend, Postmodernism breaks with the Modernist idea of progress and historical continuity, and instead, ransacks all available cultures and time-zones in a diverse exercise in collage. The *immediacy* of experience becomes the important

factor, rather than continuity with any past or projection into any
one future. Thus, an appropriate slogan for this age would be
Mutate and Survive. Nothing is finalised or formalised, but
merely re-arranged.

This is an age where magic might thrive. The search to establish magic on a solid footing, using scientific glamours or gambits to achieve respectability, can be seen as transient phases,
linguistic games for amusement, or deliberate tactics to create
free areas for the manipulation of belief and projection of image.
As a speaker at a conference on Ley Lines put it: *Stop looking
for facts, believe what you like, and have fun!* The different
strands of alternative belief may find themselves winding
together, as participants borrow ideas and tactics from each
other, rewriting them for their own specific glamours. Magic
becomes another approach for survival in the shifting labyrinth
of modern life. As much a form of entertainment as anything
else—if current trends continue, no form of human experience
will be judged to have any higher value than any other.

It can also be seen that modern imaging techniques have
acquired a magical dimension, if not a magical ethos, behind
them. Whilst there is a cultural trend towards the fleeting, the
ephemeral, the transient; and while the pace of modern life is
ever-increasing, all Control Systems are increasingly projecting
an aura of stability and foundation as part of their authority. This
reflects the rising nostalgia for common values, a shared social
past, and universal, traditional values. As the social matrix
becomes increasingly subject to rapid fluctuations, throwing out
anchors into a collectivised past becomes more prominent than
movement into a future. The desire to establish a core identity
within the profusion of styles has led to image-building to
become an industry in itself; as much reflected by the tactics of
political groups and corporate bodies, as in the fetishistic
scramble for designer labels and trendy occult symbols. Identity
has therefore become another commodity to be traded in the
marketplace. The gulf between objective icons and the illusory
has widened to such an extent that illusions come to have an
equal value.

Approaching the PandemonAeon

For contemporary magicians, the sense of being on the leading edge of cultural transition tends to be encapsulated in the concept of a new Aeon. Thus the profusion of 'new aeons' projected by various magical groups and individuals. So as not to be seen to be missing an essential item in their magical script, some Chaos Magicians have begun to project the glamour of the Fifth Aeon—the Pandemonaeon.

The concept of a new aeon has several magical functions:

1. It provides a filter through which the magician can examine current social trends, possible developments, and how they may be influenced.
2. It acts as an Ideosphere for the development of new ideas, concepts and techniques from outside the boundaries of his present Achievable Reality.
3. It can become a meta-aim to unify groups and orders towards working for a common goal, and act as a gambit to aid the design of possible futures.

Unlike many of the prevailing new aeons, the Pandemonaeon is envisaged as being different for each individual who projects himself within its frame. Just as Chaos Magic emerges from the diversity and transience of modern culture, so does the Pandemonaeon typify the trend towards individualism becoming separate from any totalizing belief or narrative, be it metaphysical or scientific. So far, it has not been projected as an overall epoch that all will participate in, but an experience of culture which embraces, rather than attempting to resist the modern condition. Thus it is likely that this aeon is merely a transitory stage itself, and what lies beyond it, none can, with any certainty, say. Some Chaos Magicians are finding that this Fifth Aeon projection is useful for going beyond current definitions and limitations concerning what is accepted as magical. The next generation of magi might well discard the concept, in favour of a meta-projection which balances their experience of culture, with what possibilities are round the corner. The absence of inevitable future projections leaves only uncertainties, where nothing is true, and everything is permitted.

Ideospheres

The Ideosphere is a non-local space entered by the magician in order to explore possible models and paradigms which may be of use in configuring the Pandemonaeon. The Ideosphere is more of an attitude; a stance from which the magician can seek inspiration from any incoming information, be it newspaper articles, cartoons, flickering media images, scientific jargon, random acronyms, or half-heard phrases from another's conversation. An idea flashes into the Ideosphere; the magician may grasp it immediately or store it for later work. The main attitude to foster is that nothing, no matter how ridiculous, bizarre or unworkable should be rejected. Working from the Ideosphere, the magician allows himself to bathe in the emanations of the mass media until, sated and bloated, he withdraws into silence to digest, regurgitate, and create new forms.

Latching onto new ideas brings forth new perspectives on existing models and techniques. It brings forth new paradigms for structuring magical processes which in turn may yield new techniques and applications. Here are a few ideas which magicians have appropriated from other sources, and made their own.

Virus Systems

A powerful source of inspiration is the understanding of, and fascination with, Virus Behaviour, whether it be the computer viruses which have revealed themselves to be the gremlins of the information age, or the biological viruses such as H.I.V, which is promoting vast amounts of research into how viruses behave. A third type of virus which has caught the imagination is the word-virus, or meme.

A virus is a set of instructions which invades larger systems, and induces them to carry out a complex sequence of replications which bring new copies of the virus into existence, and, during this process, the host system is altered in some way. This is true for computer viruses, biological viruses, and word-viruses. The emerging magical use of virus systems opens up new forms of understanding and applications alike.

The Word Virus

Like organisms, memes replicate to perpetuate themselves; like organisms they are capable of fusion, recombination and mutation. They propagate themselves by leaping between nervous systems, growing in power and infecting further host vehicles through any communications channel that can be utilised to secure them a niche. Memes compete ruthlessly with each other, for the command of the perceptual field and transmission time. The success of a meme to occupy a prominent position in the host environment is dependent on its Performance Value (Pv) and its Propagation Quotient (Pq). Performance Value relates to the degree of change a meme brings to an individual or group. If the presence of a meme brings about increased cohesiveness, ambition and confidence, then the individual or group is more likely to promote the meme. The most successful memes are those which reduce anxiety in their hosts by providing a purpose or a stable location within a social space.

Some memes survive by reinforcing each other, supporting each other's message; reinforcing the overall impact. Other memes survive by discouraging rational analysis upon their content.

An obvious example of memes in action is religion. 'God' is a meme, 'Heaven' is a meme, and the punishment of 'eternal damnation' is a meme. A complex web of memes is known as a Scheme, which are comprehensive meshes of memes that propagate themselves through any available communications channel. The religious schemes which have almost totally infected the human environment are successful as they offer varying degrees of stability, participation, and can become tacitly self-evident to the level that they become not merely the host's worldview, but the world itself. The infected hosts live entirely within the parameters of the scheme, perhaps only vaguely aware of other worlds which exist beyond the scheme. Worlds which threaten the stable order of the invading scheme must be ignored, forced back, fought, or destroyed.

Of course the spread of a meme is dependent upon the reaction of the potential host. A sense of being a unique individual with a clear purpose in life is a strong human requirement in the current age, as the sense of being an individual distinct from any cultural attachments becomes progressively stronger. The deeply-felt alienation felt by many in these first stirrings of the Pandemonaeon makes them ripe hosts for infection by memes, locking individuals into safe spaces from which they can push back the buzzing, booming confusion of the everyday world. Understanding the spread of memes leads the magician into the area of *Control Commands*—autonomic responses locked into language and patterns of thought. A growing concern for Pandemonaeonic magicians is the design of new approaches to conceptualizing, with attendant meta-languages for escaping the old habits of thinking. William S. Burroughs targets particular semantic traps which lock the human host into a narrow range of thinking: the definite article 'THE', the 'IS' of identity that does not allow for wider possibilities and assigns permanent status to verbal labels, the 'EITHER/OR' that only allows being wrong or being right. Crowley was on the right track when he urged his students to delete 'I' from their language. With no dominant 'I' there can appear a legion of selves: loose the daemons. Delete 'EITHER/OR' and open up a myriad of possibilities, none of which need to be wrong or right.

Viral Texts

One of the simplest manifestations of viral text is the chain-letter, which uses the simple, yet effective carrot & stick hook to propagate itself. A more insidious form of viral text shows up in thought and behaviour patterns. Consider the statement:

THE ILLUMINATI (x) ARE TAKING OVER (y) THE WORLD (z)

The explicit message of this statement is not important. The implied message is that group 'x' is attempting to do something 'y' to group 'z'. It is also implied that the recipients of the message should be (a) concerned, and (b) do something about it, lest they be perceived by the sender as siding with 'x'—the enemy. Beware of anyone who in all seriousness acts using viral messages, which have been one of the standby props of orthodoxy, be it political, religious, or magical. To propagate effectively, viral texts require potential hosts to be susceptible to the idea of an enemy group, action against which coheres their own sense of identity. Once a viral message is allowed to take root, then the host is open to invasion by other supportive memes—BEING RIGHT, and GETTING EVEN. Sources of much trouble and stupid, destructive behaviour.

Replicants

In orthodox magic, great store is set upon a magical object being special or unique. There are the instructions to create unique talismans, buy virgin parchment, and to create objects for a specific purpose. There is said to be power in a unique object, particularly in these times or mass production and marketing.

But wait, there is power in mass production, too. Consider the chaosphere, the central logo or glyph of Chaos Magic. It appears on books, magazines, letterheads, toy soldiers, jewelry and tattoos. It is used on rave posters and on the back of leather jackets. It has become itself a viral image. All that is required is a shift in perception and those thousands of chaospheres, wherever they are, become gateways for the ingress and egress of magical power.

Take two: A sorcerer acquires for himself a suitable receptacle for an act of magic. A three-inch high pink, plastic creature with a mane of fibrous hair, sometimes known as a 'Gonk.' There are thousands, perhaps even millions of Gonks in existence. All with a similar structure. So the sorcerer enchants upon *his* Gonk, and by the principle of Structural-Similarity, transmits that information to all the others. What he has here is the creation of a powerful Gonk-spirit, its qualities and attributions an encapsulation of the associations which are marketed as the 'image' of the Gonk. He has empowered the Gonks with spirit, and his own Gonk becomes the controller. In times of need, he can draw through his Gonk, the power of the others.

Take three: A young man is desirous of a lover. He sigilises his desire and likes the image so much that instead of destroying it, he photocopies it and disperses the images randomly. Lovers appear from all directions.

Objects need not be particularly striking or special to be magically useful. All that need happen is that the magician defines that object as magical—combining image, associations, and will. Rather than resisting mass replication, the magician turns it to his advantage.

Viral Servitors

A further application of virus systems emerging in Chaos Magic is the creation and application of Servitors which have the capacity to replicate, mutate, and recombine into new forms. Viral servitors, behaving in a similar manner to biological or computer viruses, are now beginning to propagate in virtual space, performing functions such as healing, protection, and seeding ideas into the general meme-pool.

The C.H.A.O.S Virus

In order to infuse humanity with the Pandemonaeonic currents, one must look to very basic restrictions, from which more complex bindings depend. The C.H.A.O.S Virus recovers the chaosphere both as icon of infectivity and a magical gateway for the transmission of Fifth Aeon emanations. The virus acts to bring about *change*, but at a microscopic level of processing. The intrusion of the virus into a human self-complex acts to stimulate those selves which desire CHANGE—in terms of new ideas, pleasure, intelligence, adaptability, and FUN.

Each time a self within an individual stirs towards CHANGE, then the virus copies itself. Note that much of these stirrings are likely to take place at a latent, unintentional level of information-processing. Acting over time, the virus acts to weaken ego-resistance to CHANGE, new ideas, new learning, and fun. As the virus cells propagate, they combine in groups of eight, to become the virtual shadows of new selves—potential desires, growing within the web of selves, stirring impulses from beyond the confines of the ego.

From the moment that the C.H.A.O.S Virus is projected, *every* chaosphere in existence on the planet, be it an astral form, image, or object (and any new ones which come into existence) becomes a transmission site for the virus.

The virus also prepares the host for further reinforcement which may take the form of seeded memes, enchantments, image projections, or sonic sorceries. The virus transmits itself using the principle of Structural-Similarity, so that anything resembling a sphere or circle intersected by eight vertices, will transmit the virus.

Meta-Languages

Strange languages are very much part of the overall glamour of magic, from Barbaric names of invocation to the use of foreign languages such as Hebrew or Sanskrit. All magical systems tend to generate their own technical language for describing magical experiences and techniques within a common framework. Like the technical terms used by scientists and specialists, terminology can act as a barrier for the uninitiated, if the use of special language causes description to become so opaque that no one outside the specialist group understands what is being said.

Magicians create meta-languages not only as magical tools for acts of magic, but to open up shades of experience which are difficult to describe clearly, given the current restrictions of language. The aim here is greater precision in communication. Wordless communications can be developed for experimental work in telepathy and astral magic. Experiments in these areas suggest that visual images, colours, and pictographs are easier to transmit between individuals in dream or astral space, than words alone. So attempts have been made to create communications systems based on the use of colour, spatial perspectives, and contextual imagery and settings, in attempting to establish communications in shared dreaming or attempts to link awareness in astral space.

Simulation-Visualisation

The arrival of information technology is influencing contemporary magic in different ways. Perhaps the most obvious is the use of Desk-Top Publishing and Electronic Mail which allows presentation and circulation of information. But the computer revolution is also enhancing the basic techniques of magic.

The use of three-dimension computer graphics is changing the ability to internally represent space. It has been observed that for some, the capacity to visualize objects, locations and events internally can be enhanced by playing computer games and working with computer-generated images. While visual perception is generated from the continuous tracking of images by the eyes, computer images are generated from a series of linked frames. Those who have problems visualizing can try building up a complex image slowly, using a series of stop-motion frames. By borrowing computer generated special effects, the magician can for example, zoom onto a visualised entity, or visualize an entity growing from an original cell, containing sigil-DNA, to any entity which possesses a nervous system and other desired organs.

Probability Scattering

Occasionally it may be beneficial to enchant for possibilities which do not exist as considered options within one's perceived range. Probability Scattering is a technique which enables the magician to enchant towards low-probability events which lie beyond the range of possible options perceived at any one time with reference to particular spheres of operation. For example, in works of magical inspiration, it may be desirable to enchant for fresh sources of inspiration from areas that one would not usually look towards.

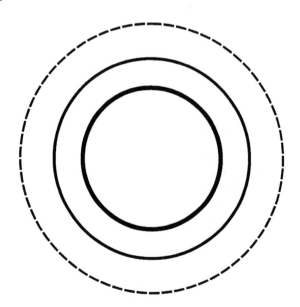

The diagram shows three bands of probability. The Outer band represents events of a low probability which have not yet become manifest. The Middle band represents events of a higher probability which are at present, conscious possibilities which have not yet become fully coherent. The Inner band represents high-probability events which from the magicians' current viewpoint, are already in the process of unfolding.

Method

Using the diagram as a free area, formulate general statement of intent. For example *It is my will to draw inspiration from unlikely sources*. Enter Gnosis by any preferred route, and make a rune-cast across the bands. Quickly scan the runes within the bands, moving from the Outer band inwards, making an assessment of what trends are indicated. Link the runes into a barbarous word of enchantment, again, moving from the outermost rune inwards, and vibrate it with all your power. Follow with immediate banishing.

This technique combines elements of divination and enchantment. Since there is no specific statement of intent, then the problem of 'lust of result' is to some extent, circumvented. It also bypasses, to varying degrees, the decision-making processes of the Ego-complex. In enchantments for inspiration, the results tend to manifest as creative ideas sparked from sources which previously, the magician has not given an attention to, due to lack of interest or prejudice.

Cut-Ups as Sorcery

From the juxtaposition of word and image, meaning is glimpsed. From the Chaos of the normal is woven apparent simplicity. All the secrets of magic are on open display. That which is truly hidden is our own resistance to this realisation. To live within the confines of Consensus Reality is to remain locked in Time: Past–Present–Future. In this sense, all magical acts are scripts for momentary *slips* through the fabric. Magic takes place outside of Time.

Through the simple technique of Cut-Up, pioneered by Brion Gysin as a literary technique, the magician can collapse sequential experience into syncretic Gnosis. The basic technique is

simple enough when applied to text: Take a page of text, cut into
4 sections and re-paste. New word lines and messages appear.
This disruption of the sequence of language creates *Tangential
Deliriums*—new messages arising from the juxtapositions of
words and the derangement of the associations this provokes.
Cut up texts on magic to discover new magick. Cut up *The Book
of The Law* and discover any amount of new chapters.

There are parallels with this method and the more obvious
tools of magic: sigils as cut-ups of desire, for example. Divination systems that cut-up a subject into image blocks, throwing up
insights, new images, gestalts. Reshuffle beliefs by deliberately
holding two contradictory belief systems—make meaning from
nonsensical beliefs. Cut-Up belief to understand its dynamics.

Third Mind

Record two different conversations. Then record them onto the
same tape. Intercut with street noises, television fragments, read-
ings from texts and newspapers. Record, replay, and intercut.
Result—a Third Mind. The 'absent' source of information which
slides in to the listeners' awareness, arises from the Time Disorientation induced by listening to the tape.

Why Time Disorientation? All routes to Gnosis act to temporarily dislocate the Ego. The Ego requires Time (sequence) to
maintain the fiction of single identity. Text and logical thinking
are sequential. One step at a time, one unit following another.
While attention is selective, the creative spark is associative and
syncretic. A great deal of magical practice rests on the ability of
the mind to make associative connections. Any stimulus which is
strong enough to evoke emotion and memory throws awareness
out of sequential Time. Smell particularly, is a hotline to memory. Instant access.

Word juxtapositions throw up new messages. Image juxtapositions open new worlds. Modern media presentations particularly in the visual arts, are increasingly utilising the Cut-Up technique: the layering of images and associations serving to collapse
Time-sense. Elements of Past, Present and possible Futures may
be evoked simultaneously in a single visual image. The news
media works to change the context of a message to create new
hidden meanings, acting under the illusion of 'objectivity.

Practical Applications

1. Divination

Create a montage of sounds, images, associations for a particular day of the week. For example, 'capture' Monday onto tape. Intercut with verbal messages which you associate with Monday; add street noises, random conversations. Intercut and playback. You have created a platform for voyages into Oracular space. Sounds, images, associations arise from the assembly. The tape can be used as a background for dream control or scrying. Stranger still, you may hear sounds on the tape that you were not aware of recording. A truck passes. Days later, you hear the sound of the truck in the street, and you are jerked sideways into oracular time.

2. Enchantment

Enchantment may be considered an act of collage. Assemble the elements you desire to affect and re-arrange. It is already done with objects and images, so why not sounds too? Assemble a soundscape as in the example above, which relates to the object of the enchantment. Recording captures the target space in the same way that a bottle traps a spirit. A recording can be taken away and altered, and then returned to the original location and replayed.

3. Emotional Engineering

Emotions can be deconstructed into three elements: physiological arousal, cognitive association and behaviour patterns. Each of these are separate tracks on a mixing desk, capable of being remixed in new arrangements. When in a state of extreme arousal (anger, sorrow, tension) the first step is to experience the physiological track apart from behaviour and cognition. Remove the identification with the source of the emotion. Still all internal dialogues, inner conversations, mental fantasies. Experience sensation without words or images. Here the magician is dislocated in Time; pure sensation without identification. In this state, any act of magic may be performed. To re-engineer emotions, experience the arousal as ecstasy. Dispassionately run the word/image track and adjust accordingly. Identify behavioural patterns and remodel them. Name the selves, capture their inner dialogues, intercut and playback.

The use of Cut-Up is naturally enhanced by keeping diaries, scrapbooks, recordings, and most importantly, being aware of what is happening outside one's immediate field of attention.

PART II

DYNAMIC RITUAL

INTRODUCTION

Aleister Crowley defined the objective of ritual in terms of the uniting of the Microcosm with the Macrocosm. This is a somewhat broad definition, but one that would be generally recognised by magicians in theistic cultures worldwide. According to Hindu magical doctrine, for example, the purpose of ritual is to use special techniques to make contact with the higher states of being which we call gods, and other supernatural beings who can guide and assist us in our efforts to progress. The different worlds are in harmonic relation to each other; and through ritual action, they can be made to respond, just as a stringed instrument will respond when one of its harmonics resounds. Ritual, a combination of sound, forms, rhythms, gestures, flowers, lights, incense and offerings carries the operator toward the world of the divine, whilst the deity, also enchanted, is brought nearer. Ritual is thus a bridge to establish and maintain this contact.

In less prosaic terms, the aim of ritual is to focus the awareness of the participants in particular ways, according to a previously-defined schema. Again, this definition is necessarily broad, since there are a great many approaches to, styles of, and categories of ritual practice; from full-blown ceremonial magic utilising robes, banners, and props carefully arranged to represent a particular magical system, to on-the-spot improvisation. The latter may be just as effective as the former; power—as arises from skill—resides in the ritualist, not the words, gestures or symbols alone.

By performing ritual, we enter a space in which all normal limitations on the barriers to what is possible are swept aside. A space in which we are reminded of all that is mysterious and awe-inspiring, if only momentarily. A space where we might conspire with Gods or dance with demons.

Are Rituals Necessary?

Whilst most magical traditions contain some element of ritual, it should be understood that ritual practice is but one aspect of magic, albeit a popular one. Like any other approach to magic, ritual can be extremely efficacious if used wisely, but equally, its effectiveness is greatly reduced if the practitioner becomes 'locked' into a repetitive pattern or approach to it.

There are arguments both for and against the practice of ritual magic. One popular argument is that ritual is unnecessary—that if one has developed magical skills, then one can "do everything in one's head," or "on the astral." Both these viewpoints contain a grain of merit. It is possible to bring about magical results without recourse to ritual procedures. This is known as Empty-Handed magic. Equally, one can enact rituals on the astral without any physical props or actions. However, such arguments often reveal more about their exponents than anything else. I often feel that arguments that you can do magic entirely in your head or on the astral reflect a certain contempt (or disassociation) from physical experience. The belief that the astral worlds are more refined, more 'spiritual' than dreary old 'mundane reality' is attractive for some people, who tend to try on a kind of magical one-upmanship. Unfortunately, if your magical work has few connections with your physical circumstances, it is all to easy to drift off into the astral dream that you are a mighty magus—as Shakespeare put it, a "king of infinite space."

For me, the crux of the matter is that ritual magic is fun. Moreover, ritual magic is a skill. A magical ritual is more than the sum of its parts. Ritual has elements of performance, and its own psychology; yet it would be a mistake to consider ritual to be merely psychodrama. Ritual can be broken down into the arrangement of sensory cues, voice technique, gesture, visualisation, movement, symbolism, role-shifting and trance induction, yet it is more than any of this. Unaccountably, rituals, when performed, create an atmosphere—a space—in which something mysterious and wonderful may happen. If nothing else, ritual demonstrates how little we know of our potential, of ourselves, and the world through which we move.

What Constitutes A Ritual?

We can identify events such as the Japanese Tea Ceremony as an example of ritual behaviour, although it is certainly different in content and purpose to the Catholic Communion Mass. The cues that we can identify in order to distinguish ritual from non-ritual

behaviour are often subtle degrees of emphasis. Changing from
one set of clothes to another can become a kind of ritual, particularly if your movements become overly stylised and you become
aware that by changing clothes in this fashion, you are changing
some aspect of your awareness in accordance with a particular
desire or aim. Hence ritual serves to focus attention. The difference between a normal gesture and a magical gesture (i.e., one in
the context of a ritual or other magical action) is one of delibera-
tion and emphasis. For a simple example, try the distinction of
simply taking a drink from a cup and then making that action a
formal toast. The action is the same—the difference comes in the
way you do it, and your awareness of the deliberateness of your
movements. To understand how group ritual can build up a particular atmosphere try the same exercise with a group of people.
First everyone takes a drink as he would normally. Then each
person in turn, makes the actions of a formal, deliberate toast.
The point is that if you do any action, however seemingly mundane, in a deliberate way, it feels different. When a whole group
of people perform that action, it takes on another degree of dis-
tinctiveness.

Another core element of ritual which is related to attention
and deliberateness is that of sequence. Rituals often follow, or
contain, particular sequences of actions and events. The repetition of actions is considered a key element in psychological
definitions of ritual. For example, repetitive hand-washing
behaviour can be explained as an unconscious ritual to ward off
anxiety. Repetition can be a powerful technique in ritual—in the
chanting of words or phrases, the repetition of movement, gesture, dance steps etc.—which I will explore in due course. For
the moment however, let us concentrate on sequencing. Magical
rituals tend to follow a pre-defined sequence, which, at its most
simplest, is a beginning, a middle, and an end. A rather obvious
point you might think, but the recognition of where and when a
ritual begins or ends is not always clear. If we recognise that a
key to understanding rituals is that they have a distinct quality of
experience to them, then we need to pay particular attention to
how the transition is made both towards and away from that
quality. It is common for modern magicians to begin rituals with
a sub-ritual (complete in itself) which marks the opening and
closing transitions of a ritual event. This is generally known as

the Banishing Ritual, and I will look at this specific form of ritual more closely later.

What can be done with ritual?

Ritual Magic can be used for:

a) Self-Change
b) Sorcery
c) Insight
d) Meditation
e) Celebration
f) Psychodrama
g) Demonstration of technique
h) Momentary suspension of embedded rules
i) Work with particular God/Goddess-form
j) Grounding oneself
k) Focusing on a specific issue/task/problem

This list is by no means exhaustive, it is simply to give you an idea of the possibilities.

CORE ELEMENTS OF RITUAL

Rituals are processes in themselves, where different elements combine to help the participant create the Free Area where magic becomes vibrant and alive. To understand the ritual process is important, so that rather than slavishly following someone else's written sequence, the magician may create his own.

1. Familiarity v. Risk

Rituals usually contain some elements which are familiar to the participants, and some elements which are new and therefore place them at risk. Familiar elements include warm-up exercises such as a Banishing, or techniques which the participants have used before. Risk elements include anything which is being tried out for the first time, and anything which requires improvisation, or freedom of action from participants. A script can only be followed to a certain point. After that point is passed, the participants must be on their toes, for anything might (and often does) happen.

The ritualist must be responsive to each moment as it happens. For example, a ritual might be designed to invoke a particular deity into a chosen person, for purposes of oracle or inspiration. It can happen that the chosen 'vehicle' for the deity does not achieve the required state—but someone else participating might.

In this example (and it is by no means uncommon), a group of ritualists who cannot move beyond their script are likely to struggle onwards, unaware of what is happening within the ritual process. A responsive and observant group, however, will be able to improvise, adapting to the new situation as it changes. This is largely a matter of confidence and hands-on experience. To learn ritual magic, like anything else, requires that the safety of the familiar be challenged with the necessity of taking risks. Of course, any ritual involves risk. The first time that one performs a ritual, one expects something strange to happen. This is usually enriched by a nagging fear of what might happen if somehow, one does it wrong. After one has done the same ritual a hundred times, one may be lulled into a sense of complacency, which is equally risky. For strange things happen just as often as when they are not expected, as when they are. The risk of ritual, is part of its glamour, and part of its power.

2. Belief Shapes the Power of Ritual

Veracity of belief is a cornerstone to ritual magic. This has several levels to it. The core belief, that Magic Works can only become embedded through experience. Another level—how far, and how much magic can work very much depends on one's dominant explanation of how magic works. Chaos Magicians have identified four basic models of how magic works. These are the Spirit Model, the Energy Model, the Psychological Model, and the Cybernetics Model. Each model has different strengths and weaknesses when it comes to explaining magical effects and phenomena. Each model also tends to develop its own terminology and frames of reference. Different systems of magic can be seen to have varying degrees of each model, and since magic, like any other field of human endeavour, follows general trends in thinking, there are different trends in magical models. Until fairly recently, the predominant model of magic was the *Spirit Model*. According to the Spirit Model, all entities (Gods, Goddesses, demons, elementals, angels, servitors, etc.) are real, and have a separate existence from those of us who would dare to deal with them. Humans and otherworld entities have a reciprocal relationship with each other.

The *Energy Model* arose in the West with the new discoveries of science (electricity, magnetism, and so forth) and the Western imports of the Eastern philosophies such as Tantra. The Energy Model might explain the discrete entities of the Spirit Model in terms of subtle energies which take the form of entities when viewed by limited human senses. So they are not separate beings which their own existence and purpose, but energies which we have clothed in form, so as to work with them.

The *Psychological Model* grew out of the rise of Psychoanalysis, particularly the work of Carl Gustav Jung, and has come to be the dominant model for explaining magical phenomena. In the Psychological Model, the Gods, Elementals, Demons, etc., have no existence beyond the human mind—they are merely symbols or archetypes of deep parts of the human psyche.

The *Cybernetics Model* is just beginning to creep in as magicians begin to speculate about the nature of magic as revealed through the lens of Information Sciences. As yet it remains incomplete, but a cybernetics-based view of magical entities might say that they are information systems which have the capacity to be self-organising, and which arise out of our participation in a complex web of systems: including personal belief, group belief, environmental systems, and the very fabric of reality itself.

But enough of theory. When, within the Free Area of ritual, it is best to believe that the elements that one is working with, be they gods, guardian spirits, allies, etc., are real. In this respect, it may be useful to ask oneself which model gives the greatest glamour of being a magician? Sending forth calls thundering through time and space to bring oneself to the attention of some mighty, ancient being, or performing a sequence of actions which allow a latent aspect of Self to rise into awareness? Which sounds more risky and exciting? If the entity being summoned is a part of the self, can much go awry? If, on the other hand, it is a being with all the powers, will, and regality of an ancient Goddess or Spirit, then how much more important is it that the ritual be performed to the height of one's ability—with style, respect, and awe. Choosing the most appropriate glamour will produce a concordant emotional intensity, and Chaos Magicians tend to the view that ritual should be intense, else all is mere play-acting. And remember, the models we create to explain the mysterious are just that, models, not the territory itself. Models cannot adequately contain the mysterious; and ritual, for all the explanations written, remains at the heart, a space where the mysterious may intrude into our lives.

3. Dramatic Awareness

This term is used to draw a parallel between Ritual and performance. Together, the performers and audience of a masque or play can build up an atmosphere which can be felt by all present.

The audience listen to what is happening onstage, empathise and react. This reaction is communicated to the actors, which in turn affects their performance. Thus an atmosphere of "Dramatic Awareness"—a shifting of awareness towards the mythic arena of experience—can quickly be generated. If the audience is familiar with the myths or struggles being displayed on stage, then the experience may be cathartic for all concerned.

Something similar occurs during a magical ritual, particularly in Group rituals, where the participation of all those within a Free Area contributes towards each individual's experience of the ritual. In ritual time, all senses are heightened, and small microscopic changes in a participants' behaviour (for example, voice tone, body language, or postural shifts) may not be obviously apprehended, but nevertheless contribute to shifts in awareness for the entire group. Very subtle cues can create profound changes in consciousness. It has been observed that ritual participants who become to varying degrees possessed by an entity display varying degrees of postural change, vocal alteration, and also, most significantly, small changes in the way that the facial muscles create the overall character that is usually associated with a particular personality. If for example, a group of ritualists are observing another person move into this state, these small signals will heighten the overall sense of Dramatic Awareness throughout the group.

Within a ritual, participants can learn to move with a quality of deliberateness to all their movements. Another analogy between ritual and theatre can be drawn, that actors make their movements with the deliberate intent of communicating something to the audience.

In a ritual space, the audience can be considered to be any participants who are not engaged in activity. On a greater level, the audience may be the entities which the ritual is designed to stir forth.

4. Coordination of Technique

Rituals often require the participants to simultaneously employ different techniques. For example, etching a pentagram in the air may require the coordination of gesture, visualisation, breathing, and colour projection, as well as the implicit belief that doing so will bring about some change within the ritual space. The successful coordination of different techniques to carry out an action within the ritual space contributes towards changes in conscious-ness. Coordinated movement, together with breathing and visual-isation, directed by the intention of bringing about a specific result creates a shift into an emotional state which a magician learns, through practice, to identify as being appropriate for that action. Emotion acts as a support to belief, and when the magi-cian feels himself move into the appropriate state of awareness, he undergoes a subtle belief shift towards the tacit 'reality' of the ritual process.

Stages in Ritual Progression

This is a basic model for ritual design which identifies five different stages in the ritual process. These stages follow the general shift in ritual awareness towards the actualization of the intent that the ritual is based around, and then back out towards post-ritual consciousness.

1. Preparation.
2. Warm-up.
3. Core.
4. Wind-down.
5. Debriefing.

1. Preparation

It is not always easy to say at what point a ritual begins or ends, since the preparation to perform a ritual can itself be elaborate: cleaning the area to be used, bathing, relaxing and meditating can be as much part of the ritual as the main event.

Fasting and self-deprivation (giving up habits and addictions) are also time-honoured methods of focusing awareness towards a particular task or goal. Especially effective are those preparations which produce changes in somatic awareness, such as dieting, sleep deprivation or reducing ones normal intake of stimulants.

If one is working within the parameters of a specific magical system, then Preparation is likely to involve assimilating the attributes, symbols, and concepts of that system. When working with a particular entity, it may be deemed useful to have had some of the ritual participants (if not all) to have acquired a knowledge of the behaviour, attributes, and qualities associated with the entity. Preparation also involves the pre-ritual briefing of participants to ensure that everyone has some idea of what is being attempted, and why.

2. Warm-Up

The warming-up elements of ritual consist of techniques that serve to raise energy and enthusiasm, and focus awareness towards the task in hand. These include drumming, dancing, meditation exercises, background music and coordinated breathing or chanting.

Not only do these techniques serve to focus awareness, they also have powerful physiological effects as well. The kind of warm-up techniques used in a ritual will help create the appropriate mood for participants. Obviously fast drumming and energetic dancing will create a different ritual atmosphere than slow moving steps, sonorous chanting and solemn music.

A Banishing, or Centering ritual is a standard warm-up precursor to most rituals, of which, more later.

3. The Core

The Core stage of ritual involves the techniques which implement the main intention of the ritual so far, which is powered by all the energy and enthusiasm generated during the rite. The content of the core stage depends on the general aim of the ritual, such as invocation—calling a specific entity into one or more of the participants; evocation—calling forth (or creating) a physical manifestation of an entity; the projection of a specific intention from the ritual space into the multiverse; the enactment of a specific mythic event; the enactment of a psychodrama designed to bring about a specific shift in awareness; or the celebration of some historical, mythic, or social event.

4. Wind-Down

This stage of a ritual marks the beginning of a return to post-ritual awareness, the 'return' being facilitated by, for example, another performance of a banishing ritual. This serves to prevent the energy and emotions generated by the ritual from spilling over into everyday life. Occasionally, light-hearted games may be used to relax participants and to discharge tension. The magical role is shed, and the mythic world bidden depart, as the participants prepare to return to everyday awareness. It is generally the case that the more intense the ritual, the more thorough the Wind-Down should be. It should be noted that not all individuals return from intense trance states simultaneously, and that careful observation of participants' return from intense ritual consciousness is often necessary. It should also be noted that when rituals are designed to bring about an intense shift in consciousness, the effects are likely to linger on afterwards. One of the strengths of magic is that it provides the individual with a framework within which to explore and assimilate shifts in awareness. It is not unknown for rituals to bring about long-term changes in an individual's awareness and life. Indeed, to do so is one of the aims of ritual.

5. Debriefing

This stage concerns the recording of impressions and insights, to be entered in the Magical Diary. The importance of this cannot be over stressed. It is surprising how quickly impressions of what transpired during a ritual can become distorted or forgotten. The magical diary is essential for the self-assessment of progress, and recording experiences for future reference. This stage also includes self or group assessment of performance on a technical level—identifying which parts of the ritual process had the most effect, and which, in retrospect, did not seem to work as well. Magicians do not, in general, enjoy having their performances criticised, but this is as much a part of the continual process of learning and refining ritual technique as any other.

Formal v. Freestyle

Formalised Ritual

I use the term Formalised Ritual to describe any ritual magic which is rooted in a particular tradition, historical-cultural epoch, or particular doctrine. Popular examples of such include: Qabalah, Tantra, Witchcraft, Voudoun, Thelema, or what has become known as the Western Esoteric Tradition. In any of these traditions, the symbolism, elements and structure of ritual are defined according to particular criteria. Magicians who study such traditions have to absorb the theory of the particular system, make its symbolism personally significant, and learn its ritual structures in order to get the most out of working with the system. This usually involves varying degrees of steeping oneself in a particular culture. For example, if you became interested in Tibetan Magic, you might well find yourself studying an appropriate language, reading the Tibetan Book of the Dead, going to listen to the Dalai Lama, researching the performance of Tibetan ritual, etc.

Freestyle Ritual

Freestyle Ritual denotes all forms of magical ritual which are not entirely rooted in one particular magical doctrine or tradition. Up until fairly recently, most people who called themselves magicians were rooted (ritual-wise) in one of the many doctrines and traditions of magical belief and structure, such as those mentioned in the previous section. Since the late 1970's however, there has been a growing interest in what can be termed Freestyle Ritual which is more open-ended, drawing on a wide range of symbolism and features, and which is highly personalised to the individual performing. The growth of interest in Self-Development, Shamanism, and the Chaos Magic Movement have helped develop this trend. In freestyle ritual, you are not constrained by any particular system of doing things, and can use elements which are not always immediately recognised as being occult.

Both these styles have their pros and cons. Personally, I feel that one of the marks of an effective magician is the ability to work within a particular system, or to be able to perform freestyle magic when the occasion befits. Freestyle ritual is particularly good for learning how to structure magical rituals yourself (rather than simply following someone else's method). If you wish to go off and spend the next twenty years or so studying the Qabalah or one of the Neo-African magical traditions, fine, but such in-depth work is beyond the scope of this book.

THE COMPONENTS OF RITUAL

I will now examine some of the different components that can be used to shape a magical ritual, and the relationships between them. Where relevant I have included a variety of exercises and techniques by which these elements may be explored. How these components are employed in devising a complete ritual will very much depend on the following:

    i) The intention, or *aim* underlying the ritual.
    ii) The particular *style* of ritual (formal, freestyle).
    iii) The *belief-system* or magical structure which the rite uses.
    iv) *Practicalities* of Time, Spatial Restrictions etc.

Ritual as Theatre

Regarding magical ritual as a form of theatrical performance is a useful way of approaching its possibilities. In modern society, theatre has become merely a form of entertainment, whilst its healing function has largely been institutionalised as forms of therapy, and its magical aspects have been driven underground. Antonin Artaud, in his classic essay *The Theatre and Its Double*, writes about a "physical language" of theatre, which is independent of speech (and hence, the waking mind), and which is aimed at provoking unconscious reactions in the audience, expressing feelings which cannot be framed into words. Such a language includes dance, gesture, mime, costume, lighting and use of props. Artaud writes that careful attention needs to be given towards these elements if the language is to be effective. This language is the same language which is used to build an atmosphere in ritual magic.

Style

The degree of adherence to a particular formal style of ritual will to a large extent determine the shape it takes. This may necessitate some degree of research as preparation, if one is aiming at reconstructing a ritual from another culture or epoch. Whilst there are a good number of books aimed at the modern occultist which purport to reconstruct the rituals of the Ancient Greeks or Germanic peoples, for example, there is equally a vast wealth of information from historians and anthropologists which should not be overlooked. How far one goes along the path of reconstruction is a matter of personal preference. Whilst one might wish to recreate the *spirit* of the ancient Greek Dionysia, it is unlikely, that one will be able to tear through one's local fields ripping livestock and passers-by apart (much as one would perhaps like to). In general, doing a ritual in a particular formal style should not, in my opinion, be seen as a restriction, but an opportunity to pull out all the stops and go for it!

One issue that relates to ritual style is that of mixing elements from different systems. There is a very vocal school within the occult milieu which holds that it is wrong (dangerous even) to mix different systems of magic. This view is most strongly advocated by champions of the so-called Western Esoteric Tradition, or the more rigid traditions of modern witchcraft. The strength of this position is considerably weakened when one considers that much of the so-called Western Esoteric Tradition is a synthesis of Hermetic philosophy, Qabalah, theosophy, yoga, medieval magic, chakras and other diverse elements. It's not so much the mixing which is the problem, but how you do it—rather like cooking. I have found, as have many others, for example, that movements borrowed from Tai Chi or Qi Gong fit very well into ritual magic sequences.

Timing

There are several considerations which relate to the Timing of Ritual. Firstly, there is the question of "When is the best time to perform a ritual?" From a purely practical level, you should perform your rituals when you know you are not going to be disturbed, for example, by children, flatmates, neighbours or people dropping by. This in itself may require alterations in your daily schedule (getting up earlier or going to bed later) which may help the ritual in becoming significant, as something special.

Some books on magic make much of the division of time into planetary days, hours, and so forth. How far you follow this is up to you, as is the performance of rituals related to the progression of astrological houses or the conjunction of particular planetary bodies. If you feel it's significant for you, then by all means do use these relationships, but equally, don't feel you *have* to do it this way.

1. Spatial Elements

This section deals with the actual physical space where a ritual takes place. Whilst some magicians are fortunate enough to be able to set a room of their dwelling aside as a magical temple, most of us have to make do with reconfiguring a room, hiring an external space, or working outdoors.

a) The Ritual Space as a Free Area

Whilst it is common for magical texts to discuss ritual space in terms of a magical circle or temple, I prefer to use the term Free Area to denote ritual space, since it covers circumstances when a circle is not necessary, desired, or appropriate. A Free Area may even denote a state of consciousness or the establishment of any physical location (however temporary) as a region where Magical Reality is dominant, interpenetrative, or highly condensed in relation to other spaces. For example, for the purposes of a ritual event, one might decide that an entire forest is a Free Area of magical intrusion and possibilities, which ends one hour after dawn or as one reaches the first visible signs of human habitation.

b) The Demarcation of Boundaries

The use of a physical magical circle is perhaps the most well-known way of marking a boundary between ritual space and non-ritual surroundings. Circles can be formed by chalk, rope, tape, sewn onto blankets or carpets or even cut permanently into floorboards. Outdoor circles can be marked out in brush, wooden ramping or turf, to give a few examples. Equally, a circle may be established using a combination of visualization, dance and a ritual sequence whereby the classical 'directions of space' (i.e., points of the compass) are set up. In physical terms this might involve the use of quarter-markers such as candles, banners bearing signs of the quarters, small altars (see below), statuettes or stangs.

The demarcation of boundaries is both physical and psychological. It focuses the attention of the magician towards the immediate area wherein magical work will take place. As Crowley points out in Chapter 2 of Book Four, the magical boundary (in this case, the circle) is an affirmation of the magician's devotion to his work.

The idea of making a boundary is also important in the sense of keeping unwanted (or uninvited) influences (i.e., 'orrible psychic entities) out of the circle, or for that matter, inviting them in.

c) The Altar

Altars tend to be the ritual furniture (often a table or box covered with a cloth) on which all the bits and pieces associated with a particular rite—pictures, incense burner, statuettes, mirror, magical weapons etc., are arranged, usually in some kind of symbolic sequence, and (hopefully) placed so that it is not in danger of being banged into in the course of the rite. Altars tend to be placed according to some structural schema, such as the 4 quarters or elemental stations used in defining the ritual space. The term altar is derived from the Latin *altus*, which means 'high' and is usually defined as a raised place or structure where sacrifices are offered and religious rites are conducted. An altar is a physical representation of sacred space, whether it be a rock in a forest clearing or a covered table in one corner of a room; it allows us to focus awareness and attention towards the sacred. In the Classical Pagan traditions, stone altars were raised as an act of recognition of the spirit of a place, the *genius loci*.

In a way, creating an altar for magical use is a process of discovering and clarifying which objects and items have a core magical significance and also, an intensely personal significance. In addition, an altar can represent both that which we are, and what we aspire towards. An altar, regardless of whether or not it is used in formal ritual, can become a place of meditation or contemplation and a reminder of what for us is significant, and of making a reconnection with that which is magical in the midst of our everyday lives. An altar need not be a large construction: one of the smallest altars in my abode is a space on a mantelpiece, on which sits a small plastic pixie. The pixie is a finder of lost things, who is rewarded by my giving him a small silver coin, lighting a joss stick next to him or just dusting him off occasionally. An altar can be as minimal or complex as you like: what matters is that *you* find it significant and empowering. Building an altar can become in itself a powerful act of magic: be it an altar that will be eventually used for formalised ritual work, or simply as a point of daily reconnection. Altars can be created for special circumstances, to commemorate special events in our lives, for example, or for specific events. Altars are particularly useful in acts of invocation, when one might create a altar to a goddess or god, or for enchantments, when a desire might be sacrificed on an altar. It can be useful to identify a few central items of magical and personal significance which can in effect, be used as a portable altar.

d) Props & Equipment

One of the most useful ritual props I have used isn't particularly magical, but is nonetheless immensely useful—a music stand. Formerly, if I had to read aloud from a book during a ritual it would be more often than not a case of standing, holding the book open whilst someone else wobbled a candle over my shoulder. With the book on the music stand, I found I had both arms free to wave about impressively, and could concentrate on my posture, voice projection, visualisation and all the other elements which are difficult to do effectively with one's head bent over a book. The music stand also has the advantage of being portable as it can be ritually unfolded and then removed when no longer needed. This is particularly useful if at a later stage, the rite is going to involve spinning, dancing or some other excitatory activity. So a prop need not necessarily be something with overt magical associations.

There is a school of thought which adheres to the belief that you cannot do ritual magic without having collected a trunk-load of paraphernalia first: the magical weapons such as cup, sword, dagger, wand, staff, pantacle, lamp etc., being of foremost importance. Whilst it is undeniable that props are nice, it's arguable whether they are essential prerequisites to ritual, and to my mind it is more useful to collect them as you go along, building them up gradually, whether by finding suitable props in second-hand shops, being given them, or making them oneself. This latter approach is for me, one of the most enjoyable by-products of ritual magic and I have found myself, over the years, trying my hand at a variety of handicrafts (including pottery, batik, tie-dyeing, candle-making, woodwork, mask-making and incense-blending) as preparation for particular rituals. For one series of workings, in which the three-pillar symbolism of the qabalah figured prominently, we found that the thick cardboard tubes which carpets are rolled around could be turned into physical representations of the pillars!

One of the early arguments of Chaoists was for a minimalist approach to ritual props, along the lines of "why use a silver-plated chalice when an old coffee mug will do?" Of course, this is a matter of choice. Whilst having special, only-used-for-ritual props can be useful, in a pinch, an old coffee-cup will serve as a chalice. It's all down to what Terry Pratchett has amusingly termed 'headology.' The other approach is the attitude of pulling all the stops out, as it were. Lionel Snell satirically championed this all-out approach to ritual in his announcement of the OTTO—the "Over The Top Order"—"why make do with an old coffee-cup when you can use a 900-year old skull-chalice from a lost Tibetan temple?"

The 'you-can-visualize-everything' brigade also tend to decry the use of props as unnecessary. This too however, can be taken to absurd lengths. Some years ago I was privileged to participate in a meditation session wherein the participants were asked to visualise themselves being in a forest. This was taking place in the grounds of an Austrian castle which was surrounded on all sides by several acres of prime woodland!

So props are useful, but not essential. If you have time and access to a working space where you can usefully deploy them, then fine—use them, but don't be tied down by them. In making props yourself, a little ingenuity goes a long way, and is part of the fun of ritual magic.

e) Backdrops

Using large backdrops on walls can be a simple, yet highly effective method of enhancing an indoor ritual space. Rituals aimed at invoking particular gods or goddesses, for example, can be enhanced by a painting of the deity in a particular aspect appropriate to the rite. Backdrops can also be painted to give the illusion of more space in a room. A living-room can be simply converted into a temple by hanging drapes of an appropriate colour around the walls, so that they obscure one's everyday furnishings. If you have access to a slide or overhead-projector, then these can be very useful for projecting images onto walls. The projection of computer-generated images is also a possibility. Related to this is the use of group-created collages and paintings as symbolic manifestations or reminders of the group's *gestalt*.

2. BodyMind Components

Under this heading I have grouped the aspects of ritual which relate to the participants themselves—such as sensory elements, movement and gesture, use of the voice, etc.

a) Visualisation

Visualisation is usually defined as 'the formation of mental visual images' or 'the act or process of interpreting in visual terms.' We all make use of Visualisation at some time or another, especially if we are mentally anticipating or rehearsing a situation which we have to deal with at some point in the future. Another good example of visualisation is if someone asks you for directions to a particular place and to describe how to get there, you try to recall how the streets and roads which make up the route fit together, and how the person trying to follow your directions would have to go.

In magical terms, Visualisation is the skill of creating and focusing awareness into these mental images. For example, a *Guided Visualisation* exercise is one where another person tells you a story in which you are participating, telling you what to imagine in the way of imaginary scenery, people, and places.

Some facility at Visualisation is generally considered a prime requisite for magical work. However, although we derive a great deal of information about the world through our visual sense, there is a good deal more to sensory experience than vision, and moreover, some people are not primarily visually-oriented, although the majority of magical/imaginative exercises are biased towards visual experience at the expense of other perceptions.

Visualisation-Related Exercises

i) Going Places

Create for yourself, a place that you can visit in your imagination. It should be a place which for you signifies relaxation and calmness. It may be a scene from your past, a place you have visited, or somewhere which you would like to visit. Give yourself a set period which you will attempt to visit this place and explore it.

The idea of this exercise is that you attempt to place yourself into this imagined setting. After each visit, note down if any particular sensory modes struck you. Is there a particular sound that you noticed? Is there a predominant smell? Can you feel a breeze, or the heat of the sun? Are there any particular emotions or memory-sensations that you experience whilst in this place? In this exercise, you are not merely attempting to visualise a scene, but to hear, feel, taste, and smell it.

ii) What's In the Box?

For this exercise you need a box of some kind, preferably with a hinged lid. All you have to do is, without making a big issue of it, occasionally go over to the box and open the lid, allowing the first thing that flashes into your mind to be in the box.

The point of this exercise is to demonstrate how we very often tend to censor the first thing that flashes into our minds, because we don't think its right, significant, or we are perhaps worried about what other people might think. So don't worry about what you 'find' in the box. What is important is that you can open the box and 'find' anything without having to consciously put it there, and that you can do this in a very matter-of-fact, down-to-earth fashion.

iii) Unconscious Seeing

This is a simple technique for seeing images arising out of everyday phenomena. All you have to do is choose some everyday object—it is helpful if it is somehow textured—such as a whitewashed window, a brick wall, a patch of moss on a stone, a plant, etc. and look at it, stilling your mind. Forget what the object is, and let forms arise out of it while you study it. This is a very ancient magical technique for allowing meaningful images to arise out of flames, the passage of birds, the swarming of bees, cloud formations, etc. Leonardo Da Vinci called it "Eidetic Vision," and it is said that a friend of his discovered the technique when staring at a wall upon which superstitious folk, particularly the sick, would stop and spit. The man is said to have gazed at the wall for hours, amazed at the shapes and forms which arose out of the blobs of phlegm. Any object which is sufficiently complex, from manufactured items to natural growths can be used in this way. I recall once becoming fascinating by the swirls and shapes seen in the remains of a plate of different-flavours of ice-cream.

b) Use of Voice

Voice is an important element of ritual—we use voice in ritual to make declarations, statements of intent, to project extended vowels or repeat mantras, and in declaiming invocations to that which the rite is focused towards (a planet, a god, etc.). It doesn't really matter how loud your voice is (a whisper can be more effective than a shout)—its the tone, pacing, and emotion that one's voice carries which is important. In ritual, both *what* we say, and the *way* we say it, can become important factors in generating the appropriate atmosphere for the ritual.

Basic Voice Exercises

i) Finding the Right Tone

Consider the following list of emotions, and experiment with ways of speaking which, for you, help project each emotion convincingly:

Showing Reverence
Being in **Awe** of Something
Radiating **Self-Confidence**
Facing something which you are slightly **afraid** of
Establishing your **Authority**
Speaking to a **Lover** or a **Loved** one after a period of absence

> Speaking to someone who one has **Admired** from afar—for the first time

It can be helpful to watch other people and listen to how they use their voices effectively in particular situations. One of my favourite examples of someone using his voice calmly, yet projecting authoritative command, is Captain Picard's "Make it So" from *Star Trek: The Next Generation.*

ii) Planetary Tones

The next step is to find a voice-tone which for you represents a particular aspect of one of the 8 planets. For example, for Mars, you might feel that the clipped, precise speech of an Army Officer is appropriate, or that slowly-paced speech brings to mind the dreamy aspect of the Moon.

Of course, speaking doesn't just involve our voices—the muscles of the face, the eyes, and limbs also follow suit. Try the above 2 exercises in front of a mirror and see how your muscular patterns change according to your use of voice.

The aim of these exercises is to help you identify and explore the ways in which you might use your voice to help focus on the particular qualities that your eventual rituals are aimed towards. This also relates to:

iii) Story-Telling

Story-telling is useful in that, as part of a ritual (or as part of preparation), relating a particular story or myth in which the chosen entity plays a starring role helps focus the attention of the other celebrants towards the qualities and attributes of that entity. This may be particularly desirable when not everyone present is fully familiar with the diverse aspects of the particular entity. Besides, story-telling is fun in itself. Some stories and myths are themselves suitable for ritual re-enactment—examples being the descent of the goddess Inanna into the Underworld, or the skull-dance of Bhairava, the wrathful aspect of Shiva.

iv) The Vibration of Names

A variant of voice technique which is often used during invocatory ritual is to divide the name of the entity being invoked into its component syllables, for example BAPHOMET becomes BAPH–O–MET and *vibrate* the name. To do this, take a deep breath and intone the first syllable, projecting it at a point a few feet in front of you. You should feel your entire body shaking with the force of the sound. With practice, you can develop this exercise so that as you continually project the sound, you feel your whole body vibrating, followed by a sense of the immediate area vibrating, then the world vibrating, and ultimately, the entire multiverse vibrating with the sound. This practice can also be used when enunciating barbarous words for invocation and evocation, in the various magical languages available.

c) Posture, Gesture, & Movement

Just as we can use our voices to project and intensify our own feelings, so too can we use bodily postures, gestures, and movements. Sit upright in your chair, tilt your head slightly upwards, fix your gaze steadily on whatever is in front of you, place your hands on your thighs, push your chest outwards, and take a deep, slow, in-breath. "What's going to happen next?" you might wonder. Just by following this simple sequence, you have *deliberately* caused a change in your consciousness, and it is this quality of deliberateness (even if it seems to happen spontaneously) which is important when we consider posture, gesture, and movement as elements of ritual magic. For example, if you were making a toast during a ritual, you would be unlikely to nonchalantly swig your drink as you would ordinarily—you'd make a performance out of it raising it as though acknowledging the presence of an audience, perhaps visualizing rays of light shining into it, or declaring that by drinking this liquid, you are absorbing the power of the planet. The point here, is that every action, within the ritual space, can be made to be significant. You may even choose to make the action of 'looking up something you've forgotten' as a performance—carefully picking up the book or piece of paper, slowly extending it before you, reading from it slowly and deliberately.

d) Body Space

Related to the above is the way in which we arrange ourselves so that our bodies take up various degrees of the space around us. A great many magical techniques are concerned with exploring our inner spaces, through visualisation, trance induction, and scrying, for example. But what of the space that is around us? Our sense of personal space is important in terms of how we interact with other people, and it is usefully to develop all of our senses as fully as possible. According to legend, shamans and sorcerers are very difficult to sneak up on, as they are aware of what is happening in their environment.

Our normal perception of Space is that it is empty and that we are separate from each other, and from objects. The amount of Personal Space that we feel comfortable with usually reflects how we may feel about different situations. The more anxious a person is, the more he will draw his body inwards towards a posture resembling the foetal position. Equally, people who are confident are much more expansive in their movements and the way they use the space around them. The way we use bodily space reflects our moods and by the same token, can be deliberately used to enhance or project particular moods in ritual. Many books on ritual discuss the symbolic associations of particular ritual postures. We should not forget that these postures also have distinct physical and psychological effects on us, too.

i) Blind Walks

This exercise can be practised individually but is best done in pairs. A group divides into pairs and one member leads the other, who is blindfolded, around an area. Shutting ones eyes automatically increases the sensory feedback from other organs.

After everyone has tried this a few times, the exercise can be modified: blindfolded members can visualise an aura about their bodies, which like a bubble or web, senses obstacles before physical contact could be made.

ii) Flowing Meditation

This exercise involves imagining space as a flowing, watery medium through which we move. Each movement causes the space around us to flow and ripple. It reacts to being pushed, and can be shaped momentarily by the hands. We are immersed in space like a fish is immersed in water, and we can use it as an additional organ of perception. This idea is used in Tai Chi for example, where one is encouraged to move as though in water, and become aware of the spaces between arms and legs. We are particularly sensitive, for example, to the blind spot behind us, and many people, especially women, can sense what is happening behind their backs—a survival sense that has remained with use from the arboreal forest to the urban jungle.

e) Lighting

When we look at lighting in respect to ritual, there are three major considerations: what *form* of lighting can be used, its *symbolic* associations, and what kind of *ambience* lighting can be used to project. Generally, one should ensure that the form of lighting used enhances, rather than detracts, from the other elements of the ritual. Whilst candle-light, for example, is generally preferred to electric lights, there should be enough light to read by—if your ritual involves reading, for example. I have participated in too many rituals where grand invocations have been reduced to farce as the ritualists declaiming them cannot see what they are reading properly. Over the last decade or so there has been a good deal of experimentation with alternatives to candle-light, using everything from coloured disco-lights to strobes and dream-machines. For both indoor and outdoor work for example, I have found that small head-torches, as used by walkers and climbers are quite useful. Even the strings of fairy lights more commonly found wrapped around Christmas trees may be used successfully.

The symbolic aspects of lighting relate primarily to the symbolism of colour which is detailed at length in many magical texts: scarlet candles for Mars, Green Candles for Venus, and so forth. There is also, however, a degree of symbolism around the form of lighting. You might decide, for example, that flaming brands, braziers, or roving spotlights are eminently suitable for a martial ritual, or that jack-o-lanterns arranged around your working space are most suitable for a Hallow's eve working.

Using lighting to project a particular ambience relates to certain arrangements. The first group rituals I ever participated in tended to have a standard arrangement of 3 candles on the altar (representing both the triple goddess and the 3 masonic pillars), as well as a candle at each elemental quarter. This was very much down to 'tradition' (i.e., "we've always done it like that"). Once I had sidled away from the straight-jacket of such an approach however, I found that you can do a lot to the ritual space by the specific arrangement of lighting in order to yield certain effects and moods. One such example is the lighting of masks by placing small night-lights inside them so as to give the appearance of flickering light coming from the eyes. Another is to arrange lighting so that whilst the altar is well-lit, the outer spaces of the area are cast into deep shadow. Candles may be arranged so that the imaginative facility of the peripheral vision is stimulated. You could even consider controlling shifts in lighting using a computer. Once you begin to experiment, the options are endless. A final thought (for the moment) relating to lighting is that of safety. If you are using candles, flaming torches or anything else which may pose a potential hazard to celebrants, be careful. The collision of candle-flame and a polyester robe is dramatic indeed, but not really the kind of drama that one is aiming for.

f) Incense & Perfumes

Smell has a very powerful effect upon us; in particular, it is a direct stimulator of memory, invoking images, associations and emotions.

Some scents have recognised physiological effects on the bodymind, and a knowledge of these can be employed when using smells as ritual triggers, adding another layer of associations to an invocation. Incense too, can have a powerful effect. Clouds of incense rising up from a thurible is not only a very ancient form of invocation in itself, but can serve to heighten the atmosphere of the ritual space.

g) Clothing & Apparel

All items of magical apparel, be they robes, jewelry, hats, cloaks or whatever, can be used as part of a 'uniform' that signifies to you (and others) that you are leaving the everyday world and preparing to do some magic. In the same way that a doctor wears a white coat or a sewer-worker puts on overalls, clothes help to focus states of consciousness and subtle shifts in reality. The classical monk's hood for example, signifies his retreat from the world. A hood is a simple, though effective, piece of magical apparel. A simple way to create a hood is to obtain (or dye) a black pillowcase, and cut a couple of eye holes in it. Wearing a hood confers a degree of anonymity, calling to mind cultural references to masked men, bandits, etc. I was introduced to the power of the hood by a female sorceress, who wore one whenever she had dealings with demons—in order, so she said, to disguise her identity so they wouldn't bother her afterwards. A hood muffles the voice and causes subtle changes in perception, without limiting one's movements in the way that a set of magical robes can. Furthermore, if you are called to perform some act of magic in someone's house, parking lot, or garden, wearing a robe can look silly at times. Wearing a hood usually (in my experience at least) looks somehow forbidding, or sinister. Some sorcerers decorate their hoods with personal symbols, or embellish the eyes to resemble owl or bat faces in order to signify that, when donning the hood, they are enhancing their ability to see (and move) into 'other' places. It all comes down to personal taste, but I feel a simple, bag-like hood is much more preferable to the tight hoods which can be obtained through the fetish-wear market.

h) Music

Musical accompaniment to ritual takes two basic forms: using pre-recorded music or live music. In using pre-recorded music, I have found that an easy pitfall is using musical pieces that, whilst appropriate to a particular ritual (or element thereof), for some have somewhat different associations for others. Whilst I find *The Sisters of Mercy* or *The Cassandra Complex* conducive to meditation, others might not so readily agree. When preparing instrumental tapes for ritual background music, I have tended to stick to fairly obscure sources, and to keep these tracks for ritual use only. A related use of tapes is to prepare cut-up sequences which can be useful for throwing out random inspirations (as in the manner of the well-known 'cocktail-party' phenomena).

Probably the most common instrument used for providing live music is the drum. Drumming is one of the most ancient and enduring methods of providing structure and accompaniment to ritual events, ranging from the use of simple beats (which is all *I* ever seem to manage) to the complex invocatory rhythms used in the Pan-African traditions of Voudou and Santeria. A general observation I would make is that a drummer can often exert undue control over the pace of a ritual such that if the drummer speeds up then the pace of the ritual will invariably speed up as well, and can occasionally lead to the ritual building to a premature climax.

i) Food & Drink

Eating and Drinking can be an important aspect of ritual. The Christian use of sacramental wine and wafers is an obvious example. During a ritual mass, the energy of a deity may be infused in a chalice of wine so that all celebrants may partake of the quality being invoked.

The Sumble

The Sumble as described by Don Webb originates from the Viking custom of making boasts and toasts prior to an expedition. It basically consists of four rounds of toasts. In the first round, all present drink to *Principles*—principles which each person present believes to be important. For the second round, all present drink to *Heroes*—people living or dead, who for those present are particular sources of inspiration. The third round is that of personal *Boasts*—each participant shares something that he or she has accomplished, and feels proud of. The fourth and final round is that of *Oaths*—each person present makes a statement of something which they are going to do. These oaths are personal; you can't make them for others.

This simple exercise has many benefits. It is useful for each participant, in helping them to identify what for them are important principles, personal heroes, or to own their own achievements before the group and be proud of them (something we often find difficult to do) and to state an intention to strive for. It also allows you to find out what other people think is important as this kind of mutual sharing and honouring of each other's feelings and achievements can do much to help building a sense of mutual confidence and commitment in a group (this is discussed more thoroughly in Part 3: Group Effects).

Another angle which can be explored (particularly within the context of a specific magical or mythic tradition) is selecting food and drink and serving and consuming it in a manner appropriate to that tradition. This can act as part of the preparation for a particular event (i.e., to get people in the mood) or as part of the ritual itself. Examples here might include anything from brewing mead as a preparation for an Othinn rite, or preparing a traditional Indian sweet for use in a ritual focusing on Ganesha.

3. The Interpenetration of Magical Reality

a) Symbolism

Every element of a magical ritual, from the props you use, to the gestures, words, colours, smells, foods, drinks, clothes etc., can be imbued with a symbolic element. It is all a matter of degree. Some 'experts' on ritual magic do hold that before one can successfully perform a ritual, one has to have absorbed the symbolism of the ritual beforehand. To a certain extent, this is the case, but it largely depends on *what* you are doing, and the *context* in which you are doing it. If, for example, you are about to perform a ritual which has been structured according to Qabalistic principles (there is an example of such a ritual given below), then yes, it does help enormously if you have studied those principles beforehand. If, however, you have designed a Freestyle ritual, then you need only be aware of the symbolism which is *personally significant*.

b) The Magical Link

In essence, the process of making a Magical Link is simple: it is the act of making a connection between one thing and another thing—in one's mind. One of the most classic examples of making a magical link is to take a wax doll, to ritually identify it as being a specific individual, and then use that doll as a focus for magical enchantment, be it beneficial or malefic. Another example is the lucky rabbit's foot. The abstract idea of good luck in itself is rare enough but when that idea is made concrete by being identified with a particular object then we behave as though the object itself attracts (and is responsible) for the luck. When we create magical talismans or amulets, we are making a *Magical Link* between the chosen object (the vessel) and the appropriate state of awareness which we have inflamed ourselves with during a ritual and whatever symbolic associations we have also attached to the object.

A further example of this process is that of making a magical toast. If you desire to drink to the health of an absent friend, you might take a vessel of liquid (perhaps alka-seltzer, Andrews Liver Salts or any fizzy liquid), and raising the vessel, strongly visualize his image reflected in its depths. You might also speak his name over the liquid, so that the sound ripples across it. Speaking aloud your wish, you then drink the liquid, and meditate for a space on inner calm. If you were to do this as part of a more intense ritual, such as an invocation of Solar power, you might visualise (at the peak of the working) the golden rays of the Sun infusing the liquid.

In one sense, when you make a Magical Link, you are bringing the object or substance into yourself and consciously bringing it into your magical awareness, or your psychocosm.

Magical Correspondences

The lists of Magical Correspondences which are featured in many modern books on magical technique are useful in that they allow us to build up associative links between a particular planet, for example, and a wide range of symbols, sensory stimuli, and other attributes. Tables of Correspondences, many of which were originally derived from books on herbal lore, have been around for a long time, and most of the ones which appear in modern textbooks are based on the lists compiled by Aleister Crowley (which were in turn based on the tables compiled by the Hermetic Order of the Golden Dawn, and the work of the Six-teenth-Century Magus, Cornelius Agrippa). It is useful to use these correspondences in devising rituals, but one should not be afraid of adding one's own links to them. Some lists of correspondences can get quite exhaustive, relating planets not only to days of the week, but also to astrological periods, hours and minutes. The key to correspondences is to use them creatively, and not get stuck into following them dogmatically. If you don't agree with a particular set of correspondences, don't feel afraid to change them! Here are some simple exercises aimed at developing personal sets of correspondences:

i) Helpful Lists

For each of the 8 planets, take a sheet of paper headed with the name of each planet, and write down as many things as possible which you can think of relating to that name. For example, for Mars, a list could include:

Mars:

> *"A mars a day helps you work, rest and play"*
> *Music from the Planets Suite, by Gustav Holst*
> *Karate Kicks, (Martial Arts), people bowing to each other before fighting*
> *Ziggy Stardust & the Spiders From Mars*

Red:

> *The Red Devils (football or parachute team)—imagine people with scarves cheering me on?*
> *99 Red Balloons—Song—Could burst red balloon in ritual?*
> *Like a Red Rag to a Bull—bullfighter—hat with horns on it— explore symbolism of bull?*

The idea is that, by writing down a few things, you can quickly build associations with other things, some of which could be brought into your ritual itself, or in the preparation for it, or re-invoking it afterwards.

ii) Posture, Gesture, Mood and Memory

Associations can become particularly powerful if we can relate them to our own personal experience. For example, one of the memories that I use to bring into focus some of the qualities of Saturn is that of being in a dentist's waiting-room. The smell of antiseptic fluid, its clinical, pristine air and my mood of "I'm not going to enjoy this but I have to do it." So, for me, the smell of hospital cleaning fluid has a saturnian association.

The first part of this exercise is that you try and recall an experience which for you relates to a particular planet. A surge of self-confidence on being congratulated for something which you did could be linked to the Sun, the memory of a particularly good conversation with a friend could be classed as Mercury; the

memory of a flash of inspiration which suddenly leapt into your
head could become the model for your Uranian state.

Once you begin to recall a particular experience, try and re-
live it as fully as possible. As you do, try and notice how your
mood effects your posture, your muscles, your voice tone, your
emotions; can you recall a particular scent, sound, taste or
colour?

The next task is to find a body posture which for you recalls
that mood and memory. You can also try and find an appropriate
gesture. It is also useful if you add to the eight planetary states a
Neutral posture/mood/gesture which can be used as an aid in
grounding yourself after an exercise. In time, the postures/ges-
tures/moods/memories can become the basis of your own
personal associations to each of the 8 planets, which will be
modified as you work with them. And of course you can use this
technique for building up other sets of personal correspondences
as well.

iii) Silly Lists

A few years ago a group of us went through a phase of trying to
place different things onto the Qabalistic Tree of Life. We started
off with characters from the Rocky Horror Picture Show (Brad
for Earth, Janet for the Moon, Frank N. Furter for Mercury, etc.)
and went on to do Star Trek characters, flavours of herbal tea,
flavours of yoghurt, curries, and breakfast cereals. Although this
is undeniably silly, it is fun, and can actually lead to useful
correspondences for ritual work. What kind of tea would you
drink before a Lunar ritual? Is there a hat that for you is Saturnian? To which planets would you classify silk, leather or
rubber? Try it out for yourself.

Magical Artefacts

What is a Magical Artefact? Broadly speaking, it is any physical
object which has magical associations for the user, ranging from
specific magical tools such as a tarot deck, set of runes, or magical weapons to items which have either general symbolic associations or those which remind us of magical moments and
evoke a particular nostalgia or mood. Whatever the nature or
history of the object, these are things which help us (or remind

us) of our magical power. Some artefacts can be classed as
generic items in that they are incorporated into our sets of ritual
props, whatever the occasion. Others may have associations
which are particular to one type of ritual, style, or system. The
wand, described below, is an example of a generic item. In *Liber
Nice*, I have described some of the magical artefacts which, for
me, have particular associations with Erisian magic.

The Wand

The Wand (also Rod, or Pointer) is the all-purpose weapon of
magic which is used to direct one's will, be it into the aeythr, a
person, or an object.

The traditional means of obtaining a wand called for the
magician to cut a forearm's length of ash from a tree (having
asked the tree for permission first!) with a single stroke, at a time
determined by astrology or recourse to the tables of planetary
hours and days. The first generation of iconoclastic chaos magicians challenged this, arguing, why not use one's finger, or a
rolled-up newspaper, or anything which is vaguely wand-
shaped? Whilst in a pinch, a sorcerer might well use anything to
hand with which to enchant his will, there is much to be said for
the traditional approach, by which one obtains a hand-made
weapon which is unique to oneself. It is, as Terry Pratchett
would doubtless say, a matter of headology.

Creating (or finding) a wand is itself an act of magic. As
noted above, the time-honoured method is to cut a branch from a
tree. Ideally, this should be a tree in a place which is significant
to you, which you have visited frequently at different times of
the year, until you have made contact with the spirit of the place,
the *genius loci*. If astrology is significant to you, then by all
means use astrology to determine the most appropriate time for
you to cut your wand. Alternatively, you could do it at a date
which has personal significance for you. Wood is only one alternative. Many magicians favour bone: for example, a bone
belonging to some animal whose abilities they wish to transfer to
themselves. Tibetan Bon Shamans use magical weapons shaped
from human bones, but this is an option which is less popular in
the West, where the traffic in murderer's index-fingers or the
thigh-bones of saints seems to have dropped off of late.

Other methods of obtaining a personalised wand include finding or being given something suitable. Some years back, I met an elder magician who had made himself a tibetan vajra, or thunderbolt, which so impressed me that, on my next visit to him, I asked him if he'd consider making me something similar. I took with me several chandelier lustres which I had found in a junk shop as a gift. On seeing these, my friend announced that we could make a vajra out of the lustres. We simply glued two of the lustres together, so that there was a point at either end, and then used a pendulum to determine which end was 'positive' and which was 'negative.' It had never occurred to me before that a wand could be made of glass. The lustres had seven notches in them, which I attributed to the seven chakras. You could peer into the facets and use them for scrying. They caught the light and created pleasing patterns in strong sunlight. By chance, I had acquired a powerful sorcery weapon. Unique, portable, and personally significant.

Obtaining the material component is only the beginning. The next step is to incorporate it into your magical universe. The most obvious means of doing this is to use it in all acts of magic, to have it present when you meditate, to sleep with it, to identify with it through meditation or visualisation. Call it to you astrally so that you can feel it's weight in your hand and feel the power you have infused it with flooding into you. Give it a name, if you so desire, and whisper to it your secrets and dreams. Keep it wrapped up, so that by the act of unwrapping it, you know that you are about to unleash the power of your refined will.

4. The Division of Roles

In Group ritual work, it's easy to fall into the habit whereby one or two people do things and everyone else stands around and watches. This can become boring, and I have occasionally found myself nodding off in long rituals! My rule-of-thumb guideline for group ritual is, whenever possible, have everyone involved doing something! For example, instead of just having one person declaim an invocation or litany, build parts into it so others can set up a counter-chant or use a call-and-response sequence. If the ritual calls for an invocation of the principle of Fire, for example, a verbal invocation can be considerably enhanced by having other celebrants dance the invocation, or use soundscaping which combines freestyle voice, gesture and movement to convey the mood being built up. Swapping roles is also highly effective—so that each participant gets a chance to perform each part of the ritual. Some groups approach role division by setting up formal roles and positions which people take on during ritual work, so that there might be, for example, an Incense-Monitor who is responsible for all aspects of the use of incense and scent; or an Exorcist, whose role is to assist people who seem to be having problems in both entering and leaving the altered states of consciousness built up during the ritual proceedings. These formal ritual roles may also be relevant for other aspects of group work, so that, perhaps, a Firemaster role might involve not only looking after fires and invoking the principle of fire during ritual, but also cover monitoring levels of enthusiasm and motivation in the group as a whole.

Hopefully the above has demonstrated the rich diversity of elements which can be interwoven into ritual magic, be it freestyle or formalised. However, it's up to you how much of this (if any) you choose to incorporate into your own ritual style. Generally, I tend to find that simplicity of style will always win out over complexity for complexity's sake. One approach I do find useful, particularly in group work, is to start with a simple ritual structure, and then progressively add to it with each working. This I find, is often more effective than dropping people into huge, cumbersome rituals.

EXAMPLE TYPES OF RITUAL

Here are four examples of different rituals and discussion of their usage. My aim in presenting them is not so much that you should try them out, but to illustrate how the elements and components of ritual discussed in the previous sections can be combined effectively.

Banishing Ritual

A Banishing Ritual is one of the first practical exercises that a magician learns. It is also sometimes known as *Centering*, which in many respects, is a more accurate term for the exercise.

A Banishing has three aims. The first is that it acts as a warm up—a preparation for doing further ritual, meditation—enabling the magician to put aside everyday thoughts—"what's on TV later," etc. It allows the magician to shift into his magician-self role, and to place himself in the metaphysical centre of his magical universe, the *axis mundi*.

Secondly, Banishing sets up the space being used for working as sacred, so that the loft, bedroom, basement or whatever becomes, temporarily, a Free Area.

Thirdly, a Banishing clears the atmosphere of the area being used from any emotional undercurrents that one usually (unconsciously) associates it with.

A Banishing can be a magical equivalent to tidying up (which should be done before working). Since most people are not fortunate enough to have a room which can be used solely for magical work, areas which are used for day-to-day living often have to be used as ritual spaces. This creates an atmosphere which can be sensed through unconscious cues, which it is well to Banish before starting focused magical work or it might well disturb the ritual. Similarly, after a working, one needs to dispel the particular atmosphere that has been created, or one might well find that it clashes with the everyday atmosphere that is normally associated with the room. On this point, it can be useful to Banish a room if there's been a particularly bad argument in it as the tension lingers, or if someone has spent a period of illness or depression there.

Most Banishing rituals have three basic components:

1. A section to focus awareness on the BodyMind.
2. A section which demarcates the main zones, gates, quarters or dimensions of the chosen magical universe—at which the magician is the centre.
3. An identification with a chosen source of inspiration— merging the macrocosm (total psychocosm) with the microcosm (self).

There follows an example Banishing ritual that illustrates these three sections.

Octomantic Banishing

This is a banishing sequence based on the Eight rays of the Chaosphere as facets of self/magical expression, showing eight different areas of magical activity (see *Liber Kaos* by Peter J. Carroll for a further exposition of these themes). Follow the sequence in the diagram. The direction of Magic can be taken as East.

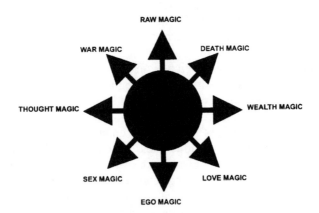

1. Begin facing East and stand, arms by your sides, head tilted slightly upwards, breathing slowly and regularly. Clear your mind of thoughts. Reach upwards with your right hand breathing

in, pause, and then bring it down the centre line of your body whilst breathing out, visualising a beam of white light passing down through your body, from above your head to below your feet.

Next, turn your head to the left and point with your left hand, then turn to your right and stretch your right arm out, forming a Tau Cross. Breathe in, hold, and breathe out, visualising a ray of white light running across your body, from left to right.

Then, whilst breathing in, bring your arms across your body so that they are stretched out in front of you, with hands reaching out at chest level. Exhale, and visualise a circle of light around your body.

Then, inhale, bringing your hands backwards and fold them across your chest. Breathe out, and visualise a sphere of white light expanding around yourself. Feel yourself to be super-charged with energy, yet at the same time, calm and ready for further action.

This completes the first stage of the Banishing, serving to direct attention to one's BodyMind and internal states.

2. Establishing the 8 directions of magic. For the first ray, breathe in, and on exhalation, snap fingers or clap hands, visualising a chaos thunderbolt (or dorjes) flashing forth, and declare:

"Raw Magic," making an appropriate gesture & hurling it outwards. Continue until you have established all 8 'rays':

- Death Magic
- Wealth Magic
- Love Magic
- Ego Magic
- Sex Magic
- Thought Magic
- War Magic

This section serves to establish the 8 directions, demarcating the sacred space, and placing the magician at its centre.

Then, facing East, raise arms in gesture of invocation and declare:

"These are my weapons
Expressions of my will
I grasp them lightly
I stand poised, at the centre
The Universe dances for my pleasure."

To close, run through the sequence again but with each intake of breath, visualise the thunderbolt returning to you.

For greater effect, each thunderbolt may be given its appropriate colour. Also, each thunderbolt could evolve into a chaosphere, or a personal servitor-entity which is emblematic of that power for you. If you wish to experiment with this Banishing, you should develop it into a form which works best for you.

This final declaration is the magician informing himself (and any others who may be listening in) that he is at the centre of his magical universe.

When working, Chaos Magicians choose one direction as 'metaphysical' east as the beginning point of any ritual which involves a progression through a series of directions. As a rule-of-thumb, I often take 'metaphysical east'(when indoors) to be any wall with a window in it.

Practice

A chosen Banishing can be done as a daily practice on awakening, and before retiring. It should be used to open and close any magical activity. In time, one will find that the ritual can be done almost on autopilot, and the associated feelings arise without conscious effort. It should be taken as an encouraging sign if one starts having dreams about Banishing. On a personal note, I find that whenever I dream of doing a banishing ritual, despite having developed a wide variety of personalized ones over the years, it is invariably the first one I learned (the Golden Dawn Lesser Pentagram Rite) which features in the dream.

Ritual Mass

The key element which is shared by both a religious (i.e., Catholic) Mass and a Mass performed by a magical group is the calling into the Free Area of the power of an entity, and the sharing of the power of that entity by all participants. In a Catholic Mass, the focus of the ritual is the miracle of Transubstantiation: the conversion of wine and host into the body and blood of Christ, which the participants consume. In a magical Mass, the modus for sharing the power may be much wider. The chosen entity is invoked into a chosen priest or priestess, who then becomes that entity (with varying degrees of possession). The entity may then deliver a litany, which can be scripted, or be an improvised oracle. The entity may be questioned by those attending, and may answer in any way it chooses fit. It may choose to lead the participants into acts which it sees as appropriate, or empower a prepared sacrament with its energy so that all may partake of its power. Or it may choose to share its power with those present in other ways.

In a Mass, it is occasionally useful to have ritual officers who are aware that it is their task, should it be found necessary, to banish the entity from its chosen host. It is not unknown for entities to resist departing from a space that they have been called into. When an individual has become deeply possessed, it is sometimes necessary to restrain him, and recall him to waking consciousness by forcefully banishing the possessing entity and making the host recall his own identity and whereabouts. In extreme cases, a lustration of water may be necessary to bring him out of the possession trance.

A less-than-serious example of a ritual mass follows.

Chaos Mass 'H'

Discordians have long identified Harpo Marx as a modern avatar of Harpocrates, Egyptian God of Silence. This Chaos Mass serves to manifest the power of HARPO, as Lord of Silence, Trickster, and Sacred Clown.

Preparation

The individual acting as Priest is given a woolly wig, Top Hat, and horn. Other props for use by HARPO can be placed on the altar.

Statement of Intent
"It is our will to invoke HARPO, Sacred Fool and Lord of Silent
Mockery, that the glamours of magic be dispersed, and Laughing
Anarchy enter our Hearts."

Priest: "Let the Pomposity begin."

The assembly then proceed to strut about, making self-impor-
tant proclamations about the 'serious' and 'sacred' paths of
magic, and that as mighty magi, they should be respected and
admired. They should declaim that magic is not a subject for
levity, that it should be taken seriously, that there is no room for
clowning about and being silly.

As the assembly do this, Priest begins to whirl and leap about,
making the appropriate gestures and facial patterns of Harpo,
silently invoking the name HAR-PO upon himself until the
Avatar, summoned to a room of high pomposity and seriousness,
manifests.

As the Priest feels himself swept into possession, he bran-
dishes the horn and gives the litany:

"Honk, Honk, Honk, Honk, Honk-Honk
Honk-Honk-Honk-Honk-Honk-Honk-Honk" (ad infinitum)

At which point the assembly freeze into statues of pomposity.
HARPO then has free reign to play whatever tricks and poses he
wills, his aim being to banish self-importance, and reduce the
assembly to laughter. (Note: a feather-duster, used as a tickling-
stick can be a very helpful prop here.)

HARPO then takes up a large rubber glove, fills it with the
chosen sacrament (milk?), makes a pin-prick in the index finger,
and proceeds to squirt it into the mouths of the Assembly.

He may then cut any capers and poses he wishes, until all
traces of self-importance and ego-attachment have been banished
from the assembly (if only temporarily).

Closure

Priest should be captured, divested of his ritual garments, and coaxed from silence into speech. Once he has made a few sensible remarks, the entire assembly break into raucous laughter and cheering.

Notes

Obviously some familiarity with the Marx Brothers' films is a prerequisite to the enaction of this rite, as is having a group of people who are willing to play at being pompous assholes, and indeed recognising how easily magicians can become pompous assholes and the need for banishing pomposity and self-importance. Rites which have a silly theme are no less important than those which are serious.

Ritual Invocation

The ritual below is an example of the invocation of a specific quality of energy (metaphorically speaking) to power a particular statement of intent. It was originally devised as a group rite but is suitable for modification into a solo ritual. One of my initial motivations for writing it was to demonstrate how the symbolic structures of the Qabalah lend themselves to practical ritual magic. In its original use, it was preceded by the celebrants spending a period meditating on the 4 Five cards in the Tarot and The Tower of the Major Arcana—these cards relating to the action and symbolism relating to Geburah (i.e., Mars).

Geburah: Invocation Of Martial Power

Possible Applications

1. Increase of Will, Confidence, Purpose
2. Initiating New Projects
3. Enhanced Sexual Vitality
4. Increase of energy, Courage
5. Destruction of Obstacles (internal & external)
6. Charging of Talismans
7. Charging Magical Weapons

Props & Artefacts used

1. Geburah/Mars incense
2. Scourge, Chain, Sword
3. Anointing Oil (Juniper)
4. Tarot cards: The Tower, Adjustment, The Emperor
5. Bell, Gong, or Drum.
6. Five Scarlet Candles
7. Fiery liquid (sacrament)
8. Focus—pyramid solid constructed from Red card, on which are painted in black the planetary symbol of Mars, the Elemental symbol of Fire, and the signs of the Planetary Spirit, Seal and Intelligence.

Preparation

The Altar is set up on a cloth of scarlet. It should comprise the five candles, the Tarot cards, the magical weapons, instruments and focus.

Ritual Officers

Master of the Temple (bearing Sword)
Priest (bearing Sword or dagger)
One or more Assistants wielding Scourges.

Sequence

1. Banishing Ritual
Following the Banishing, celebrants are arranged in rows as though they are soldiers on parade. The M.T and assistants stand facing them.

2. Statement Of Intent
"It is our Will to Invoke the Powers of Geburah for..."

3. Purification
M.T and assistants may inspect the celebrants. The bearing of all is that of a military formation. Then each celebrant is brought before the altar and scourged five times, then returned to his place in the formation.

4. Invocations
First Invocation
   M.T then directs celebrants to form a circle around him.
This is done so that the assisting Priest who bears a sword
stands facing the priest.
   All celebrants come to Attention and look upwards. MT leads
them in the invocation of the God-Name of Geburah:

   "I call upon the mighty one ELOHIM GIBOR, god of
strength.
   Above our heads there swirls an Orange Mist, and dimly, a
shape forms in the mist—the image of a mighty king; he stands
in a chariot, arrayed with chains and shields. He is armed with
Spear, Scourge and a bright sword hangs from his belt. He is the
embodiment of Law, Power, Discipline and Strength."

Second Invocation
   M.T raises sword and begins invocation of KHAMMAEL:

   "I call upon the mighty Archangel KHAMMAEL, the Burner,
the Wrathful One. He who destroys and purifies. He who
cleanses all decay and stagnation from the universe. KHAM-
MAEL, the embodiment of Power, of Will, of Purpose, of
Courage, of Self-Scrutiny and Discrimination. KHAMMAEL
mighty Archangel of Mars, bring your force and flame into our
hearts."

   Whilst the M.T delivers this invocation, all visualise the mist
swirling, forming a vortex. From the eye of the vortex there
descends a beam of laser-thin scarlet—it strikes the tip of the
M.T's sword and throws a corona around it. The M.T closes the
invocation with a sharp "Hah!" which signals the next phase of
the rite.

Flashing Power
   M.T draws down the sword and thrusts it towards his assis-
tant, blasting him with the power of Khammael. The assistant
spins around deosil and then hurls that power to the celebrant to
his right. This continues around the circle, until the Assistant
returns the power to the M.T by projecting the power back at
him.

Third Invocation
M.T raises sword and summons the SERAPHIM:

"See the brilliant scarlet flames dancing upon this weapon.
I now summon the SERAPHIM, the Fiery Serpents of Purification and Correction, to manifest our Will (all visualise the
Fire-Serpents entwined around the M.T's sword)—visualisation
of desire-forms can be made at this moment.
M.T spins and projects power outwards with cry of "Kia!" All
visualise Serpents streaming forth and give sharp cry of exulta-
tion.

Closing

Banishing Ritual

MT: "Atten-Shun!"
      "About-Turn!"
      "Stand-At Ease!"

"Stand Easy—Banish with Laughter."

Notes

This ritual demonstrates how the careful arrangement of props,
symbolism and actions contributes to the projection of a particular mood or atmosphere within the ritual space. The ritual is
structured according to the dictates of Western Qabalah; the
invocations act to draw power through the astral zones, the
spheres of Gods, Archangels and Angelic powers, enabling the
celebrants to identify with these forces both individually and
collectively. The Flashing Power exercise is used to distribute
the force of Khammael between the participants, by turning
deosil (clockwise) they take the force within themselves and
project it outwards and thereby enhancing it. If this rite is used to
project a common intent (i.e., increased confidence) the combined power of the rite is projected outwards, into the participants' immediate future. Alternatively, to charge a magical artefact, it could be directed into that artefact.

A Ritual Enchantment

As I have previously remarked, it is not entirely necessary to use a formal ritual format for the purpose of casting an enchantment. It may sometimes, however, be deemed to be desirable—for example, as an element of a group meeting or during a period of magical activity which is centred around a specific theme or idea. The ritual below was devised whilst I was undertaking a six-month period of working with the Norse god, Thor, and had been asked to demonstrate a practical application of these researches to a group of which I was then a member.

The Hammer-Cast

This ritual uses the mythic structures and symbolism of the so-called Northern or Germanic Tradition. It uses an invocation of the mythic qualities of the god Thor, enabling the participants to identify with the powers and qualities of the god in order to create the appropriate mood and atmosphere for hurling forth an enchantment. Anyone familiar with Thor from either Norse Mythology or Marvel Comics will recall that his hammer, Mjollnir, always returns to him, reinforcing the idea that the participants of the rite will achieve their desire.

Requirements:
A Statement of Intent for creating a sigil—which can be visualised or used as a mantric word of power. The Sigil should be prepared beforehand, in a manner that it can be easily recalled during the rite.

0. Rite begins with the *Statement of Intent* (given by the leader in parts—all repeat).
"It is our will to cast forth a desire, in the name of the Thunderer."

1. Deep Breathing
Leader demonstrates posture which all adopt. Leader begins 9 slowly-paced inhalation/exhalations. Whilst breathing, celebrants visualise lightning bolts crackling around their bodies, especially between their hands.

2. Stance

Celebrants take up Thurisaz runic-posture and focus upon their sigilised desire, whilst leader declaims the litany (see below). Celebrants visualise themselves as holding Thor's Hammer in their right hands. The sigilised desire is focused upon the hammer.

3. Remaining in Posture, leader initiates paced Vibration of THUR-IZ-AS x9

4. With a wordless scream, celebrants hurl the hammer forth.

THE LITANY
(variations on this basic theme)

"Mighty Thor, champion, defender of Asgard,
Lend us your strength
Indomitable one, slayer of giants,
May our aim be true,
Sky God, Judge of men,
Let our Will be pure,
Dweller in Thrudheim, wielder of Mjollnir
Let the cast fly true,
Storm-god, Son of Earth,
Look well upon us.

INVOCATION

Invocation basically involves calling upon an entity and thereby identifying oneself with it, to the level that one apparently merges with it. This technique can have profound effects, both emotionally and physically, and like any other powerful magical technique, it can be tricky if not given due care and attention.

Why Invoke?

For what reason might one desire to bring a Goddess, God, or other mythic entity into oneself? The multiple entities found within polytheistic and pantheistic systems each encapsulate different attributes and qualities. Thus one might desire to invoke Baphomet for inspiration, Pan for ecstasy and heightened sexual arousal, one of the Nornir, for knowledge of the future, Ra-Hoor-Khuit to give a 'hawk's-eye view' of a situation, or Kali, to consume some aspect of self which one wishes to loosen from one's ego-complex. Through invocation, one might make modifications to one's selves, seek inspiration, or specific knowledge about a certain event or item; develop powers of heightened perception or feel oneself to be charged with power which can be used for further magical tasks.

Invocations tend to result in an ecstatic state, whereby the recipient is so passionately swept up into trance, that some quality or attribution associated with that entity manifests in the person, such as enhanced oracular perception or knowledge of hidden lore. While this ability may be developed by anyone who practises magic, most people don't do it, and thus a magical practitioner may be asked to act as the incarnation of a particular entity as part of an event, or to bring about a similar experience in another person—'invoking upon someone,' as it is known.

Invocation serves to heighten dramatic awareness to the extent that the magician, who is identifying (or being identified as) with the mythic figure in question, gains both access to abilities associated with that figure, and temporarily is able to perform acts beyond his or her normal capacities. Actors often report a similar experience of becoming so caught up in characters they are portraying, that they find they can sing, dance or perform feats of agility which, while appropriate for those particular characters, are beyond their own normal range of ability. It seems that, given appropriate conditions, we are capable of much more than we usually allow ourselves.

Designing Invocations

Source books of Magic abound with examples of invocations, but, for now, it is the processes underlying invocations which are to be considered. Firstly, it is essential to build up a framework of symbols which can be employed to focus awareness onto the subject of the invocation. This is where the symbolic media and tables of correspondences mentioned earlier come in useful. If for example, a magician wished to invoke Star Trek's Mr. Spock, then the first thing to do would be to research Spock's mannerisms, gestures, posture and Vulcan inscrutability, and adopt these as part of the ritual. As a further aid, a pathworking could be devised based around the image of Spock walking through the corridors of the USS Enterprise, until the magician felt sufficiently composed as Spock to undertake an appropriate task, such as debugging a computer program, which often requires unswerving logic, patience and calm—all qualities for which Mr. Spock is well-known. Logical?

Background Research

It's generally thought to be a good idea that before you embark on an invocation, you need to know something about the entity you are going to invoke. Background research basically takes two forms: using other people's material, and finding information yourself using magical approaches. Some authorities have it that the more you know about an entity, the more effective your invocation will be, but this is not always possible. Sometimes, all you may have to go on is a name and a vague association. So appropriate magical research might include meditating on the name of the entity; using mindscaping techniques in order to meet that entity on the astral plane; using divination techniques to try and draw out more information, or trying to relate the entity to particular tarot cards or runes; use of dream magic techniques to try and 'dream' the entity, or perhaps visiting a locality which is associated with the entity and meditating there. Reading fiction, myths and folk-tales wherein the entity features can also be an excellent way of getting into the right mood. Indeed, invocation is basically concerned with getting yourself into the right mood for a particular entity. Hunches and synchronicities relating to your interest in an entity are just as important, if not more so, than literary research into the entities' history and characteristics. I think what is important is that however you go about it, you begin to build up a feel for the entity, be it goddess, god, daemon or a little-known local spirit. It doesn't matter if you can't quite put your thoughts and feelings into words.

Non-Verbal Invocation

The basis of non-verbal invocation is to bring forth in yourself the right mood in order to feel the presence of the entity within or around you. I occasionally find that this mood is something which wells up inside me, perhaps as response to other things which are happening in my life. A few years ago I had reached a turning point in my magical direction as it were. I didn't know quite what was happening, but I knew I wasn't happy in my current situation. The stress of trying to resolve the issue was winding me up something rotten. The situation was complicated by feelings of both personal, organisational and business-related loyalties which I felt would make it difficult to make a clean break. This all peaked up one evening at a Seminar. Feeling sick and twisted up inside, I walked across the venue's grounds and found a tree well away from the main building, where a riotous party was going on. Sitting down, I began an impromptu puja and invoked 'Pasupati,' the Tantric deity who is the herdsman, one of whose functions is to remove 'that which binds.' I'd never worked with this god before, but emotional intensity (born out of overwhelming need) enabled me to achieve the appropriate state of devotion, and I was stunned by a vision of Pasupati, blazing with white light, staring back at me. In retrospect, it was the white-hot intensity of this moment which allowed me to let go of the bindings that I felt entangled in. The effect wasn't immediate of course, but that, for me marked the change-point. It wasn't so much a conscious decision to invoke Pasupati, but more that it felt right at the time. There are many different techniques which

130   *Phil Hine*

can be combined for non-verbal invocation. Dance is one very popular approach, though admittedly not my particular forté. Many of the elements discussed in the section on elements of ritual can be utilised. Perhaps one of the simplest, yet most effective techniques, is the identification of particular emotional states with entities. For example, I have a Pan-mood which often manifests as the desire to go off on my own into the country, or a general horniness which I can enjoy without necessarily feeling that I have to do something about it. Equally, I have an Isis-state which feels like a frosty regality occasionally reflected back by watching 1930's Hollywood movie queens. Whilst these states could be intensified through formalised ritual proceedings, it's nice just to experience them from time to time.

Non-verbal invocation can also be effective using dance and music. In a group setting, this might comprise of the individual calling the chosen deity into himself by dancing, whilst others invoke that deity using either stylised or freeform dance and music. Dance styles can be drawn from various magical traditions or created for a particular deity by the group.

Verbal Invocations

When designing verbal invocations, it is important to consider *Delivery*. The way we speak is a powerful way of projecting our intentions. The delivery of a speech quickly transmits to both self and audience one's degree of confidence. A fine invocation may be written, but can quickly be rendered ineffective if it is read out in a deadpan voice and punctuated by 'ers' and 'ums.' Words can be paced, so that speech can excite or relax the listener—which can be oneself or others. A good delivery of an invocation serves to raise dramatic awareness in both self and others. If you think of it in terms of a feedback loop, then the more enthralling the speech, the more intense the degree of dramatic awareness, and the more people will become caught up in the ritual atmosphere. When one person, for example, is performing an invocation, others present may temporarily become the audience—and participants can shift between active and passive involvement throughout a ritual. The key to remember is that, if such be your intent, then everything that happens inside the ritual space can be used to enhance the atmosphere. Try exploring the effect of pacing your speech, deliberately breathing louder, and, when reaching the climax of the invocation, becoming breathless and adding a bit of tremble. You don't have to shout to be effective, a whisper or can be just as effective (if not more so) than a loud voice.

If you can successfully use your voice to project emotional tones—such as awe, reverence or passion—then those listening; both yourself and others, will pick up on the emotive undertones and become drawn into the atmosphere you are generating. As people enter different stages of trance, their voice pattern changes.

Others present pick up on this, if only unconsciously, and so the atmosphere of dramatic awareness is generated. In a ritual sequence, all speech can be used to project appropriate feelings which generate the group atmosphere. This is best performed when the people speaking are confident and relaxed about what they are saying. Hence the problem with (a) reading from textbooks and (b) using very long speeches. If possible, it is preferable to either learn a speech so that one needs not to look at bits of paper, which tends to be bothersome (especially when reading someone else's writing in a dark room or wind-swept moor) or improvise something at the spur of the moment. Like all practical techniques, being able to do this is simply a matter of practice and confidence. Unless one is doing something that is particularly stylised, simplicity is usually the most effective approach.

Structure and *Rhythm* are also important. An invocation to a particular figure is often based on a resume of the qualities and energies associated with it, or referring to legends or deeds associated with it. The rhythm of speech, is also important. The rhythm given to words when delivering an invocation can quickly generate appropriate moods in those using or hearing them. An invocation to Pan, for example, might have a fast and frenetic rhythm which leaves the speaker breathless, bringing to mind the wildness of Pan; whilst an invocation to Cronus, God of Time might be slow and ponderous. Rhythms are known to have distinct physiological effects, serving to relax or stimulate breathing and heartbeat.

It should be noted that an invocation may not necessarily read well, but all the same can sound excellent when chanted.

The classic form of invocation has three distinct parts to it. In the first, the deeds of the figure are given, spoken in the third person; in the second, the qualities of the figure are spoken in the second person; and finally, the powers of the figure are spoken of in the first person. Thus the process of identification with the figure becomes more intense throughout the invocation, uniting self and subject. Thus, as the speech proceeds, one is moving from a position of describing that figure as a separate being, and becoming identified with that figure to the extent that (for all ritual intents and purposes) you become that figure. Following which, for the rest of the group, you are the earthly avatar of a Mythic figure.

Having taken on the role, you can now act, using the power and attributes of that figure, which can range from delivering an oracular speech to leading a frenzied dance. In the Western Mystery tradition (such as it is), it is usual for one person to act as vessel or channel for a mythic figure, and other participants to take on the role of celebrants (or congregation).

However, in other cultures, it is not unknown for several people at once to become possessed by the same deity. In Haiti, there was once a celebrated case of about 300 people, all possessed simultaneously by the God Legba, who marched in protest at the political situation to the presidential residence!

In western magic, people tend to stick to one approach which is usually what they've been taught in a group or coven. This is often a pity, because there are often good alternatives to be found in, for example, the study of drama or oratory. One useful element to look at is the idea of Status Shifts. We move through status shifts as a consequence of social interactions, along a scale of low to high Status transactions. These transactions also occur during rituals. During a vocal invocation, you might begin with the status position of a supplicant reaching up to a deity, and eventually act with the status of that deity, whilst others will (or should) regard you appropriately. This often leads to a confusion of roles, as some people find it hard to distinguish between the role someone might take within a ritual setting, and how he behaves outside of it. Someone who becomes a goddess in a ritual should not be treated like one after the ritual has been concluded! Hence the prime danger in identifying oneself with

Mythic figures is one of blowing up one's ego to massive proportions. If you continually identify with a figure who reinforces some idea which you have about yourself, all you will do is imbalance yourself towards those particular tendencies. I have known at least three people become quite seriously disturbed because they worked exclusively with lunar, oracular figures who accentuated their predisposed tendency to slip into passive, oracular trance states. As in all practices, an understanding and continual assessment of oneself in terms of strengths, weaknesses, and ego-identifications is necessary, especially if you are working with others in a teaching or group leader role.

It's fair to say that the more that is put into an invocation, the more intense the effect will be. There are more elements to consider, such as the use of gestures to reinforce speech; the use of lighting and props; smell, taste, music and stage-setting. Of course the absence of speech can be as equally effective, as can be the use of grunts, howls and cackles. Having an infectious laugh can be a very useful skill, as well; you can literally laugh your way out of some situations. Humour is an important element of ritual, which is often neglected by some of the ever-so-serious people one runs into occasionally.

One approach to experimenting with invocations is to assemble a variety of speeches written by other people and try reading them aloud until you hit on a delivery that feels effective. It can be useful to tape such experiments, and even use them as background effects in ritual work. Using appropriate music can also be productive. While it's useful to look at other people's written invocations—so you can grasp the way that structure and rhythm can evolve through the way lines are delivered—it's generally considered better to use your own attempts at invocation. Not only does this build confidence and give you a good feel for what works and what doesn't, but it allows you to build up a close contact with the figure you are identifying with. Generally, it's easier to invoke human figures than non-human ones. Using the same principles in approaching shape-shifting, it would be appropriate for you to observe a particular animal: look at its characteristic postures, facial expression, its vocalisations, and characteristic behaviours. You would become the animal by close identification with its characteristics. The intensity of trance would probably much depend on the degree of abandonment that you allowed yourself to have.

Overshadowing and Possession

Invocation often results in a state of awareness which has two extremes: Overshadowing and Possession. Overshadowing is a trance state where the recipient of an invocation—the person who is acting as a 'channel' for the invoked entity—feels imbued with the power of the figure which has been invoked. He may also feel varying degrees of detachment from what is going on around him, but without losing any sense of volition. People who have been overshadowed by an entity tend to report feelings of having an altered perception of bodily shape, and sometimes are able to distinguish a dissonance between what they 'as the entity' wanted to do, and what they 'as themselves' wanted to do.

In the case of possession however, the personality of the magician is almost submerged (sometimes totally) by that of the mythic figure which has been invoked. It is not uncommon, when this occurs, for the individual involved to have only a partial recollection (if any) of what happened during the possession state. For example, Maya Deren, author of the classic *The Voodoo Gods* (1953) found that on several occasions on viewing Voodoo rituals in Haiti, she herself became possessed. On one occasion she awoke from trance to discover that she had been mounted and ridden (possessed) by the Goddess Erzulie, and had led the ritual. Individuals who become deeply possessed can often do things that, under normal circumstances, would incapacitate them. People possessed by the Loa, for example, are able to place hot coals in their mouth without getting burnt, dance manically for hours, and consume large amounts of rum without becoming drunk. They may also display a knowledge of subjects which they would not normally be able to discourse upon.

Possession is a wide-ranging phenomena which is probably the most popular form of union with the divine in human history. Possession-oriented rituals are apparent in ancient Egypt and it has been shown that the earliest forms of Qabalistic practice were oriented towards this type of experience. Possession was a recognised phenomena in ancient Greece, two examples being the Delphic oracle, and the practices of the Theurgists, defined by Proclus as, *"...in a word, all the operations of divine possession."* Possession is a central feature of Voudoun, Santeria, and Macumba, religions which are gaining increasing popularity, and is apparent in most tribal cultures, from America to Australasia.

Possession also appears in early Christianity—particularly with the manifestation of speaking in tongues which remains popular in modern-day forms of evangelical Christianity. St. Paul's dramatic experience on the road to Damascus bears all the hallmarks of a sudden divine possession, yet he was worried by the phenomenon, and found it necessary to lecture the Corinthian Christians on the need to carefully manage speaking in tongues: *"If therefore, the whole church assembles, and all speak in tongues, and outsiders or unbelievers enter, will they not say that you are mad? ...do not forbid speaking in tongues, but all things should be done decently and in order"* (I Corinthians, 14).

An indicator of the possession experience is that the person affected shows physiognomic changes, such as altered voice pitch, facial expression, postures and gestures. Occasionally the facial muscles re-contract into different patterns, demonstrably different to the persons' characteristic facial expression. These changes can act as signals to other members participating in such a rite. They signal the arrival of the invoked figure, and serve to heighten the dramatic awareness of the whole group. Once one person has become possessed, it is easier, should this be desirable, for others to become so, too.

Possession enables an individual to let go of normal limitations and perform feats which are normally impossible, or forbidden by society. Possession in Voodoo and similar cultures is an expected and sanctioned occurrence (though often by no means pleasant) whereas in the West, such an extreme form of disinhibition is usually frowned upon, and very much regarded as demonic by many people. As such, possession is a much rarer occurrence in Western Magic than overshadowing, although in recent years it has become a more common practice amongst Chaos-oriented magicians.

The ability to lose control appears to be a key factor in the possession experience. I have seen people who, upon attempting to take on a manifestation for the first time, clearly lose the trance when their inhibitions over what is acceptable behaviour conflicts with the persona of the entity they have taken on. Expectations over how to behave, even within the free space of a magical ritual once they have been built up, are difficult to shed. The ability to release one's inhibitions and go with the possession takes time to build up for many people, though it can equally be the case that individuals who seem otherwise, to lack charisma and confidence, can sometimes very quickly let go and enter possession trance. One explanation is that the possession experience gives participants permission to act out of character. As a voudou celebrant said to S. E. Simpson (author of *Religious Cults of Caribbean: Trinidad, Jamaica & Haiti*, 1970)... "What a person is afraid to do, he does when possessed." Permission to act in a manner appropriate to the God is effectively sanctioned by officiating officers, celebrants and audience. However, in modern rituals, the limits of permission are not always clearly defined. Anthropological accounts of possessed persons seemingly going out of control agree that any relating violence is approved of and expected—part of the play of the ceremony. In teaching others the trick of becoming possessed, it is essential to convey the message that the individual is not responsible for the behaviour of the spirit. Once one understands that all present are able to divorce the behaviour of the individual from the presence of the God, the need to hold fast to one's personality diminishes.

It should be understood that possession is not merely a matter of entity and vessel, but an experience that arises from the total interaction of those present. In some senses, possession is a form of theatrical performance. Accounts of possession ceremonial by Deren, Seabrook, and others indicate that the interaction between performers (those possessed by spirits), audience, ritual officers and the Master(s) of Ceremonies co-creates the possession experience. Of particular interest is the role taken on by the Master of Ceremonies or officiating Priest.

Keith Johnstone (*Impro*, 1981) notes that in Voudou ceremonial, the officiating priests have high status, yet are "indulgent" to the possessed participants, who often exhibit child-like, or playful behaviour. Another useful analogy is the idea of the MC as 'ringmaster,' coaxing the possessees towards the ecstasy of gnosis and whipping the audience on. A good MC ensures not only that the spirit behaves (or misbehaves) appropriately, but also that the audience participates in the performance. All too often, I have seen the 'audience' in a possession working standing uneasily round the possessee, and occasionally, being berated by the spirit for their lack of participation. Invocatory rites are similar to evocatory rites in that they are context-derived. In my experience, the successful appearance of an evoked goetic spirit depends very much on the ritual space—the use of appropriate props and paraphernalia. In the same fashion, good possession working requires a clear context that is known and understood by all participants. Conflicting expectations often give rise to results which are at variance with the participants' intentions. This is not, of course, an issue, in ceremonies where the entire assembly knows what to expect of the entity manifesting. William Sargant gives an account of a Voudoun ceremony he witnessed in Haiti, where two girls became simultaneously possessed by Ghede, a loa who is known to be particularly sexually active: *"They half stripped each other and one girl symbolically raped the other with a masculine type of pelvic approximation. It ended with the total emotional collapse of both participants."* Sargant goes on to say that the group was somewhat amused by this episode, and that the girls, who were normally restrained and quiet, had no memory of what they had done. He notes that the only people who were upset by the incident were the boyfriends of the girls, but that they could say nothing, as it was the manifestation of Ghede. This in itself is an important point. In many possession-oriented cults, there is a tacit understanding that whatever possessed persons do, it is the action of the indwelling entity and as such, they cannot be faulted. Furthermore, after the people come out of possession, they are not told how they behaved.

It has often struck me that the size of the group participating in a possession working can also contribute to the depth of trance on the part of the possessee. Whilst work in small, close-knit groups allows a strong atmosphere of trust, confidence and relaxation to build up, which is conducive to possession taking place. However, large groups, particularly frenzied workings involving strobe lights, massed dancing and screaming, allow a celebrant to achieve a deep possession relatively quickly. Again, the effect of being in a crowd enables the dominant personality to be shed quickly. Also, the fact that the vehicle for possession is the focus of attention for the entire group brings on an excitatory state of arousal, kicking in the fight-flight autonomic reflex, washing away the borders of self-image in a flood of adrenaline. Rhythmic drumming, dancing and chanting are three of the most popular means of creating a possession experience, to which modern magicians have added the use of strobe lights and audio effects. The use of Masks, and other ritual props, is an important feature in possession. In some cults, when a celebrant begins to display the symptoms of possession, the character of the incarnating entity is discerned by the officiating priests, and that individual is given the appropriate props for the particular god or goddess. In Western approaches to possession, it is more likely that the vehicle visualises himself, or is already dressed in the appropriate garb. In contemporary magic, the vehicle for possession by a particular god tends to be chosen before the ritual proceeds, rather than, as in Voudoun, being spontaneously ridden by the loa. Masks are particularly useful in conferring a degree of anonymity to the wearer. Masks which are particular to a certain spirit tend to exhibit consistent behaviour, no matter who is wearing them. As has been noted, spirits tend to a certain conservatism and the invading spirit may be defined as a mask, an arising character which has its own behaviour and personality, as defined by belief and context. This may not, however, be the case for 'unfinished' gods, that is, entities who are not reinforced by an informing tradition, belief system or even a general expectation of character formed from the pool of celebrants' experience. This appears to be the case for entities such as Baphomet.

Whilst in a religious context, the direct experience of the indwelling entity serves to validate belief in that religious system, possession can occasionally be problematic from a magical perspective, where certain, unshakable belief is not quite viewed in the same light. While within the ritual space, it is important to invest total belief in the possession experience, the continuance of uncritical belief outside it can become dysfunctional. This, however, calls into question the function of possession-experience, particularly within the context of Chaos Magic. I have often heard an incarnating entity utter oracular or prophetic statements during possession workings. In a context of generalised belief, one assumes that the results of possession workings would be integrated into the successive experience of the participant. I often wonder how far this is the case in Chaos Magic, where consensual belief in the reality of the experience may be shed as soon as one leaves the temple space.

A second problem which relates to possession is that of knowledge of the entity. It may occur that an entity manifests within a vessel that is unprepared. By this, I refer to an individual who has no prior knowledge of the entity, in terms of its character, mythological associations, or relevant behaviour. This is particularly relevant when we consider entities that have knowledge of specific areas. In possession-oriented cultures, it is usual that entities who can offer diagnostic advice manifest through healers or witch-doctors. It would be difficult for someone with no knowledge of such specialisation to give a coherent delivery, even if he was possessed by the relevant spirit. A related problem is that individuals who are new to the possession experience may not have the skills to accurately deliver a message. Again, the ability to let go, as discussed above, is relevant.

Thirdly, there is the problem of fixation. Some magicians appear to become fixated on manifesting a particular persona, often to the point that regardless of the character of the entity, the same behaviour and persona is apparent. Arguably, this is not true possession, but an expression of ego-reinforcement in front of an audience. This can result in obsessional mania, as the self being continually reinforced dominates the magician's behavioural repertoire, to the point where it is difficult for any other selves to manifest, and the individual's beliefs and behaviour are limited to that of the dominant self. There is often a deep-rooted insecurity behind such fixations.

A fourth problem with possession is related to the idea of banishing or earthing. It is not unusual for individuals to remain possessed even after a rite has been concluded. There are instances of participants in such workings becoming spontaneously possessed hours or even days after the event. In the religious context, this tends to lead to conversion experiences. Some psychological models of possession relate the experience to the release of accumulated tension, and if the experience does not culminate in exhaustion (it's own banishing) or collapse, then the effects of it may linger. Those who wish to make use of possession-oriented work would do well to bear this in mind.

Like many other types of magical experience, possession is a learned response. When an individual first experiences possession, it may have far-reaching consequences as a life-changing agent. It may occur suddenly, or gradually, and in some accounts of possession, it can be agonizingly painful. The degree of resistance to the experience is interesting in this light. William Sargant notes that often, the more one resists the onset of possession, the more intense the experience actually becomes. I have noticed that, in my own experience of being possessed, whenever I have consciously tried to limit the depth of possession, it has in fact, proved to be much more intense than I expected. With practice, one may achieve a state of possession relatively quickly.

Whatever the setting or the context, the key elements of possession remain similar. Warm-up rituals such as banishing prepare for the main event by helping the celebrant to focus attention on the entity to be manifested. The use of excitatory gnosis such as drumming and dancing place the body under stress, allowing awareness to be inflamed with the image of the incoming entity. Individuals may spontaneously become possessed, or the possession may be directed into one individual chosen specifically to be the vehicle. Whilst it is possible for someone *other* than the chosen vehicle to be possessed by the entity, it appears rare that entities *other* than those being invoked manifest. As Sargant says, Christian revivalists do not become possessed by the Goddess Kali. Since the gods have a certain amount of regality, they often react badly to being commanded, yet can be steered by weaker commands. Hence the indulgence on the part of officiating priests as noted by Keith Johnstone. It is often the case that the God is reluctant to leave the vehicle. In modern magic, this tends to be dealt with by placing the celebrant under further stress by capturing them (if necessary) and calling them out of trance until the invading persona has departed.

Possession remains a powerful form of magical work. It can be used to derive oracular information (as used by the Greeks and Tibetans), to charge magical weapons, to share in the power of the God (as in ritual Masses) or 'live' a particular mythic transformation. In constructing possession-workings, it can be useful to examine magical and religious paradigms where possession is a recognised and culturally-defined technique. The experience itself can be related to wider phenomenon such as religious conversion, hypnosis, and abreactive therapy. As with all types of magical technique, it's use requires careful analysis and evaluation if it is not to devolve into a habituated limitation. In general, magical possession is both useful and enjoyable, if a little hair-raising at times.

As ever with magic, the more the care is given to the ingredients, and the skill with which they are compounded, the more intense the experience will be. No amount of theorising can put across the actual feeling of what possession is like. It needs to be experienced, and practised, to be fully understood.

Devotional Magic

In his *Liber Astarte*, Crowley offers a more complex schema for invocatory design, which involves seven different stages: one begins by addressing the entity as would a slave to one's master, then as a vassal to his lord, then as a child to its parent, a priest to a deity, as one sibling to another, as a close friend, and finally, as a lover. This particular schema requires that the magician make appropriate paradigm and status shifts, and is particularly useful when embarking upon a magical 'monasticism'—a period of days, weeks or months during which one particular deity is invoked progressively, on a daily basis, sometimes referred to as a *magical retirement*. Progressive invocatory work of this nature can yield up a great deal of information about the nature, qualities, or aspects of a particular entity. It also allows the magician to create a personal relationship with a particular entity. Other useful approaches to devotional invocation include:

(a) Behaving in a manner which you feel would please the entity throughout your daily life.
(b) Discerning the 'hand' of the entity stirring events in your everyday life.
(c) Establishing a personal shrine to the entity and regularly giving offerings—money, incense, flowers, sweets—whatever you feel is appropriate.

(d) Devising personal prayers, visualizations, mantras, meditations etc., that can be used anywhere in any place. For
example, at one place of work, I had a large image of
Ganesha depicted as the lord of scribes on my computer,
thus allowing me to offer devotion to Ganesha both easily
and unobtrusively.

In terms of devotional magic (and I feel this is also true for
any magical activity) it matters little whether you are doing
formal ritual or informal, off-the-cuff actions, so long as what
you are doing is genuine for you and from the heart.

EVOCATION

Evocation is concerned with the calling forth of an entity into a defined space (such as a triangle, crystal, bottle, etc.), within which it can be bound to carry out a specific task, or a series of tasks within a particular sphere of influence. The practice of evocation has tended to receive less emphasis than invocation in modern magic, as it has acquired a sinister glamour through association with popular grimoires such as the *Lesser Key of Solomon the King* and popular films such as the Dennis Wheatley classic, *The Devil Rides Out*. Also, those magical paradigms which have an undercurrent of transcendentalism, tend to de-emphasise the technique, as self-development is held to be the goal of the magician, rather than merely manipulating the physical world.

However, for the pragmatic sorcerer, evocation may be an immensely useful technique.

Evocation has a very wide range of applications. Evoked entities may be sent forth to perform specific results-oriented tasks such as healing, protection, giving inspiration, operations of an offensive nature, etc. They may also be employed to modify one's own behavioural and cognitive patterns, act as guides for dream-work and astral magic explorations, and can be set to patrol a given area, such as one's house, possessions or an outdoor space. A popular contemporary use of evoked/created entities is to place them as site guardians at areas that are environmentally at risk.

The Dynamics of Evocation

Regardless of the language and glamour that one uses to describe the practice of evocation, the basic technique consists of the following stages:

1. An Entity is either chosen from an existing grimoire of spirits, created by the magician, or otherwise contacted (i.e., through dream-work, trance, or scrying).

2. This entity is then called forth into a defined space. The parameters of this space depend very much on the system or glamour that the magician chooses to work within. Thus a magician using the *Lesser Key of Solomon* would use a triangle inscribed with the symbols of that system, command the demons into appearing, subjugate them into obeying his commands, and then send them forth. Alternatively, a magician working within a shamanic-oriented paradigm might first embark on a psychoactive-assisted vision-quest, during which he meets the spirit, learns its name, shape and form, and upon returning from trance, calls forth the spirit from the otherworld into a prepared receptacle such as a bottle, stone, crystal or mask. The terms and techniques may differ, but the underlying procedure is the same.

These two phases may be further examined as:

1. Identification
Here, the magician is concerned with discovering/creating the entities' name; shape; number (if appropriate); form, and perhaps even persona. That is, the magician defines the entity as an individual unit, and relates to it as though it were so, for the duration of the working. The paradigm that one is working within will provide the belief buffer as to the nature and aetiology of that entity. By allowing the entity to have, to varying degrees, a socially-defined mask or independence, then the magician is able to interact with it as if it were an independent being.

2. Environment
The environment of the entity can be understood to be the general paradigm which the entity is being worked within; from background belief to the very parameters of the ritual being used to establish the entity as a discrete unit, allot it a task, and send it forth. During this stage, the magician can also decide upon any specific qualities, symbolism, or organs that are appropriate to the nature of the entities' task.

3. Data
This stage covers the isolation of any variables concerning the operation, such as a time limit, a particular window of opportunity, optimal conditions for success, or if the entities' operation is to be linked to specific cues, such as time-periods, astrological conjunctions, moon-phases, or command words used by the

magician. For example, an entity whose task is to seed the magician with new ideas could be brought into operation whenever the magician vibrates a particular word or phrase.

4. Procedure
This final stage concerns the construction of the Statement of Intent: the encapsulation of the task that the entity will perform and when, where, and how.

These four stages are taken from the procedure of writing a computer program in the COBOL language. To further the analogy, one may consider that an evoked entity is a program shell, with a particular name, identity, functions, and the ability to process variables. The magical operation serves to launch the program, and set it working upon a user-defined operation. The magician acting within the ritual procedure to summon, bind and command the spirit, forms the input device. The output device, is the world (or worlds) into which the spirit is launched.

An entity which is specifically created by the magician to perform a set range of tasks is known as a Servitor (derived from Latin, it means, "a male servant"). Servitors can be created to perform a wide range of tasks, from the specific to the general, and may be considered as expert systems which are able to modify themselves to take into account new factors that are likely to arise whilst they are performing their tasks. They can be programmed to work within specific circumstances, or to be operating continually. There is some evidence to support the proposition that evoked entities tend to operate according to the ritual process and background paradigm that they have been created within. If, for example, a magician working within the paradigm of classical Goetia believes that its demons are dangerous and prone to become uncontrolled, then it is likely that such will be the case. Whatever the paradigm being used, it should be borne in mind that there are always likely to be hidden variables in any such operation, and that due care and attention should be paid to all aspects of the operation. There is a good deal of magical apocrypha relating to the notion that bound entities may, at some point, become uncontrolled. Despite the anecdotal nature of such stories, it is only common sense to act with care, when utilising this technique.

The very act of Evocation begs the question of the nature of such entities. A Pantheistic perspective would have it that Spirits are real, and have an independent existence from humanity. Those of a religious persuasion would probably agree with this view, adding the rider that only their gods are real, and that the others are all demons. In contrast, a Psychological explanation might be that all the gods, devas, allies, demons etc., are aspects of the human psyche—that gods are expressions of a Higher Self, while demons are expressions of a Lower Self.

A third model for the understanding of Spirits is the Interactionist Perspective. This model proposes that Spirits have some of their origin in the human psyche, but also have an independent existence from the psyche. Spirits may be generated by an act of will, or unconsciously. We may give them shape, form, identity, qualities, and powers to act, and they are seemingly able to act independently of their original makers. Over time, they may become independent, and have the appearance of sentience.

Regardless of the explanation, magicians relate to Spirits as though' they are real and independent entities. One may consider that Spirits are everywhere. It is a limiting trap to fall into the limitation of viewing Spirits only in classical magical terms. A behavioural habit, addiction or obsessing fantasy can be understood (and hence worked with) in terms of being a form of magical entity. One might choose to look wider than the classical division of Elemental powers and consider the Elementals of petrochemical reactions, electricity, or nuclear fission. There is much magical writing about the Spirits of Nature, but who considers the spirits generated by life in the large urban sprawls where most of us actually live? Is there some form of machine-elemental arising from the tendrils of the worlds' computer networks? If so, can magicians interact with it?

Imagination is a key factor in dealing with Spirits. Out of belief imagination, and time-sense, the 'movie-director' faculty in the mind creates its own special effects, which may be dimly glimpsed from the corner of one's eye, or faintly seen within the heightened tensions of a magical operation. If one sets up the conditions where one person can 'see' an entity, then it becomes more likely that other people will be able to see it, too—as indicated by numerous 'UFO & Monster flaps.' Parapsychologists have written fictional biographies of spirits which have enabled test groups to 'receive' information from the spirit.

The dynamics of human-Spirit interactions can also be modelled as an Ecosystem. It is not so much a case of one factor, but many interwoven factors which conspire to create and maintain the experience: from electromagnetic shifts to increased levels of neurotransmitters; from embedded belief to the history of a given place; from local myth to expectations. For the Chaos magician though, the experience is more important than the explanation. Explanations and models arise from personal experience, and models allow us to work with Spirits in areas which have been previously untouched.

Evocation & Cybersorcery

To Extend the cybernetic analogy further, there follows an approach to evocation which diverges from the approach outlined above.

Generally, the approach to Sorcery & Results Magick is to take one particular variable in a situation and magically nudge it so that the situation develops in a way that turns to one's advantage. This can be likened to flicking just the right pebble at the top of a mountain, to produce an avalanche in a certain direction. Microscopic (unnoticeable) changes build up into a macroscopic event. This approach however, uses the technique of writing a program which can handle a series of diverse variables and conditions at any one time. Each stage of the program is assigned a spirit to oversee the development of a specified condition. The spirits work in co-ordination, with an overall controller, to carry out the overall operation. The various stages in the program are presented in the form of a flowchart of events and levels of operation.

Flowchart Design Sequence

1. Define General Magical Intent with respect to the situation.

2. By intensively analyzing the situation, identify as many different variables within it which can be used to influence it in the desired fashion. It is important to consider how changes in

these variables may affect the development of the situation. The SWOT Analysis pattern may come in useful at this stage:

Strengths:

Here we look at data which enhances your position, such as information, being able to visualise the target, astrological conjunctions, or anything else that you think will help effect your intent.

Weaknesses:

Now we look at factors which go against the success of the operation. There's no point trying to conjure for something which you haven't any pathways for it to manifest along.

Opportunities:

Here we look at what long-term consequences are expected if the operation is successful, at time factors and anything else which should be considered.

Threats:

Here we consider what happens if the operation goes wrong: could you be compromised by it? What happens if one of the variables you are trying to effect changes very quickly? How do you cope with new events appearing?

Any schema which enables the magician to break down an overall situation into different elements will be useful at this stage, such as using divination systems to gain a broad overview and identify points which might be usefully tweaked magically.

3. Once the situation has been thoroughly analyzed, one may begin to design the program's flowchart. Examples of levels of operation may include: Cognitive behaviour, Behavioural Patterns, Self-Referential Statements, Emotions, wild events (that is, generating a sphere of availability for appropriate external variables to arise within the situation) Time factors, the appearance of specific cues and signals, and events beyond the immediate parameters of the program.

Once the flowchart has been created, it can be sealed in an envelope and forgotten, for example, by being filed away.

Alternatively, a working may be devised to ritually, fire it into operation. Experience with this approach has shown that it is not necessary to ritually assign a spirit to each stage in the sequence (though this could be done, using for example the hierarchy of Spirits in the Lesser Key or generating specific entities from the Enochian tablets). It is the process of analysis and flowchart construction which suffices to create a sequence. The sequence may be fired by any chosen factor: from astrological phases to a command word or behaviour from the target of the sequence.

The advantage of this approach to evocation has is that it acknowledges the complexity inherent in any life situation. If nothing else, the rigorous analysis of hidden variables which might arise in any given situation allows the magician to build a much broader perspective on a developing situation than might otherwise be the case with the single-shot approach. A simple example of this kind of approach is a discussion I had with a colleague concerning his efforts to magically affect his chances of promotion at work. Following a lengthy analysis of his work environment, we decided that simply enchanting for better pro-motion chances was not likely to yield results unless there was the possibility of an empty slot in the hierarchy for him to step into. Accordingly, we decided that a more effective approach would be to work to give a fellow worker a step up the ladder first, and then for my colleague to form a good relationship with the person who had been promoted in order to become his assis-tant. In general I find that the more rigorously one analyses a situation, the more one is likely to discover a novel approach (or three) which supplies the key to twisting it in the way one would like it to unfold.

ASTRAL MAGICS

The astral plane. Is it real, or what? It's the place where your astral body goes when you're dreaming or having an Out-of-Body Experience. It's populated by demons in the lower regions and angels in the higher levels. The dead can be found there, too. Once you're there, you go anywhere in time and space. It's an extension of our imagination and a region of consciousness. These are just some of the properties that are popularly attributed to the astral plane. Astral experiences can include flights of fancy, dreams, mind-wandering, near-death experiences or even encounters with ghosts or aliens. There are a vast number of explanations of how it operates, from the Theosophically-derived multitudes of planes, to those which attempt to set the astral plane on a scientific footing. Personally, I find that trying to explain astral experience rationally does my head in, and as with many other facets of magical experience, I have stopped trying— at least on paper. Thankfully we have the work of Aleister Crowley to turn to as a source of much clarity on this often confusing subject. In his essay, *Liber O*, Crowley warns the reader against attributing either "objective reality" or "philosophical validity" to the experiences one might have therein.

Not only are there allegedly a multitude of astral zones to contend with, but it is also believed that the astral plane is coterminous with physical reality, to the extent that everything on the physical has an astral counterpart, and that intentional actions cause ripples or echoes on the astral plane. Thus if I raise my arm and draw a pentagram, visualizing it blazing fiercely in the air before me, that pentagram exists on the astral, and can be perceived both by entities which dwell on the astral and human beings with clairvoyant talents. So it is often useful to bear in mind that when you are doing rituals on the physical level, as it were, you are also operating on the astral level, too.

Astral work can be one of the most troublesome areas of practical magic. It's not that it is particularly difficult or dangerous, but one does need to get to grips with the whole question of veracity of the experiences one has while there. Some years ago,

I met a woman who told me she'd made astral contact with the shade of Samuel Liddel Magregor Mathers, one of the leading lights of the Hermetic Order of the Golden Dawn. "And how did you know it was him?" I asked. "Oh," she replied, "he spoke with a strong Scottish accent and he signed his name Magregor Mathers." Somewhat bemused, I replied that Mathers was a Hampshire man, and that it is on record that he only visited Scotland once in his life, to inspect the Golden Dawn. Amon-Ra temple in Edinburgh. I could see that the woman was rather proud that Mathers had singled her out as it were, for contact. I don't think my comment about Mathers not being Scottish troubled her for a moment. Now while it is easy to dismiss this sort of thing, she did go on to tell me that Mathers had instructed her to find out about the Qabalah, which he said was important for her spiritual progression. Naturally I pointed her in the direction of Mather's fine book, *"The Kabbalah Unveiled"* which she wasn't aware of.

There are 2 points to be made about this example of an astral event.

1. An individual encounters a spirit which gives them a pointer to information.
2. The individual accepts the reality of the event at face value. The spirit presents its credentials and they are accepted.

The first point relates to the process which is apparently occurring. The second point relates to the question of the 'veracity of the experience.' How much credence the individual gives to the surface 'realness' of the experience.

Crowley points out that the danger of the astral plane is that it presents experiences that conform to one's phantasies and offers up ego-inflating delusions. It can be understood as a feedback loop: if you secretly suspect that you are a great magician, then you may well have astral experiences which serve to reinforce your belief about yourself. In simple words, all astral experiences should be taken with a pinch of salt.

What is commonly termed as the astral plane can be understood as a metaphor for a wide variety of experiences which we don't quite understand, but tend to accept with varying degrees of validity. Whatever the surface experience seems to consist of, be it meeting spirits in dream or vision, clairvoyantly perceiving entities, meeting people (be they friends or dead Magi), or journeying to bizarre and magical landscapes and conversing with strange denizens, it is important to be able to look beneath the surface of what appears to be going on, and be aware of what is occurring in terms of the dynamics of the experience. Thus, to go back to the example given earlier, it is not so important that the woman of the example met up with Magregor Mathers. What is important is that the experience prompted her to investigate what was, for her, a new branch of magic. In an earlier edition of this book, I tried to discuss astral experience using the metaphor of Virtual Magic. In retrospect, this doesn't work very well, though what I was trying to get at was that, to some extent, we create and contribute towards our astral experiences in ways that are not always immediately obvious.

There is a famous example of a dialogue between a student of Zen and his teacher. The student says, "Master, whenever I meditate I have a vision of the Buddha." To which the master replies, "Oh everyone gets that. Just breathe deeply and it'll go away." This is the kind of attitude which is helpful when one approaches astral work.

Mindscaping

This is a very common technique whereby the magician uses a set of cues (usually visual or oral) to focus attention onto a particular facet of experience, which is then entered as a discrete astral space. In a guided-journey or pathworking, the user might be presented with a written narrative which he or she reads through or listens to (read by someone else or taped). In much a similar way that we become totally absorbed in a novel or television programme, the user is caught up in the narrative. Journeys are often written so that they provide not only visual cues, but also cues for all other senses and feelings, in order to enable the participants to feel themselves to be there as much as possible. Some journeys are purely passive in that the participant goes along with the story, whilst some are interactive in that they allow varying degrees of freedom for the participants to have their own unique experiences within the narrative. Journeys can also be based on images: tarot cards are often used for example, as a basis for setting the scene for a journey.

There are some similarities, I feel, between participating in a guided journey and participating in fantasy role-playing games. An observer, watching a Fantasy Role-Playing Game in progress might see only a group of people, surrounded by pieces of paper, rolling dice, and moving a few props around. The participants however, have, from a magician's viewpoint, transferred some of their attention into a virtual enclave wherein they can experience their larger-than-life roles within a defined and constructed space. Any physical props act as reference points; the flow of the game provides a contextual narrative, and group collusion supports and maintains the fantasy (virtual) reality. A good role-playing game session requires both a supportive narrative and a degree of 'freedom' for the game characters to interact within, and explore the game world. To play a role successfully depends not only upon learning a script, but also entails drawing on your own experience thereby showing aspects of yourself through the character.

Role-playing can often lead to surprises as the roles which we engage in help us to define ourselves. Assuming a role which is outside of your normal repertoire can lead to the discovery of unexpected capacities. Often, these are latent possibilities which we have rejected or repressed as incompatible with our self-image. Role-Playing can itself be a useful magical exercise, done as a group-defined fantasy in which participants meet aspects of themselves in specific situations. The same dynamics that maintain a fantasy game can be used to create a group mythos which can then be explored and modified according to the participants' experiences.

Mindscaping has a wide variety of uses. One might decide to journey into the landscape of the tarot card, The Tower in order to gain insights into the meaning of that card. Alternatively, one might construct a journey to visit the Goddess Freyja in order to ask her some pertinent question. It's common for psychologists to get people who are nervous about social situations to rehearse situations prior to going into them in reality in order to reduce stress and anxiety. If effective, a journey will evoke emotions, insights and even revelations which are concordant with the theme of the imagery used. In meeting Freyja during a journey, one might be moved by the experience and be given an answer or perspective on a particular issue which so far has escaped one's attention.

Mindscaping is also useful in that it can help develop imaginative spontaneity. The mind has a wonderful capacity to create virtual realities internally and very quickly. Confabulation is a psychological defence mechanism whereby the mind can quickly construct false realities to cope with a situation of anxiety. Such false memories, which are often highly detailed and consistent, sometimes appear when a subject is questioned while under hypnosis, and emerge, depending on the situation, as memories of UFO abduction, past lives, or involvement in satanic rituals.

A Group Astral Temple

The creation of a group astral temple further enlarges the spatial significance of the group as individuals contribute to the formation of a shared dream-space for exploration and group magics. An example strategy for creating a group astral temple follows:

The initial considerations are two-fold. How to create a shared astral space, and how to create an astral event whereby participants can interact with each other within this non-local space. The following design was drawn up for a group of three people to work with.

Spatial Design

A black, square room, with doors in the W, N, & S walls, and a large, circular 'black mirror' set into the eastern wall. From the centre of the ceiling, there floats a black chaosphere—ready to act as focus for power and energy as an aetheric lamp for the temple. On each of the doors is etched, in glowing light, the sigil of one of the members of the temple. On the floor of the temple is a glyph which is made up of each member's individual sigil, set in an interlocking pattern.

This design is quite simple in the initial stages of practice, so that each participant can easily visualise it, and attempt to project themselves within it. When all members can accomplish this easily, the group may add further rooms, corridors and points of egress into other dimensions. To the basic elements of design may be added sensations such as smell, touch, humidity, colour, sound, etc., to create the internal representation of the area.

To begin this experiment, each member of the group would agree to attempt to enter the temple, and record their experiences therein (having perhaps chosen common times and dates to try the experiment). These can be later discussed, and any common details can be taken as a success.

Techniques to assist Entry

In this example, the following techniques can be used to assist the projection of awareness into the temple space.

a) Scent as a memory enhancer.

A specific perfume could be created, and used within a ritual designed to promote group trust, empathy and bonding. When used individually for projection into the virtual temple, it can act as a memory enhancer for the appropriate emotions and images.

b) Photographs to aid visualisation

To aid the individual visualisation of other members of the group, photographs of each member, in their ritual garb, can be prepared.

c) Mantra tapes

A standard mantra to be used by all participants can be prepared. All make an audio recording of themselves performing the mantra, and exchanges them, re-recording them into a cut-up sequence so that each person could can the audio illusion of the other members joining in with the mantra.

To enter the temple, each member visualises the Temple's sigil and sees himself stepping through the appropriate door, seeing the others also stepping through their doorway. Each member then sends a bolt of energy into the Temple's Chaosphere, which activates it.

The conditions by which this experiment could be judged successful can be agreed, initially, as reported experiences wherein each participant entered the temple space and saw the other members there. Once this has been achieved, other conditions can be set, which include, for example, one member giving a signal to the others such as a particular gesture, or the telepathic projection of an image or emotion.

Further experiments can be attempted whereby two members use the temple to 'draw' another member into it. This can be attempted by having one member of the group meditate passively, whilst the other two enter the temple space and enact a virtual ritual:

Astral Tractor Beam Exercise

1. Participants begin in Astral Temple, having charged Chaosphere.

2. Statement of Intent:
   "It is our will to send power to ...(name)... to aid them in transferring awareness to this space."

3. Participants repeat Temple's power-mantra, whilst projecting pure Octarine (magical) energy into the chaosphere. Gradually the chaosphere becomes orange, the colour of mercurial (communications) magic.

4. The participants visualise the face of the person they wish to draw into the temple, and begin to chant "...(name)... be here now."

5. They visualise a beam of Orange energy extending from the Chaosphere and striking the body of the target. The beam then draws the target person towards the temple.

6. Participants concentrate on the door bearing the person's individual power-sigil, and chant "...(name)... you are here now." Until they 'see' the person appear through the appropriate doorway.

Other suggestions for experiments within the virtual space might involve one person, using the temple's dark mirror, firstly attempting to project messenger-servitors into another member's dreams, and later, to project themselves into the other's dreams.

PART III

GROUP EFFECTS

INTRODUCTION

Magic in the twentieth century has been characterised by the formation of both small groups and large organisations, over the pursuit of magic as a purely individual stance. A group setting provides a source of social support for an individual. It also enables the individual to participate in a cross-fertilisation of different ideas, skills, and techniques which he would not be able to access if operating on his own. Groups can command more resources in terms of space, information, and materials with which to operate. Working in magical groups can also be great fun!

Having spent a good deal of my magical career working in groups (ranging from small groups to large magical organizations) I am admittedly biased towards the desirability of magicians becoming involved in group work. For me, the prime benefit of working in groups is a sense of community, of belonging and participating in a group where my own ideas can be validated, tested or challenged, in an atmosphere of acceptance.

What is important and valuable about being in groups is often very tenuous and difficult to get to a handle on. In an attempt to get to grips with this, I asked a few friends who are all part of a group what was, for them, important about the group. This particular group has been running for 3-4 years, and meets twice or three times a year, usually at campsites. There is a core membership of 8-9 people with others who attend meetings more infrequently but remain part of the overall contact network. Most of the people in the group have known one another in varying capacities prior to the groups' inception. The group is not focused around any one particular system of magic, and its ritual events are celebrations of free-form dance and music, arising organically out of the interactions of the members, rather than using any predetermined patterns.

> *T: Gossip! There's no point in being in a magical group if you can't have a good gossip!*

> *C: I don't work in groups normally, but being in our group, I find there's a feeling of family. For me its about*

being with folk who I don't have to pretend to be anything else with.

T: I wonder whether the feeling of family came with the group or it was there already, and the group became an expression of it that we hadn't had before. And that within the group, the sense of family grows.

It's also the chance if you're a solo worker to work in ways that you can't do on your own. All our music and dance stuff. It's so nice either to be dancing with other people or to be listening to other people playing. Much better than banging a drum on your own.

C: Also, in our group, there's a trust that you are safe to be whatever you are, and I don't feel judged on it.

T: You're right. There's also earwigs. Cream teas. Cuddly toy rituals that you can't do on your own. Shopping expeditions.

L: There's also something about not having to be vigilant. Not having to constantly put up barriers. You can also rely on other people to take care of things.

T: Yes, you can trust people to be looking after the practical bits, like looking after fires or getting the kettle on.

L: And that people can handle that themselves; you don't have to look after them.

C: I did several years in one group and that was sometimes really frustrating and at other times really empty and at other times really full. There was always a purpose, and sometimes you weren't in the right space to be there for that. We'd have meetings before the ritual to discuss what we wanted to do and they were often the more comfortable. It was very social and there was a lot of interaction rather than just a need to come together to perform. Those times were sometimes brilliant and sometimes just damned awful.

P: I think some groups get very task-oriented and the socialising is seen as somehow less important.

T: But then if you ask people why they are in a group they'll talk about community, even though the group may be very task-oriented. I think it's one of those illusions which people are fostering that you don't need to socially interact with others. If you're with somebody once a month and you do your job and then you go away, then you're part of a community; ignoring the fact that communities are much more about the social side. Because if the social side is good then you can work anytime, but if the social side isn't sorted the work won't, in the end I don't think, last, because of all the stuff which isn't resolved.

L: What's good about our group is that we get together for a weekend.

T: Whips & chains & scorpions!

M: Yes, because we get together for a weekend or sometimes a week, it just flows really naturally; it all develops and at some point we'll say "Oh yes, now's the time to dance and drum." It's not organized or regimented. If someone does try and organize too much, its like we're all not interested.

C: I think the thing about actually living together for a few days is, again, about community. And it's really nice to unzip your tent and see who's face is poking out of theirs.

T: You can see who didn't get their paint off the previous night.

Again, this is part of the way our group is. Without having to have a development plan, we either talk through things or sense what's changing in the group. People are talking now about having time where we've got two nights to play and dance, rather than one night and then go. One of the others was saying that he's feeling us all—the whole thing—moving on as the energy gathers, into a stronger space every time. And that's something that we're not planning. It happens because of the sense of community.

P: We give each other time to get to know each other again at each meeting. You don't always get time for that at a two-hour meeting. You don't always get time to find out how other people have changed since the previous meeting. What I like about our group is that we have time to settle back into each other.

    C: Yes, that's what happened sometimes with the other group I was in. We'd come with stuff which wasn't part of the ritual: who we were, what was going on for us. Sometimes it could be left, sometimes we met at the right point, but when we didn't, things felt weird, false. I felt discomfort. In any group you're going to get some who socialise better than others. Some people are going to socialise more outside the group than others. In the working group I was in, there was one person who continually tried to sabotage the group and felt the need to control the others. In the end we just had to finish. That was not a nice situation.

    L: Our group isn't as important as the individuals in it. Its very nice that there's a strong sense of everyone's individuality. I really enjoy conversations and finding more out about each person.

    P: When a group subsumes individuals so that they feel powerless—that their voices are not heard—then you get problems.

    C: If you're working in a magical group—whatever form that magic takes—I think you have to have a trust in others, but its not always there. There's something about that lack of honesty that undermines everything else. In another group that I was in for a while, one person wanted things this way, another person wanted things another way, and they didn't trust each other at all, but they never communicated that. Consequently, every time we got together and tried to do anything, nothing worked. And people are in groups for different reasons, and that's something else: why people are in a particular group and what they want from it. That's something that came up in one group I was in: why were we together; what were our objectives; what did each person expect from it. These questions don't always get sorted out, agreed upon and in

*some way or another made clear. So you get hidden agen-
das that sabotage everything that you do. If you're not
clear on things within the group, you go away with feelings of dissatisfaction.
We don't have a common way of working in our group
now.*

*T: There isn't a common mythos. We're not claiming a
single tradition—just claiming insanity.*

*L: Again I really like the individuality of that. It makes
for a creative tension.*

T: A very exciting synthesis.

*P: There's nobody who wants to force their way of
doings things onto everyone else.*

C: Maybe we should all have tantrums next time.

T: Yes, a Tantrum Afternoon!

To create an effective magical group requires more than a
room full of people, a few props, and an elaborate charter from
any Secret Chiefs. There must also be some awareness, and
attention to, the dynamic processes of group behaviour. Also,
just as *Know Yourself* is an important dictum for the individual
magician, then *Know Each Other* is equally important for a
magical group. Furthermore, it should be recognized that groups
are complex entities, because people are complex entities. On the
surface, magical groups look deceptively simple. People turn up,
do whatever magical work has been arranged, and go home
again. If things are that simple, why then do problems arise?
Groups require *work* from each member if they are going to be
effective in fulfilling the needs of each participant. To be effective in groups, we need to be aware of how we behave in relation
to other people, and vice versa. I also feel it is useful to gain
some insight into the dynamic processes which underlie group
behaviour. Working in groups requires particular skills. It
requires both personal and interpersonal skills and an awareness
that this kind of learning never ends and that what might work in
one situation does not necessarily carry over into another. When
we look at how we have behave in groups, we also have to
acknowledge that despite having spent years assimilating the

complete works of Aleister Crowley or probing into hidden astral dimensions, we might still be somewhat deficient in the getting on with other people department.

WHAT IS A GROUP?

Groups differ according to size, duration of existence, objectives, activities, significance to their members, formality, and internal structure. Generally, there are five key points which distinguish a group from a collection of individuals. These are:

a) Interaction
b) The sharing of common Goals
c) The presence of group Norms
d) The development & recognition of Roles
e) Cohesiveness

Interaction.

Group activities and goals are reached by the interaction of members, necessitating a degree of interdependence between them.

Common Goals.

It would be difficult to conceive of a group where there was no drive amongst members to achieve a common goal. Having said that, common goals may not be clearly explicit within a group, and participants' individual perceptions of what the common goals are may vary widely and become a source of conflict. When the goals of individual members are wholly homogenous, the group would be expected to run smoothly. However, in magical groups, this is often not the case. Individual members may well have conflicting agendas and there may be a certain degree of conflict between an individual's own magical exploration and the general direction which the group has taken or chosen. This situation is further complicated by individual's expectations of the group and its perceived purpose. Also, different levels of magical ability and interest within the group are also a further complicating factor.

Norms.

Groups develop normative values concerning what is appropriate and inappropriate behaviour within the group. Norms are thus group rules—ideas which the members hold about what should be done and what should not be done by members under certain specific circumstances. It should be noted that these norms derive meaning not from a particular act in itself, but from the significance that the particular act has for the group. For example, studies of work groups in factories shows that there is often an implicit norm that workers should not exceed a particular production quota, and act to regulate new workers who work faster as it is perceived as being detrimental to the work group as a whole.

Norms may be made explicit by members of a group to each other, but it is often the case that they are implicit (that is to say, under the surface) and may only arise when a situation occurs which one member is felt to have broken or transgressed them.

Norms tend to arise slowly—they are not usually formal rules which members consciously decide upon. Rather, they can be understood as shared values relating to what is appropriate behaviour within the group.

Roles.

Group roles may be formally assigned (Magister Templi, Archivist, Insubordinate are formal temple roles within the IOT Pact, for example), but most roles are assumed (often unconsciously) as a product of interaction. Questioner, critic, enabler, tension-breaker, arbitrator, are some of the informal roles which individuals may take on temporarily, or habitually assume. Of group roles, the most important is that of the group leader. Leadership is a complex issue in itself, but it should be noted that there may well be a distinction in a group between the assigned leader and the real leader. Since groups need to maintain themselves and also to accomplish their tasks, it may well be the case that different individuals fulfill the different styles of leadership role necessary.

Cohesiveness.

Group members recognise that they have shared experiences together which creates a difference between them and others who have not done so, giving rise to a sense of cohesiveness. This latter point is a key feature in magical groups. Cohesiveness is what binds the members together and gives the quality often referred to as 'we-ness,' where group members feel united by common interests, shared experience, and reciprocal sympathy. It also includes the feeling of morale: the *esprit de corps.* Belonging to the group is expressed by the frequent use of "we" and "us." The importance of cohesiveness in determining the effectiveness of a group cannot be overstressed. Groups become more attractive where there is increased cooperation and participation in activities. Members become more inclined to remain with a group as they get to know other members and mutual trust arises. The stronger the feeling of 'we-ness,' the more likely it is that members will accept the groups' norms and participate in its activities. There is a positive correlation between the sense of cohesiveness in a group and the intensity of interaction between members. This is an important point. Some groups shatter when conflict arises as members are unwilling to bring up tensions and problems within the group. What tends to happen is that these conflicts are nurtured by individuals or cliques within the group until they pass the point of being resolvable *within* the group. The result being that members either leave, or tensions within the group render it ineffective. This often results in group members complaining about each other behind each other's backs or to friends. Also, it is not uncommon for individuals to scapegoat the group as a whole *"It's all your fault"*—rather than admit personal responsibility in conflicts. When cohesiveness is strong, group members feel safe enough to explore areas which have previously been avoided. This also contributes to self-disclosure as each member tends to reveal more in order to clarify his own position.

Cohesiveness is particularly important for magical groups. Not only is cohesiveness an important factor in group magical events, but it also contributes to self-exploration and self-disclosure for each individual in the group. When members feel that they belong to a group and feel supported by it, they are more likely to open up to others about how their magical work is affecting them at a deep, personal, spiritual level. This may well involve taking interpersonal risks within the group, for example telling another person how he feels his relationship towards them has changed over time. It also becomes easier to offer critique of a particular approach, technique or belief without fear that the critique will be taken as a personal slight on behalf of the other. Magical groups use ritual and celebration to promote cohesion, examples being initiations which act as a rite of passage of demonstration of commitment to the group ethos and Events for celebration as in births, marriages, deaths and seasonal changes. Not only are such events important for fostering a sense of 'we-ness' between group members, they also reinforce the feeling that the group recognises each individual's unique experiences outside of the immediate group and values that uniqueness, whilst creating a space for the group as a whole to share significant personal events for each individual.

What is a Magical Group?

Groups of magicians vary from small, informal groups to large Magical Orders. Most magical orders are subdivided into small groups, whether they be dignified by terms such as Temples, Working Groups, Lodges, Power-Zones or Encampments. In the present context, a magical group is a small group of people who meet regularly to practice and discuss magic, whether independently or as part of a larger overall structure. Whilst magical groups are subject to the general principles of group dynamics, they also have unique features (and problems) which distinguish them from other types of small group, such as therapeutic or work groups.

The Magical Group is a Primary Group

The term 'Primary Group' was first coined by Charles Cooley in 1965. Technically, the feature that distinguishes primary groups from other types of group is that the interaction between members takes place on a face-to-face basis i.e., directly, rather than indirectly.

Members of primary groups share a distinct psychological unity which arises from this direct, face-to-face interaction. I feel it is appropriate to consider magical groups as primary groups, as magical work necessitates a good deal of self-exploration, If "Know Thyself" is an injunction for individual magicians, then "Know Each Other" is the corollary for magical groups. As such, members will, to varying degrees, be engaged in deep levels of self-exploration and self-disclosure on an interpersonal basis.

The Importance of Self-Disclosure

Self-disclosure is an important element of interpersonal dynamics. Self-disclosure is generally understood as the revealing of personal secrets or some significant experience in a person's life. Studies of groups have shown however, that there are both appropriate and inappropriate forms of self-disclosure, and it is generally considered by social psychologists that the most appropriate form of self-disclosure in groups occurs when members disclose themselves as a reaction to what is taking place in the group in the here and now. It is not enough to simply reveal intimate details of one's past history alone, but to do so in order that other members might understand how this disclosure is relevant to one's reactions in the present. Self-disclosure is not merely the revealing of facts, but of the self at the present moment. If facts are revealed, it is in order to support the revealing of self.

Social psychologists studying self-disclosure in groups have made a distinction between 'history' and 'story.' In 'historical' disclosure, a person may relate many facts about his experiences but does so in such a way that his self remains hidden. In contrast, 'story' is an invitation for dialogue. It is not merely a recounting of facts, but a demonstration of how selective facts reveal the person as he is *now* through his experiences.

Such self-disclosure can only take place in an atmosphere of good interpersonal relationships within a group. As this latter can only form gradually, then it follows that self-disclosure is also a gradual process, acting in turn to strengthen relationships and the group as a whole.

Group members are often wary of people who jump into self-disclosure too quickly. It may be that too much self-disclosure, as much as too little, may be a sign of underlying disturbance. Inappropriate self-disclosure can sometimes be understood as an exhibitionistic tendency on the part of the individual. It can occur, for example, in discussions of particular magical techniques, that one person recounts a personal instance that he feels is appropriate to the discussion. Others may see this as a chance to score points by recounting their own experiences, until the discussion devolves into a mass of anecdotes where the implicit aim is for people to top each other's accounts. Thus, one person's 'story' can incite others to proclaim their 'history.'

A colleague once remarked to me that "magical groups are not therapy groups." In the present context, this relates to the fact that some people will use a magical group as a vehicle for exposing themselves psychologically: to use the group as a sounding-board for their own problems and opinions, in order to satisfy themselves, rather than contributing to the group development as a whole. Group leaders need to be aware of the dynamics of disclosure, in order to be able to judge whether or not disclosure is appropriate to the circumstances of the group. Whilst acknowledging the point that magical groups are different in character and objective to therapy groups, it should also be noted that magical groups do necessitate close interpersonal relationships and depth of feeling between group members. Magic is not merely an intellectual pursuit, and whilst it is often presented in the same factual light as the exoteric sciences, it touches us on deep, intensely personal levels. It should also be recognised that group members will not move towards self-disclosure (or for that matter, any other group stage of development) uniformly.

Just as self-disclosure is appropriate when it takes place within the context of interpersonal relationships, interpersonal relationships can only develop through mutual, appropriate, self-disclosure.

The benefits of self-disclosure are firstly personal ones. Lack of self-disclosure tends to result in limited opportunities for reality testing as this lessens opportunities to obtain valid feedback. Individuals who never disclose themselves to others lack self-awareness, in the sense of self-knowledge or insight into self. Self-disclosure is, therefore, necessary for self-knowledge in that, in communicating with others about ourselves, we also communicate with ourselves. Self-communication is not merely the recitation of personal facts, but concerns the impact which these facts have on our lives and the ability to allow our feelings into consciousness and to own these feelings as parts of ourselves. This alone is an important point in respect to magical groups. One of the main strengths of a magical group is that it allows members to confront their own magical experiences and beliefs with those of others. This provides an unparalleled opportunity for the reality testing of one's magical world-view. All too often, magicians who work entirely alone become prey to obsessional complexes wherein they become powerful, superior beings who, despite a complete lack of social skills, are merely one ritual away from becoming all-powerful adepts. In a group situation however, it is more likely that anyone displaying the symptoms of Magus-itis (see *Condensed Chaos* for a further discussion of this), or emotional and behavioural obsessions which are the consequences of continually invoking a deity which boosts one particular self to the detriment of others, is going to have this pointed out to him. Through feedback from shared magical experiences, one may come to know oneself better. This feedback is also important for behavioural change. If individuals do not have (and use) opportunities to reveal to themselves how they see and do things, they are unlikely to receive feedback information that will enable them to decide whether they want to make changes in attitude, belief or behaviour. Since magical development as it is generally understood implies (and demands) behavioural change as a result of one's practice, the relevance of the above to magical groups should be obvious.

STAGES OF GROUP DEVELOPMENT

Since the 1940s, a number of models which account for stages in group development have arisen. A great deal of research into group dynamics has been prompted by the popularity of psycho-therapy groups, self-help groups, consciousness-raising groups, counselling groups, the human growth movement, etc. This diversity of theories provides a rich framework for analysing group behaviour. Some models of group dynamics propose that groups move through a series of linear stages, whilst others point out that particular phases in a groups' development may recur throughout its life. This is a particularly important point. The assumption that, once a particular conflict or issue has arisen and been resolved by a group, then it will not recur again, is a common fallacy. It is more realistic to say that groups learn that problems and conflicts will reappear, and that the effective group will accept this and work through them, each time at a deeper, and more satisfying level.

A much-quoted model of the developmental processes under-lying group behaviour has been proposed by Bruce Tuckman. Following an extensive review of research into group dynamics he has proposed the following stages: Forming, Storming, Norm-ing, and Performing.

Forming

Groups start in a wide variety of ways and individuals have many different motivations for joining a magical group, some of which may be unconscious. These include: the need to confirm one's ideas (including self-image, both positive and negative), the need to belong (security), enjoyment, and achievement. The state of members in this first stage is, to varying degrees, one of uncertainty and anxiety to the unknown—this being the inten-tions of the leader, and other members of the group. Perhaps most importantly, members will need assurance of being accept-ed and recognised. This anxiety is likely to be heightened if there is no sense of direction in the group, if the leader assumes a non-directive role. A common coping strategy which members fall back on is to limit themselves to polite social interaction. Relationships at this stage tend to be formal and cool as members try and present a good impression of themselves. Members who know each other from outside the group will tend to interact with each other more frequently than new members.

A deep level of self-disclosure is not expected to take place at this stage. Indeed, any such disclosure may not be appropriate, as one person doing so may well scare others who do not feel settled enough in the group to go so far themselves. The expression of deeply personal values does not tend to occur until people are sure that these values will be accepted by other members of the group.

Storming

The storming phase begins when members begin to come out from behind their formal masks of politeness. In a new situation, this gives rise to feelings of vulnerability, and thus gives rise to tension. Also by this time, members will have an increased knowledge of each other (through both verbal and non-verbal communication). They will have decided who they like and who they don't like within the group. Being vulnerable in the presence of people whom one is not sure of is also scary. Increased interaction throws up differences and incongruencies that will not be acceptable to all, in the same way. Another source of conflict is the tension between individual and group. In accepting the direction of the group as a whole, some members may feel that their sense of identity is being subsumed by the group and that they are sacrificing their sense of identity to it.

Conflict with the leader

The storming phase is also characterised by tension between the members of the group and the leader. For example, if a member feels his own sense of individuality to be threatened, he may attempt to counter this by becoming hostile to the group leader or other members. This tendency may be heightened if there is a perceived lack of direction or structure in the group. Polarisation can occur when some members try to play it safe rather risk confrontation and challenge.

Norming

Once the immediate concerns over authority and intimacy have
been resolved, members accept the idiosyncrasies of each other
and of the group as a whole. At this stage, group norms and values start to emerge as an expression of the groups' cohesiveness.
Group values reflect the mutual desire for tolerance, support and
openness. As the group moves out of conflict into cohesiveness,
members will become more involved and committed to the
group, placing it higher in their personal scale of commitments.
However, the response to earlier conflict in the group is often
expressed as a need to maintain harmony at all costs. So the
sense of group cohesion is fragile. There is sometimes pressure
expressed towards members who do not conform to the norms
emerging in the group. Gradually this gives way to tolerance.
Related to the development of norms is the identification of roles
within the group. This is not about the formal roles, but the
informal roles such as who is best at clarifying issues, who gives
support, who questions best, who acts to mediate between others,
etc.

The Leader becomes an Equal

This phase is also characterised by a shift in attitude towards the
leader. The leader is no longer seen as an expert, authority figure
imposing his will onto the group, but as an equal member, whose
input is sometimes useful, and at other times, not.

Performing

During this phase, the group is oriented towards its task.
Members will adopt roles which enable them to accomplish the
group's activities, having learned to accept and relate to each
other as social entities. The group functions as a whole and
members acknowledge each other's individual differences and
allow them to emerge within the group. During this phase, the
possibility for positive confrontation emerges. Members become
relaxed enough to challenge both the group and each other
regarding decisions and choices in an atmosphere of mutual
respect.

The above model provides a useful device for exploring and interpreting group behaviour. It should be remembered that there is unlikely to be, in any one group, a clear transition from one stage to the next. A group may periodically cycle through these patterns, for instance, as a consequence of new members joining the group, or changes in the external social environment. Whilst a group is *forming*, it will also be *performing*, and vice versa. During the *forming* phase, *performing* will be overshadowed by *forming*, and during the last phase, it will be mainly *performing*, and *forming* to a lesser degree.

The strength of this model is that it provides useful guidelines for group facilitators and leaders. For instance, inexperienced leaders are often taken aback when conflict towards their role is expressed. They tend to take this hostility personally, and become defensive. A common attempt to alleviate this hostility is to become non-directive or increasingly authoritarian; either approach tends to increase tension rather than reduce it, leading to emotional explosions which further damage the ability of the group to move towards cohesiveness. Similarly, leaders need to be aware of the dangers of attempting to maintain an illusion of harmony within a group at the expense of acknowledging underlying problems and conflicts. If tensions are not acknowledged within the group, members will tend to express them amongst themselves—with friends and in small cliques. If resentments are not allowed to emerge, individual members tend to foster them alone, until they display them aggressively or leave the group (often both). This also tends to give rise to a feeling that leaders do not care about member's problems, or that whatever they say will not be taken as being important. Members who express unresolved issues are often made into scapegoats by the rest of the group. Members may be relieved that a problem has been brought up, but also scared about the disruption to the (apparently) smooth function of the groups' activities.

The Group and the External Environment

Groups do not operate in a vacuum, they are also influenced by the surrounding environment. For example, there are great differences in the group dynamics between people who live in a village as opposed to living in a large city. Some magical groups exist within a larger organisation and may well be influenced by tensions between the immediate group and what is perceived to be the rest of the organisation. The history of the group itself may be considered part of the surrounding environment as this is ever-present and influences its behaviour. What is perceived to be the group tradition might, for example, become a rigid norm which prevents adaptation and flexibility giving rise to the view that "we've always done...that way." There is also the factor of cross-membership with other groups to bear in mind. In a provincial town, the magical group may well be the only game in town and henceforth be of primary importance to an individual who wants to work magic in a group. In contrast, large cities (such as London or L.A.) might have a great many groups operating, and it becomes easier for individuals to move to another group. An individuals participation in a group is influenced by the importance that he attributes to the features of that group in relation to the importance attributed to other groups of which he is also a member. In other words, when members belong to several groups simultaneously, they will tend to prioritise participation in one group's activities over another, based on the importance of those groups to them, and the level of satisfaction that they obtain from participating in these groups. This is a problem for group leaders to be aware of for, after all, it is difficult to resort to draconian tactics such as insisting that members put one's own group first (I have seen this done, with the effect that the person immediately reduced his membership of different groups by leaving the group concerned with his commitment to them).

Glamour Projection

Modern magical groups are as much concerned with creating an overall image as any other group in society. This image may be projected through the use of distinct symbols which have particular associations. The Chaosphere has, for example, different associations than the inverted pentagram & goat's head.

Some groups promote a certain style in terms of dress, haircuts, and membership through particular behaviours and codes. The secret signs and signals employed within magical organisations become part of this overall glamour, which is as important for participants as its overall relationship to other groups. There is always a certain degree of tension between the desire to project such a glamour on a wide scale, and the point where the glamour becomes a fashion which is distinct from the original group, and will be taken up by others outside of the group's immediate membership.

ISSUES SPECIFIC TO MAGICAL GROUPS

Perceptions of Magic

Individual members of a magical group are highly likely to have vastly different perceptions of what magic *means* to them. To a large extent, this factor is related to the consensual belief system shared by members of the group. For purposes of discussion I will make the distinction between *loose* and *tight* consensual belief systems. An example of a tight consensual system would be a Wiccan group wherein all the members share the overall belief system known as Wicca. In contrast, a Chaos Magic group could be generally characterised as loose, in that members would be much more likely to have divergent personal beliefs, and loosely agree on a few principles. This is an important issue as engagement in a shared tradition or belief system can be a contributing factor towards group cohesiveness. Where beliefs are convergent, members can feel assured that their personal feelings are more likely to be shared and therefore, understood by other members. When beliefs are divergent, members will have to explain themselves more and therefore incur risks with each other.

The Challenge of Change

Similarly, a group will be affected by the *divergence* of belief which arises out of its performance. It is in the nature of magic that as individuals progress with their own work, and in the work of the group as a whole, their attitudes, beliefs and values relating to magic change. This change may be gradual or sudden, as in the case of members experiencing spiritual revelations, illuminations, or initiatory periods as exemplified by what St. John of the Cross termed "the Dark Night of the Soul." It should be obvious that these changes can lead to conflicts and tensions within the group. In a tight-belief group, the expression of changes of belief can become problematic, particularly if group norms consider the tradition of belief to be inviolate, that is, not open to question or change. Even in comparatively loose-belief groups, apparent threats to the groups' established norms may be met with hostility. This is particularly apparent in groups where allegiance to the groups' tradition is given a higher normative value than that of individual flexibility. Hence the phrase 'magical differences' which is often used to explain the reason why individuals leave a group.

Conflicting Values

This issue is further complicated by the tendency for group members to assume that the group as a whole shares the same general beliefs and attitudes towards aspects of magic that they themselves adhere to. A prime example of this occurs in sorcery workings, where a member proposes that a healing or cursing operation take place, assuming that other members share the same values relating to these acts. This can become a problem when the assumption is challenged. When a group norms have been established (usually implicitly rather than explicitly), on the lines that all members' contributions are valued, and that all members should support each other's magical work, members whose proposals are challenged tend to feel personally slighted. Equally, members who challenge are likely to feel uncomfortable in interrupting the group task, in having to disclose their personal values, and challenging another member. This kind of situation is accentuated when the group is under a time restriction. Often, it is felt that it is easier to go along with a situation which one is not entirely comfortable with, rather than rock the boat.

Related to this is the consensual belief, often held to be factual that magical workings by a group are somehow more powerful than solo workings. When a member asks the group to support a working, there is usually an implication that it is of great importance, therefore a challenge made concerning the value, subject, or morality of the working is more likely to be taken personally. Confrontations of this type challenge the assumed 'we-ness' of the group but also provide a focus for the elaboration of personal differences and divergent opinions within the group. This requires careful management. Group members need reassurance that the challenging of one particular instance of their ideas is not—as it is often taken—a challenge of their entire historical input to the group. Phrases such as "we all feel..." or "we all should..." are often used to make all-inclusive statements which, whilst appealing to the mutual sense of 'we-ness' in the group, also use that 'we-ness' feeling as a block against being challenged.

One effective approach is for the leader to draw attention to the divergent beliefs and interests within the group at an early stage and encourage discussion of this diversity, perhaps suggesting that the group could spend a period exploring any specific interest areas in turn. This provides an opportunity for members to appreciate each other's magical backgrounds, to find out where each individual is coming from, and in what directions the group can move. This can be effective if each individual is willing (perhaps with assistance) to lead a session exploring his own interest areas. It is of course useful if group members can discuss issues relating to personal and shared values prior to actually engaging in magical work which might relate to those values. It is also useful for the group to discuss a general proposition that, whilst members are encouraged to support the work of the group as a whole, they each have the right not to participate in activities which they find repugnant on the grounds of taste, ethics, or personal preference. If a member of the group doesn't wish to participate in a particular ritual or event, they should be able to say so, without feeling that they are letting the group down or causing problems for everyone else.

Contribution to the Group Process/Task

A common source of conflict which can arise in groups is that of perceived differences in individuals' contributions to the overall group process and its tasks. This tends to be voiced by phrases such as "I do all this...and I'm not appreciated by you" or "Without me the group couldn't function." Individuals who put a lot of effort into a group may at some point come to expect an unrealistic level of appreciation from other members, which is often related to issues around respect for their perceived status within the group. When their views or ideas for the group are challenged, they become defensive and threaten the withdrawal of their input, often citing their historical contribution to the group in order to illustrate the unfairness of how they feel they are being treated. There is thus a misperception on the part of the individual that their high level of contribution to the group affords them a higher status within the group as a whole, so that they do not expect to be challenged about their ideas or behaviour.

Magical groups often attract dynamic individuals who will quite happily take on set tasks within the group but also see the need for other tasks which have not yet been identified by the group as a whole and throw themselves into creating them. For example, a member might feel that the group needs a newsletter, a historical archive of member's magical work, or an extensive range of props for ceremonial or ritual use. These ideas are usually met with approval from other members. The problem here is not so much that individual members want to do more work for the group, but that having decided to take these additional tasks on, members may well come to have unrealistic expectations about the consequences of their additional input, leading into the scenario outlined above.

Related to this is the issue of tangible, as opposed to intangible contributions to the group process. Members who make tangible contributions—the newsletter, magical archive or elaborate ritual props—to the group may discount the contributions of group members which are less apparent, such as the individuals who manifest the roles of 'supporter,' 'questioner' or 'joker' within the group.

Conflict over this issue can result in the aggrieved individuals leaving the group. It becomes extremely difficult to resolve the situation unless those members become willing to examine their own personal motivations which underlie their impetus towards making contributions over and above the norm as it were. Such individuals need reassurance that their contributions to the group are valued, but also need to acknowledge that they should not expect a higher status within the group as a direct consequence of their extra efforts. This can be particularly difficult when it is felt by such members that the rest of the group is not giving sufficient support to a project which they have started on their own initiative, so that it becomes the fault of the group, for example, that the newsletter is not being supported. It is often easier for the aggrieved member to blame the group for not supporting their project rather than saying "well perhaps we don't really need a newsletter." Again, this relates to the perception of common aims and values within the group. Support or tacit agreement by the group as a whole of an individual member's project does not necessarily mean that the rest of the group will automatically give the same level of importance to the project that the member who initiates it does—though this is often assumed to be the case.

Orientation of tasks within the group can require careful management. If, within a group situation, the major contributions to its work is continually coming from the same people, they are likely to very quickly become bored with continually supporting the others. Unless a magician is purposely seeking to have a group who entirely follow his ideas and plans, this is a very unsatisfying situation for all concerned. Task orientation needs to be formalised, to varying degrees, and set up on a rational basis. Ability, interest and responsibility are the main criteria here. Giving someone a task to perform because he is liked or disliked does not serve the interests of the group in the long run, nor does continually giving someone a task that, in time, becomes his exclusive property alone. Everyone within the group should be given the opportunity to develop the skills necessary to perform appropriate tasks.

A simple example of effective task orientation is in regard to organising a seasonal celebration. This can be broken down into particular tasks, which might include:

Finding a suitable site
Organizing transport and routes to the site
Preparation of incense and lighting
Preparation of any props required
Selecting individuals to take on distinct ritual roles
Writing and distributing an appropriate ritual format for the event

Each task may be assigned to a particular member, and then rotated for successive events so that each member gets the chance to have a go at different tasks. This useful in a group situation as it promotes cohesiveness and commitment. If people feel that they are essential to the success of the group, then they are more likely to show commitment to meetings. Furthermore, this can aid the process of members forming friendships which go beyond the immediate group meeting place. I have found that in general, group members who restrict their interactions with other members to formal group meetings find it harder to participate in the more intimate aspects of the group's experience.

Challenges to Authority

Magical groups often attract individuals who desire to be perceived as authorities on the subject, by virtue of their professed expertise, or having attained some particular degree of initiation. Such individuals may not be formally recognised or designated as leaders in the group, although they may be accorded a high status within the group if other members collude with their identification of being authorities. Conflict can arise within a group when an authority or other members feel that the position of the particular authority is being challenged.

The legitimisation of authority is a complex issue. It can be that the perceived authority is held to be the most experienced person in the group. Alternatively, the 'Star Syndrome' denotes individuals who become authorities by having gained some degree of notoriety or having written x number of books. There is also the issue of authority which stems from so-called 'spiritual' initiation. The problem with 'spiritual' authority is that it is rarely open to close inspection by others, and it is fairly easy for a charismatic and forceful person to claim moral superiority to others on the basis of a higher initiation which is not, *a priori*, open to inspection. Such was the position of some of the leaders in the Golden Dawn, and many of its imitators since. Anyone may make the claim that due to a divine illumination, he has a mandate to lead and inform others but of course not everyone is in a position to carry it across in a group. The magical group, of course, is often the ideal place to make such a claim and make it stick, and so a good number of would-be gurus and magi have managed to fool at least some people, for quite a long period of time.

The problem with having, as it were, "God on your side," is that it tends to inspire the individual with a tendency towards absolutism. Paranoia is an inevitable consequence, probably due to the feeling that anyone who dares to criticise or merely express a different opinion is also calling into question the very authenticity of the person's initiation, and therefore, authority.

In the present context, perceived challenges to established authorities within the group can easily become a conflict which polarises the group into 'followers' and 'heretics.' This can lead to dissatisfied members leaving the group, or schism within a larger organization. Internal schism within a group is, in a way, self-regulating, in that it makes a further polarisation between 'followers' and 'enemies.' Having a group of ex-members that the group can categorise now as enemies tends to bond the members together again, using the glue of mutual paranoia and ruffled feathers. The next course of action is all too familiar: psychic attack, magical battles, sniping through the pages of the occult press and so forth. If the members feel that they have 'Truth', 'God', or 'The Great Work' on their side, then the perceived enemies automatically become black magicians or satanists. The threat of dealing with internal contradictions within the group can be brushed aside as the membership roll their sleeves up for the important task of defending Cosmic Truth against Ultimate Evil, just in the same way that adroit politicians use wars to distract the populace from trouble at home. Studies of groups such as religious cults indicates that groups are remarkably resilient in upholding their shared beliefs in the face of threats to their continued existence.

Authority in a group is very much a two-way process, dependent as much on how group members perceive authority figures as on how those who desire to be taken as authorities present themselves.

Transgression of Group Norms

Group normative values tend to be implicit rather than explicit and one often doesn't find out what they are until one unwittingly transgresses them. I have met people who have been censured by the rest of their group for actions as simple as laughing during an invocation or lighting a cigarette after a meditation. In magical groups, simple transgressions may become elevated due to the magical/spiritual context against which they are interpreted by others. Thus laughing during an invocation may become 'being disrespectful to the Goddess' whilst lighting a cigarette can be turned into 'desecration of the circle.' Often, such transgressions are not voiced openly and the maldoer gets the cold-shoulder treatment from other members and is left to work out himself what he has done wrong.

Sexuality in Groups

It's undeniable that some people seek out magical groups with a hopeful eye on getting laid or finding a magical partner. Of course, this will be the case for *any* type of group. It is also, sadly, the case that the leaders of some groups tend to view new members as new sources of nookie. Of course, this is rarely stated boldly, and so new members to magical groups are sometimes informed that they have so much potential that they are going to be immediately given a higher initiation which involves sacred (of course) sexual intercourse with the leader(s) of the group or that they were soulmates in a previous incarnation. Sexual behaviour between group members, like any other form of behaviour, gets justified on the grounds that it is somehow magical which means that normal discrimination, preferences or feelings ideally, shouldn't apply. The argument one often hears is that magicians should be able to rise above personal feelings when one learns that, for example, the High Priest of the group has been shagging your partner for the last two months. That members of magical groups should experience strong feelings for each other, which may or may not manifest as sexual activity, is unsurprising. What makes all the difference of course, is how the individuals concerned, and to some extent, the group as a whole, handle it. Like other group issues, this is often tricky, particularly as we tend to think of our sexual lives as personal and no one else's business. It is naïve however, to believe that sexual interchanges that go on between group members will pass unnoticed by everyone else. Its as well to be aware that personal feelings, fears, attitudes, inhibitions etc., do not simply go away when the circle is cast or the Temple door closed.

Magic, as seen through the lens of the popular media, is very much associated with sexual orgies. It may be paradoxical then, when we consider that even though magicians acknowledge the power of sexuality, its group effects have received little attention. Group sexual gnosis tends to manifest only in fairly well-defined spaces and usually at times when normality has been suspended, to avoid later conflict and repercussions. Use of sexual gnosis in a group situation does not necessarily imply an orgiastic free-for-all, merely the awareness that sexual behaviour is a powerful route to ecstasy. Again, sexual gnosis can appear as a feature of mind-control groups, but while group sexual gnosis can be a powerful conditioner, it may also be a powerful De-conditioner. To be utilised successfully, it requires careful group management, prior, during, and after any operations. It is imperative that participants feel emotionally secure with each other and that a high level of trust has been secured. However, it should also be noted that when the focus of a group's behaviour becomes entirely based around sex, it tends to lose any wider impetus.

Running Groups

Before I get down to practical issues, the first thing to look at is one's own motivations to run a group. Personal motivation to get something going can be complex. It may be, for example, that you suddenly perceive a need for a type of group in your area, and with the absence of anyone else willing to set something up, decide to take the job on yourself. When it comes down to it, setting up and managing any kind of group is hard work. Also, I would stress, it can be fun, rewarding, and instructive. It can be rewarding, in that it helps get your name around the occult scene, which can be valuable if you want to build a reputation as someone who Gets Things Done. It can be both rewarding and instructive in that managing groups requires a variety of skills, related to Organization, Promotions, and People Management, all of which are readily transferable into other Life Areas, and which are difficult to acquire passively. Also, if you are involved in any kind of Group where learning is going on: transfer of skills, theory, practice, etc., then you are widening your capacity for experience in these areas.

This latter point is particularly relevant for magical training groups and workshops. While some magicians start groups to dispense their Occult wisdom among those less fortunate, others run groups so that they can share information, skills, resources, etc., to the mutual advantage of all. One of my own primary motivations for running a magical group is that it provides the impetus to do things that otherwise, I would probably not set aside time for.

Working with people in groups can enable you to learn a lot about:

Yourself
Other People
Group Dynamics
Organization & Management
Shared Magical Experience

Of course, if you are setting up any kind of magical teaching group, then the responsibility for teaching rests with you. Teaching others practical magical skills can be either boring or highly rewarding and instructive. It can be boring if you find that you are the only person in the situation who voices an opinion. On the other hand, it can be rewarding and instructive for you, if the people you are working with are lively, committed to their own magical development, eager to try things out and experiment past magical dogma, and can come up with their own ideas.

Teaching is also useful because it necessitates that you revise what you already have assimilated and, by preparing Teaching material in a variety of formats, you can often discover aspects of it that you were not quite, previously, aware of. Also, if you can successfully transmit an idea or skill to others, it demonstrates that you are:

Confident of your own ability
Able to communicate successfully
Able to organize yourself and your resources.

To be a successful teacher requires that you develop the ability to organize the way you express your ideas, in order that others can understand them. This is particularly useful when it comes to turning feelings into words.

Practical Considerations

Aims & Objectives

Obviously, before one proceeds to start a group, it does help if one has defined clear aims and objectives for the group. This is tantamount to defining your *Statement of Intent*. Of course, this is also something which may well change, especially when other people get involved. Being clear of your own aims and objectives is good, if only because nothing looks worse than getting a group of people together and then being vague at them. However, it is possible to go overboard on this. I have occasionally met individuals who have produced huge charters and lengthy dissertations about what their group will be about. This, I find, is not terribly effective. Firstly, if you present a group of prospective members with a lengthy essay on what the group is going to do, then it tends to come across that you are not leaving people room to give their own ideas to the development of the group. Secondly, you're setting yourself up for disappointment, since the more fixed ideas you throw up about how the group should operate, the more likely it is that people will disagree with you. Like a magical Statement of Intent, keep your initial aims/objectives clear and simple.

Spreading The Word

Letting people know about your Intent is the next step. This can range from Word of Mouth to cards in shop doorways, posters in alternative/occult shops, listings in occult magazines to even adverts in local papers! Obviously, how much advertising you do depends very much on the type of group you want to start, and how widely you wish its existence to be known. It also helps if you have some idea as to who the target audience is for the group you have in mind, and what kind of publications, for example, it is appropriate for you to use.

Points Of Contact

Also at this point, it is useful to consider how people can get in contact with you. Assuming that you don't want your home address available to all and sundry, you should consider what other options are open:

Telephone

Whether or not you give out your telephone number depends on (a) how much privacy you want, and (b) if you're sure that no one else will object to strange people ringing up. Not therefore a good idea if you live at home or in a multi-occupancy dwelling.

Box Numbers

Getting a Box Number is generally considered the best way of ensuring a Contact Point with a reasonable degree of anonymity. The main two sources for Box Numbers (in the UK) are the Post Office, and British Monomarks. There are also various companies who provide Accommodation Address Services (forwarding mail, taking fax messages etc.), and some news agents and alternative businesses also provide box number services. The Post Office Box Number service has several drawbacks. The first of these is that you are assigned a Box Number in the nearest Sorting Office to your home address. If, for example, you don't work near to where you live, then actually collecting your mail regularly can be a problem. Also, there are two different tariff scales according to whether or not you want to receive letters and parcels, or just letters in your box. A third issue is that if any official bodies ask the Post Office who uses a box, they will instantly give out your details. Finally, when you are going to collect your mail, you should take some form of identification along. Since the last wave of bomb scares, the Post Office have become more security-conscious and you might well be asked to prove your identity. If you don't think any of the points raised above will affect you, then a P.O. Box might be just what you require. You have to pay for the box on a yearly basis.

British Monomarks are a London-based company who are behind all those BM/BCM addresses used by a wide variety of groups and publications. You pay a flat rate for a BM number, and any mail that comes to your number is then forwarded to your home address (which you are also charged for), or, if you can, you can go and pick it up from the office. Unlike the Post Office, British Monomarks don't start getting awkward if several people seem to be using the BM number at once.

Personal Referral

This means that you meet people on the basis that someone else either recommends you to them, or them to you. If for example, you regularly turn up at some open function, then someone else may be pointed in your direction, or equally, you could be pointed in theirs.

Finding A Venue

Another fairly practical consideration is the Venue for your group. Again, this depends on the type of Group. Socializing-based groups tend to meet in corners of Pubs, or peoples' front rooms. Discussion Forums tend to be found in hired rooms in Pubs or Hotels. If you are running this kind of group, then establishing a good relationship with the management/publican is a priority. If a pub landlord knows that an event will bring in at least 20 people who will use the bar (i.e., not sit crowded around one glass of mineral water all night) then he may let you have a room for free. Hotels tend to be less keen on making this kind of arrangement.

If you plan on doing something a little more practical, then you need to find somewhere appropriate. Assuming that you don't have access to a ruined castle, stately home with grounds, decent-sized cellar or any other space where you live, then here are some options to consider.

Local Community/Adult Education Centre

These places often have rooms to hire for a fairly cheap rate, especially during the evenings. Some give access to useful facilities like coffee or licensed bars, photocopiers, etc. Beware of prowling caretakers and lost people looking for their word-processing or quilting class. Check out any possible drawbacks. One Centre I used for group meetings rang the fire alarm 10 minutes before closing time, which did on one occasion, shatter the carefully built-up tranquillity of a Pathworking Session.

Drama/Dance Studio

If you can find such a place that isn't booked up until next year or horrendously expensive, then this can be an excellent choice for a working space since a lot of shouting/weird noises/thumping etc., as well as people dressing up in odd costumes is likely to be easily accepted.

Rehearsal Studio

A favourite of chaos magicians in London. Again, they tend to have a high tolerance for weirdness, and can often be hired for a reasonable price. A problem can be that the hour-blocks that rehearsal spaces tend to be booked for do not always suit the needs of the group. Other considerations are that your rites will tend to be accompanied by the sounds emanating from the band in the studio next door, and also it has happened that the group who have booked your room next may decide (especially if they can't hear music from within) to wheel in their amps, etc., at the most inconvenient moment.

Therapy Space

These can be expensive, and many are run by groups of politically-correct New Agers who might well object to their space being used to summon demons.

Outdoors

Working Outdoors has obvious advantages, but can require a lot of planning. These include:

- Insuring privacy from wandering dog-walkers, drunks, policemen, etc., both noise and vision should be considered.
- Getting there—and Getting back—especially in darkness. I have found in general that people who are charged with the job of driving the group car or minibus back to base after a rite tend to have a bad time of it, particularly if they're still a bit gnosticated from the rite.
- The Weather (time to get good at weather-magic?)
- Fires. Firewood can be gathered in the daytime, and then hidden, ready for when you get to the site in the evening. If you work outdoors regularly then you might consider making a portable fireplace; for example, half an oil drum with 4 holes in it. You take the drum with you to the site, then after you have finished, extinguish the fire, slide two poles through the holes and immerse the drum in water, then carry it back with you.
- Tidying the site up afterwards, unless you want evidence of your ritual circle to suddenly appear in the local paper as 'Satanic Ritual Sacrifice in local Wood.'
- Site preparation: clearing a working space.

Nom de Plumes

If you're considering hiring somewhere to use as a Venue, then you might want to make up a cover name for the meeting. The word "Folklore" is much used by various socializing and Discussion Forums, while magical working groups tend use names which include terms like "Experimental Drama." Examples of this are: *Personal and Cultural Transformations*, *Isle of Thanet Drama Group*, and *Drama-Experiment-Movement-Origination-*

Network. This sort of thing will only work if everybody in the group knows what the *nom-de-plume* is.

Booking Rooms

Most places that hire rooms will require money up front the first time, or at least a deposit. Bookings can be done by telephone, but it's a good idea to go down and, if possible, have a look at the space you'll be using. If for any reason, you have to cancel a booking, give the venue's management as much notice possible. Good venues can be hard to find, so if you do find somewhere suitable, its good to keep a friendly relationship with the management.

People Management

Running a group requires some skill in the arts of People Management. What this involves, again, depends on the kind of Group you are setting up. For example, an open social forum, where people turn up to socialize and meet each other may only require 'loose' management in terms of the group environment, for example, introducing people to each other for the first few meetings.

Leadership

The first point to mention is that in Pagan/Occult circles, people often don't like the idea that groups need leaders. This has given rise to some spectacular mangling of the English language, and much talk of Organisers, Facilitators, and so forth. When all's said and done, groups require that someone initiates decision-making, and sees to it that things get done. The larger the group, the more necessary this is. Another issue to bear in mind is that if you set up a group, then you are to some extent responsible for how that group develops, and are likely to be perceived as being so by other members.

Critics of hierarchical magical groups (which use a system of magical grades to denote positions of responsibility within the group's structure) tend to accuse such groups of being 'top-down' structures, they complain that decisions come down from above and lower-grade members do not participate equally in what goes on in the group. The antidote to hierarchy is proposed as being the so-called 'Structureless' or Consensus Group. The Consensus Group, it has been argued, is non-competitive, leaderless, loose and informal. In terms of Group Dynamics, the idea of a structureless group is something of a contradiction in terms. Any group of people meeting together over time, will inevitably structure itself in some fashion, regardless of the intentions of its members. If no formalised structure has been laid down, an informal structure will arise, which may be even more open to abuse than a hierarchy, as its implicit rules are not open for all to be aware of. What we should remember is that any group is much more than its overt structure; hidden hierarchies of status can arise quietly in loose networks, and what seem on the surface to be hierarchical groups can behave as networks. In my experience, formal position in a hierarchy is not as important in the long run as being in with the right people. A general point about all complex group structures is that they are not static and they change as people move in and out of them, as ideas and concepts change, and the members who remain committed to the organization develop new patterns within it.

When examining the role of group Leader it can be useful to break it down into a series of appropriate tasks and functions, and then look at who performs these tasks and how. Magical Groups and Orders often run into problems as their leaders tend to be charismatic personalities whose influence over the group as a whole is not balanced by their being accountable to the group members. Just as a group leader may criticise the performance of a group member, then a group member should be able to criticise the performance of the leader without the whole thing devolving into personal or magical differences which lead to schism or a split in the group. Knowing when to act, when not to act, and how to act as a leader is a delicate art in itself.

There seems to be a general assumption within the occult milieu that, as Antero Alli has pointed out, someone who thinks of himself as a good magician automatically tends to assume that he will automatically be a good leader. Implicit in this assumption is that both magicians and leaders are born rather than made. Aside from being somewhat judgmental, this assertion is not supported by research into the dynamics of leadership, into which there has been a good deal. Leadership is one of those complex skills which can only be learnt 'live,' as it were. However, one can learn a great deal from both observing other leaders in action and reading about the various approaches, strategies, and theories of leadership.

A first general point to consider is that leadership is *contextual*. That is to say, the role of leader is only relevant within a particular social context. In a magical group for instance, the leader may well take charge within the context of formal group proceedings, but in a more informal social meeting, taking charge may not be entirely appropriate. Problems can occur in a wider social setting where the status which the group gives the leader might not be recognised by outsiders. Leadership is also contextual in that whilst an individual may be given the formal title of leader this does not necessarily mean that other group members will automatically regard him as such. So giving someone the title of leader is not enough for him to be regarded as a leader. In a sense, the group as a whole gives permission for one individual to act as a leader.

This brings me to a second general point: that effective leadership is *responsive* to the needs and situation of the group as a whole. There is a popular idea that leaders act to impose their will onto the group regardless of other people's feelings. This can only occur, however, when other members of the group *collude* with the leader. If they come to feel that they are not supported or recognised by the leader, they are likely to withdraw their support. A common occurrence is that group leaders, having set up a particular agenda for the group to work through—for example, a series of rituals—attempt to work through that agenda, sometimes overlooking or ignoring indications from others that the set programme is, for whatever reasons, no longer appropriate. Whilst one of the functions of the leader is to direct the group towards performing its formal tasks, the leader also has to be flexible enough to discern when it is appropriate to direct the group to its task, and when it might be better to do something else instead. This requires an appreciation of the subtleties of group mood, which more often than not, is not so much discerned through direct questioning of people, but through observing body language, and not so much what people say, but how they say it. People might well voice assent for going along with something, but there's a whole world of difference between someone saying "Okay, let's do it" enthusiastically, and just going along with what the leader is suggesting.

This also brings up a third general point: that the leader must effectively *express* the norms and standards of the group. Although a good magician does not necessarily equate with a good leader, a good leader in a magical group context must be perceived by the group as a whole as a good magician. This in itself can lead to problems arising. If there are, for example, unrealistic expectations about what constitutes a good magician—that adepts are wise, superhuman beings incapable of error—then the leader is likely to be judged unconsciously by this standard and any mistakes or errors in judgement (which are inevitable) are likely to be viewed as serious transgressions of the standard, rather than forgivable mistakes. A colleague once remarked to me that being the leader of a magical organisation was rather akin to sitting on top of a stepladder at the business end of a firing range! In a magical group, a leader may be perceived both as an exemplary role-model and at the same time, become the target of member's feelings and projections concerning authority and parental figures. I have tended to find that those who most fervently deny that they have the authority or status of leaders within the group are, nevertheless, perceived by others as being leaders, perhaps due to virtues such as age, experience, or sociability. Refusing to recognise this can be as damaging to the well-being of the group as much as attempting to grasp too tightly the mantle of leadership.

The Three Circles Model

The above diagram shows the interaction of three areas of need within a group: Task Needs, Group Maintenance Needs, and Individual Needs. These three areas of need are interdependent. For example, if there is a lack of trust and mutual understanding within a group, this will affect both task performance and individual needs. If individuals within the group do not feel that their contributions to the group as a whole are valued, then they will be less likely to contribute to the group's common task, and the 'we-ness' of the group will also suffer. Conversely, if a group has a well-developed sense of team spirit, it is more likely to rise to the challenges of its chosen tasks, and individual members will feel more personal satisfaction from being involved with the group. The question for the leader is, how to contribute to these three areas of need? To be effective, the leader must firstly, be *aware* of what is going on in the group (both on the surface and the underlying dynamics); secondly, have an *understanding* of what is required at any given moment; and thirdly, the *skill* to put what needs doing into effect. The effectiveness of the leader's actions can be evaluated on the basis of how much the group responds. In terms of the 3 circles, the leader's task is to (a) achieve the task (b) build and maintain the team (c) respect and develop individual members.

Clarifying

A primary responsibility of a leader is to ensure that the group achieves its common task. The phrase *common task* should be stressed as, if group members cannot relate to a task or see that it has value for themselves, the group, or some wider whole, they are less likely to give it whole-hearted support. Whether the task is the planning and execution of a series of rituals, a performance for others or a skill-sharing session, it should be meaningful to all concerned. In order to achieve this consensual clarity, the leader must be able to communicate effectively. Communication is not only being able to outline your ideas to others, but being able to elicit from other people their understanding of what you are saying.

It is also necessary to be able to take something which is quite general and vague, and turn it into a series of specific steps and, in turn, be able to relate the particular to the general. An effective leader is therefore aware of both the big picture, and all the little details in-between, and how they relate to each other. The leader has not only to be able to say what has to be done, but why perhaps, it has to be done in a particular fashion. Clarity about the task is essential if it is going to be achieved successfully, and the leader has to be prepared to reinforce clarity whenever the need arises.

An example of these leadership functions in action might be the performance of a group ritual where many celebrants may be working together for the first time. Here, the leader's primary task is to ensure that all participants know *why* the ritual is being performed (this includes understanding of any general and specific objectives related to the ritual), *how* the ritual will be performed and *what* is expected of individuals during the rite and, perhaps most importantly, if anyone requires *clarification* or further explanation of any aspect of what is going on, be it practical or theoretical.

Planning

Planning comes in answer to the question, "How does the group go about achieving it's common task?" Planning can sound boring, but it need not be. For me, being a member of a group that is actively and enthusiastically planning a ritual or event is just as exciting as actually enacting that plan, if not more so. Plans develop from ideas, so perhaps an important aspect of the leader's role in planning is in ensuring that as many ideas come forth as possible, whilst at the same time, being able to take divergent ideas and thread them into a whole. In order to be able to do this, the leader needs to be aware of resistance to new ideas. One of the most common forms of resistance to new ideas is the "Not Invented Here" syndrome, which can manifest in forms such as "If I/we didn't think of it, it can't be any good" or "That's not part of our tradition." I used to be surprised how easily people, who were otherwise open to magical ideas, could quickly reject new ideas which came from another direction—be it science fiction, dramatherapy or psychology—precisely because those ideas weren't obviously 'magical.' Group games such as Brainstorming have become popular methods of getting people to generate ideas whilst suspending judgement, but leaders can also use other methods to stimulate idea generation:

a) Encouraging members to bring in outside experience to the present issue.

b) Taking one person's suggestion as a start-point and inviting ideas to build on it.

c) Developing a team solution by including different member's suggestions into the emerging plan.

d) Being positive about all suggestions. This latter is significant. Someone might, for example, come up with a plan that is unfeasible at the present time. Acknowledging that the person has made a good suggestion, but that you feel it is unfeasible for the present ('perhaps we'll come back to it later') is a better strategy than dismissing it out of hand. A leader needs to help others feel that their contributions to the group are valued, regardless of whether or not they are acted upon. Its better to have people coming up with wild and wacky ideas than to have your request for input met with sullen silence.

It's also worth bearing in mind no matter how much you tweak a plan, it's never going to be perfect. The more complex a plan for something, the more likely things are likely to go awry. This is particularly relevant to the planning of complicated ritual events, if only because the goddess Eris might be watching, and wants to see what happens if someone drops a sword at a critical moment, scattering burning incense onto bare feet and furnishings! Plans should be flexible, so that if, at the last minute, Frater Implausible fails to turn up with the ritual props, the rest of the group is not stuck there standing around looking sheepish. When I was trained in the running of groups, I was taught to have a 'plan B' ready waiting in the wings if need be, and beyond that, have a set of stand-by exercises that I could draw on if I really needed them. In short, plans may look perfect until they come into contact with other people.

Planning is also necessary for effective communication. In the above example of a leader seeking clarification from celebrants prior to a ritual performance, the leader needs to be able to think ahead and plan what he or she is going to say. The message needs to be clear and understandable. People who are new to group rituals often feel insecure and it certainly does not help when leaders explain rituals using complex or obscure terminology. Complex procedures can be clarified by breaking them down into a set of points. In addition, the leader needs to not only transmit facts, but also enthusiasm for what is about to be done. Using colourful language, non-verbal cues and humour can be helpful here, but this requires confidence to do effectively, which in turn takes practice and planning. This kind of planning really involves developing a general skill which has an almost limitless range of applications. If you can plan what *you* are going to do in a situation, you can go on to plan how you might try and affect a group situation in order to promote teamwork, creativity, or encourage particular individuals. As I have said, plans rarely survive contact with reality, but you are only going to find out what works, and what doesn't, through experience.

Invisible Leadership

A leader is best
When people barely know that he exists
Not so good when people obey and acclaim him,
Worst when they despise him.
Fail to honour people,
They fail to honour you;
But of a good leader, who talks little,

When his work is done, his aim fulfilled,
They will all say, 'We did this ourselves.'

— Lao Tzu

There is a common idea that leaders impose their will on the group, and that the group does what a leader tells them. An effective group is, to a large extent however, self-determining, regulating its own performance by its own standards and norms. The more the leader has clarified the group's common task in terms of what needs doing and how, then the more likely it is that each individual member will share that clarity. It may be that a leader needs only to intervene in the group process gently, rather than heavy-handedly. A quiet word or even a glance can be more effective than coming on strong as the leader. Developing the ability to quietly but firmly silence someone, and the ability to equally quietly test for consensus (without making group consensus a big issue) is more useful in the long run, than being overbearing and bombastic.

Motivating

If you are setting up a group which will require other people to take on distinct roles or jobs, then one of your immediate concerns will be the ability to motivate others. It is essential, in this kind of scenario, that once you have delegated a task to someone, that it gets done, and that you don't end up running everything yourself, which is an easy situation to get into. Often people will volunteer themselves for jobs without really thinking the matter through. I tend to look at this on the basis that people get one (maybe two) chances at doing a task and if they don't actually do it, then (regardless of their excuses) that's it as far as I am concerned. Having said that, if someone does volunteer to do something, then you should check out if he has (a) the resources necessary (Time being an important one) and (b) the requisite abilities. If he doesn't ask you exactly what the task entails, then you should tell him and giving out a checklist of tasks is often a good idea. It's a common enough scenario that managers give people a job to do without actually saying what the job entails and then complain because it hasn't been done to their satisfaction. People who know exactly what they're supposed to do (and how to go about it) are usually much happier and more likely to be self-motivated about going out and doing it. So if you want to motivate people into helping you then support them. As Ralph Waldo Emerson put it, "Trust men and they will be true to you. Treat them greatly and they will show themselves great." Equally important in motivating others is the leader's ability to recognise other's achievements. This needs to be done equally across the group. In any magical group, particularly the larger orders and organizations, there will be individuals who excel at edging themselves into the limelight. If the group is to maintain a strong sense of 'we-ness' however, it's important that everyone and not just the high flyers can feel that his achievements (no matter how small) are recognised (this is where techniques such as the Sumble discussed previously can be helpful).

Self-Assessment

Being an effective leader is not something which happens overnight. Like any long-term magical endeavour, it's something that you grow into. Whilst reading books and going on courses in leadership can be helpful, it's something that most of us tend to pick up as we go along. Just as developing interpersonal skills is important in being able to relate effectively to other people, as a leader you must be capable of assessing your own performance in that role. Of course, the ability to assess oneself, in terms of feelings, experiences, behaviours, ideas etc., is fairly central to magical development. It is particularly important in group work though, and even more so if one is a group leader.

Bringing People Into the Group

Who Gets In, And How?

These considerations are pertinent for the more practically-oriented group, such as a small Magical Working or Training Group. Firstly, I'll look at some approaches for candidate assessment.

Interviewing

An interview is probably the best way of finding out whether someone is suited for the group, both in terms of what he has to offer you, and letting him know what your group is about. If you arrange the meeting in a public place, and he doesn't turn up(which is often the case), then you can take this as a very clear message about the sincerity of his intentions. Interviews can be done on a one-to-one basis, or by a panel of existing group members. If this is done, you at least have the benefit of other people's opinions of the candidate, and, someone to talk to while you're waiting for them to turn up!

Letters

Often, your first contact with a potential candidate will be a letter. The contents of the letter can tell you a great deal. Do they enclose an SAE? If the letter is an illegible scrawl written on a scrap of paper the size of a bus ticket, do you think they are the sort of people you want in your group? Look at how the person presents himself. Does he give any details which helps you get a picture of what he could be like?

What Next?

Assuming that the candidate has got past the first stage of your induction procedure then the next step to consider is bringing him into the group. You could, for example, invite him to a meeting of the group and afterwards, invite comments from the established members, or bring him in on a trial period, as is done with the Year-and-a-Day waiting period between working with a Wicca Coven and being Initiated into the group proper. It is not unknown (though hardly good practice) for candidates with certain recognized physical attributes (i.e., girls with big bazooms) to bypass the usual procedures and quickly become high degree members. However, if posing as a Magister of a magical order is the only possible route you have of getting laid, then you are a sad person (Note: the occult world is full of SAD persons).

As to Who Gets in: this very much depends on what you're looking for in your candidates. If you are seeking magical sycophants or people sad enough to think that opening their legs for you will give them the keys to the universe, then so be it. If not, here are some considerations worth bearing in mind:

Can you get on with them as people?

This is at the top of my list as a candidate might well know Crowley's *Liber 777* backwards but if he manages to piss everyone else off within ten minutes of meeting, then he might well be a problem.

Do they strike you as interesting, with something to offer?

Regardless of magical experience, or lack of, if someone comes over as being enthusiastic, and can converse readily and easily then the fact that he hasn't read loads of books shouldn't matter. In fact, I tend to find that people who aren't well-read—magically speaking—tend to come up with some very innovative ideas about magical practice as they don't know any 'better.'

What can they offer the group?

Here, you should take into account skills and resources that the candidate has. This puts me in mind of one applicant I interviewed who, although a complete beginner to practical magic, drove a large van, had a room suitable for meetings, and could light bonfires in the pouring rain!

What do they say to you?

This is often neglected, yet important. People who are merely 'head nodders' to what you tell them, tend to become 'head nodders' in a group. A person who, at an interview, makes intelligent comments about what you have to say is likely to take the initiative when prompted, or often, without being prompted at all.

Any prior magical experience?

This may be a benefit, but much depends on what type of experience they've had, how successful (in their terms) it was, and whether they can accommodate themselves to the working style of the group, or whether their experience is such that they feel that they have to point out that what you're doing is WRONG because their last High Priestess/Magus/Guru said so.

Is it better to only have people you know personally in the group?

I was asked this in regard to group management recently so here goes: if you know enough people who are serious about doing magic to start a group then all well and good. Even if I knew someone well, and knew their magical history too, I would still have a formal (or semi-formal) chat with him about joining the group. But bear in mind also, that if things don't work out, you may have to ask him to leave, which can have damaging effects on a personal relationship. At some point, I think you'll have to consider someone you don't know well (if at all)—hence the suggestions above, which are information-gathering strategies to help you make the necessary decisions.

Does Size Matter?

It is generally agreed that the optimum size for a small magical group is 8-12 people. For any other type of group, number is often determined by the size of the venue you are using for meetings.

Refusals

Refusals can be tricky to deal with. A great deal depends on the type of group you are running. I have heard, for example, of cases where open discussion groups or workshops have been declared single-sex only, as it was the only way they could avoid having one particular person turning up and disrupting proceedings. This may well be the reasoning behind some women-only groups—avoiding the situation of having a male who is a known sex-pest/pain-in-the-neck turning up.

Another tricky situation is one where you as group leader might get on well with a particular person, but no one else does. This is particularly important when it comes down to magical groups. It is all too easy for a leader, when faced with other peoples complaints about someone else in the group to make excuses because he personally liked the person being complained about. If X and Y have a problem, then it is not just a matter between and Y, but also your problem. Deal with it objectively and fairly, and this will come across to your members. If the problem can't be easily sorted out, then at least your members can see you are taking all viewpoints into consideration.

Whatever the case, refusals must be dealt with firmly and fairly. Give people a good reason (the truth is often best), and if you handle it well, then they are less likely to become embittered and go around spreading malicious rumours about you and your group.

The Lemming Effect

It is worth noting that if people are not happy with a situation regarding a group, they will usually vote with their feet and leave. Occasionally, it may happen that if X leaves, then Y, Z, and W (all friends of X) might leave also. This may not sound like a huge problem, but it can happen that people suddenly decide to leave without giving a reason. This happened to me once when four people in an open group left in two weeks, and I didn't find out until much later that it was due to an offhand remark made by another group member (who remained).

Expulsions

Barring someone from attending a meeting, or expelling someone from a magical group, is usually unpleasant, but often necessary. Expelling someone might well be a last resort, but it should never be done in desperation. A colleague and I had to expel a person who, despite verbal assurances of commitment, was consistently late or failed to turn up at all for meetings which, since we only had a two-hour work window, caused some disruption to the progress of the group. After three verbal warnings, we called a group meeting and threw the miscreant out. All the other members were present, which reinforced the fact that this was a group decision, and not just the decision of the group coordinators alone—though of course we delivered the judgement.

Again, this area of group work requires careful management. I feel that honesty is the best policy, and if the expulsion has been prefaced by giving the offending person due awareness of the situation, then if he hasn't made any effort to sort himself out, then he cannot really complain.

PART IV

LIBER NICE & LIBER NASTY

LIBER NICE

All Hail Discordia!

The phenomena which has come to be known as Discordianism is of even more recent origins than the Cthulhu Mythos. Much of the mythic origins of Discordia have been popularised in Robert Anton Wilson & Robert Shea's *Illuminatus!* trilogy, and in Malaclypse the Younger's *Principia Discordia,* which sets out the basics of what appears to be, at first glance, a religion centred around the Greek Goddess, Eris.

According to Classical sources, Eris was a daughter of Nox (Night) and the wife of Cronus. One of the primal Titan Goddesses, she gave birth to Sorrow, Forgetfulness, Hunger, Disease, Murder, and Lies. She figures in the story of the Judgement of Paris, as it was she who caused the argument between the Goddesses Athene, Hera and Aphrodite, by casting a golden apple, inscribed with the word KALLISTI ("to the prettiest one") into the banqueting hall where the Olympians were feasting. All three Goddesses claimed the apple as their own, which led to the Judgement of Paris, the outbreak of the Trojan War, and a major turn in Greek History.

It is related, in *Principia Discordia,* how Eris made an appearance in the early 1950's to two young Californians, who as a result became Omar Ravenhurst KSC, and Malaclypse the Younger. Eris appointed them 'Keepers of the Sacred Chao' and gave them the message "...tell restricted mankind that there are no rules, unless they choose to invent rules." After which Omar and Mal declared each other High Priest of his own madness, and declared themselves to be a Society of Discordia, whatever that may be.

Thanks to the Discordian tactic of declaring everyone on the planet to be a Discordian 'Pope' by using 'Pope Cards' etc., anyone who wants to be a Discordian can declare themselves so. But acting from a Discordian stance is very much a Social Perspective.

Discordians tend to be known through their actions, which, from an archetypal point of view, are related to gambits of

207

'sacred clowning' or poking fun at authority figures and injecting a much-needed dose of humour into any dimension. It was Discordians who pointed out that amidst the massive lists of categories and dualities drawn up by magicians, the duality of humour-seriousness had too long been absent. Discordians thus tend to be engaged in placing humour into areas which have hitherto, been perceived as entirely serious areas. Using techniques borrowed from Surrealism, Dada, Pataphysics and Situationist Agi-Prop, Discordians may adroitly put across a message wherein humour and seriousness are indivisible elements.

Key elements of the Discordian stance can be seen in the historical processes that generated this meta-movement. This includes: the endemic paranoia of the fifties; the optimism of the sixties turning to cynicism before the end of that decade; the growth of conspiracy theories entwining everything from the Kennedy assassination to UFOs in a tangled mesh of suspicion and myth. The death of 'truth' as reality becomes increasingly magical, manipulated by the mass media to serve up the hidden agendas of the multi-corporations and government cliques. The Discordian perspective prompts a reaction of humour to the perceived banality of Consensus Reality, and the desire to prick at the bubbles which the façade of normality form.

From a magical perspective, Discordian elements enter magical processes to demonstrate the danger of taking oneself, or one's enterprise, too seriously.

Erisian Sacred Weapons of Power

Here are my weapons of power (and some other stuff) that I associate with Eris. Of course Eris doesn't need any weapons of power dedicated to her, being mostly too busy causing chaos and confusion to bother with what her worshippers are doing.

Dice

Dice are of course associated with chance, gods of the long shot and taking risks. I got into dice-magic after reading Luke Rheinhardts' classic novel, *The Diceman*. The basic method here is that you select six courses of action or behaviour and then decide which one to do on the roll of the dice. There are also divination systems based on dice, and the cube itself has a lot of

magical associations, though offhand I can't recall any of them.
Rolling dice is a good time to ask Eris to look favourably upon
you.

The Ego-Hammer

At least two partners have threatened me with hammers when I
started to rant/lecture/pontificate on subjects they were not really
into hearing about at the time. The original ego-hammer was a
10-pound lump-hammer but it has since been replaced with a
large, brightly-coloured inflatable hammer. This is used with the
power-mantras "Bonk" or "Biff" and a suitable litany such as
"Lo, you are talking through your bottom—Again."

The Chaos Grenade

The Chaos Grenade is an etheric weapon formed by compressing
Murphy's Law, Heisenberg's Uncertainty Principle or anything
you like into a ball. To activate, take it in one hand and make the
sacred gesture of pulling the pin, and then hurl it into any space
or group that you feel would benefit from an injection of Erisian
wackiness. To activate it upon yourself, simply hold the ball and
throw the pin and you will be illuminated. Or not.

Smartie Servitor

The Smartie Servitor is a ritual aimed at increasing the level of
'nice weirdness' in your town. Smarties, for those unfamiliar, are
brightly-coloured chocolate drops which come in a tube. Since
the mid-70's, the television advertisements for them have been
markedly psychedelic.
1. Statement of Intent:
   "It is our will to make (your town) more fun!" If you like, at
this point, you can all visualise a Discordian Chaosphere. (A
Discordian Chaosphere is just the same as an ordinary one, but
the central bit is a smiley face and the arrows are wobbly.) It
represents the happiness which can be found when you accept
chaos into your lives and understand that Eris has a hand, or
maybe a finger, in everything that happens to you.)

2. "Airburst" Group Visualisation:
   a) Group sit in a circle, arms linked, breathing deeply and rhythmically.
   b) Feel a circuit of energy build up, running between group members.
   c) Each member projects a cord of energy flowing from himself into the centre of the circle.
   d) These cords entwine about each other, forming a column.
   e) The column is visualised as free-standing. It pulses with rainbow-colours.

3. When the ritual leader feels that the visualisation has been established, the group begins to summon the four avatars of Chaos: HARPO, CHICO, ZEPPO, GROUCHO by chanting their names and visualising waves of power expanding the tube until it extrudes a wobbly sphere (this can be accompanied by a slow drumbeat, gradually becoming faster.

4. Chanting becomes progressively faster, as does the drumbeat. The leaders begins countdown 10–1, shouting "BLAST OFF!," at which point all visualize billions of brightly-coloured Smarties, each with the word FUN written on them, spurting out of the tube and raining down upon **** , showering cars, people in offices, policemen, children—all radiating the weird glow of magical possibilities.

Banish with Laughter.

Spiral Pentagrams

The traditional five-pointed star or pentagram is a very solid geometrical figure. Whilst in a phase of magical work with Eris, I began to wonder about using a pentagram made up of curves. The result of a few minutes with a compass can be seen below. It is much more organic. When using this pentagram in rituals, visualisations, etc., I visualise the outer petals spinning clockwise, and the inner petals spinning anti-clockwise, the whole figure becoming a 3-dimensional tunnel, twisting into infinite space. This seems to me to be appropriate for the ritual invocation of Eris, and I've also had them turning up spontaneously in dreams as astral doorways. To seal them I simply reverse the direction of the spin, visualising them becoming flat figures again.

Erisian Theurgy

For Discordian magicians, the Goddess Eris may be seen as the hidden hand of Chaos. She is the prime instigator of weird phenomena, coincidences, Fortean events, and fortuitous occurrences. Her flipside manifests as the patroness of Bureaucracy. All these are organising structures which eventually lead to an increase in chaotic behaviour amidst a maze of rules and regulations. She is related to the happy anarchy of children, clowns and fools, as opposed to the primal Chaos associated with the Great Old Ones of the Cthulhu Mythos. She may be understood to be present in all events which defy rational explanation.

> *"The past knows me not. Each moment is a new beginning. The future is traced by the folds of my gown. And I have shed my gown, the possibilities of all things not yet born."*
>
> — Eris, The Stupid Book.

Eris may be invoked for inspiration, information from an unlooked-for source, or to increase the general level of synchronicities within an unfolding event system. Be warned though, devotees of Eris report that though affable towards humanity, she displays a bizarre sense of humour towards those who would propitiate her!

The popular appeal of Eris has paved the way for a proliferation of thoroughly modern deities which have arisen from the contemporary mythical landscape. These include cartoon characters such as Hiroshima the nuclear goddess, archetypal tricksters such as Bugs Bunny and Wile E. Coyote, and characters from pop music or Rita, goddess of parking, all being examples of this trend which I have came across. Grant Morrison, (creator of DC's *Invisibles* series) has also elevated John Lennon himself to god-hood and, hence, a subject for magical invocation.

The appeal of these new gods is that one does not have to have bought into the general belief system of the occult to appreciate them. In the mid-eighties I helped orchestrate a series of open Erisian events. Most, if not all of the people attending them, were not interested in magic or the occult per se, yet they were hip to the idea of a wacky Chaos goddess stirring up eddies of events around them.

An argument which is often raised against these modern gods is that fictional entities are not as valid as properly historical gods and goddesses. This is very much the same argument which says that for a magical method to be valid, it must be old. It also presupposes that the mythological deities themselves are somehow, unchanging. Underlying this argument is the assertion that magical beliefs and methods are special and divorced from any modern practice, no matter how similar it looks. For exponents of this view, a magician in a ritual space invoking Isis or Pan is a magical event, but a teenager surrounding himself with posters and icons of his favourite pop star, and modelling himself on his or her appearance before going out to a gig, isn't—even though the underlying intent (behaviour change and empowerment through identification with a larger-than-life mythological figure) is essentially similar, and the effect no less (perhaps even more) efficacious and perhaps more so. For me, the only real difference is that the magician has had to learn how to invoke, while the teenager just goes ahead and does it.

Humour, enjoyment and celebration are key elements of historical paganism. Newcomers to the occult milieu might be surprised by this, given the number of injunctions that magic is a 'deadly serious' affair and that in some circles, humour aimed at the gods themselves tends to be met with apoplectic accusations that one is behaving inappropriately. There is an inherent tendency for modern magicians to be terribly respectful of their gods, in a way that is somewhat reminiscent of Christianity. After all, it's difficult to imagine Christians joking about Jehovah in the same way that the Nordic peoples told amusing stories about Loki getting one over on Thor. The idea that a God or Goddess is 'sacred,' yet at the same time we can laugh about their doings, is almost taboo in some modern pagan circles. Personally, I have always warmed to gods who like a good laugh— even if at times it is at our expense. Yet the myths of the gods resounds with the laughter of their ancient worshippers. It's difficult not to smile at the thought of Thor sitting in a dress, seething whilst Loki extolled the virtues of the 'bride' to the Giant groom.

Magic is itself a form of playing around. For me, one aspect of the statement "Nothing is True, Everything is Permitted" is the proposal that magic is as much related to the domain of play, humour, and entertainment as it is to 'serious' endeavours, be they scientific or otherwise. Despite the tendency to undervalue play and entertainment, they are probably two of the most significant human endeavours. There is no doubt that play is the source of much of our learning and development. Both magic and play share the common feature that both are defined in terms of their contrast to the 'ordinary' world. The various forms of entertainment—poetry, painting, sculpture, drama, etc.—do, at the same time as providing entertainment, serve to formulate, clarify or advance magical themes. Both magic and entertainment serve to draw the participant out from the 'ordinary' into the mythic, or larger-than-life world. Furthermore, for the majority of people who are interested in magic, it is a leisure pursuit, rather than an active engagement. Numerous forms of divination have game-like aspects, such as Tarot, I Ching, etc., and likewise, games can be turned into divination systems. Further, one of the central themes of modern magical exploration concerns the nature of personal identity. Play and entertainment also trade on this theme, particularly comedy, where several core themes revolve around the disguising or confusion of identity. There is also an overlap between folklore—which is both instructive and entertaining—and the anecdotal narrative which is the basis of most reported magical experience. The history of magic is also replete with hoaxes, and the trickster figure, from sacred fools to Aleister Crowley. If magic is entertaining, the sceptics are merely those people who refuse to join the fun. Can we see magic as a form of Comedy? Banish with laughter! On a practical level, magic as Play can be appreciated when we examine the technique of Invocation. Modern magical theories relating to invocation tend to both explain and distance the individual from the entities being *played* with. There is much talk of subpersonalities, archetypes, etc., which, for me, intrude on the magic of the experience itself. From the play perspective I would much rather interact with deities on the level of what we might term imaginary friends. From the viewpoint of a child, imaginary friends are more significant than parents and peers. The technique of Evocation can also be viewed in this light and when we're evoking something, we're clothing something indefinable in the bright colours of our imagination.

Magical Misdirection

Magical misdirection is concerned with the obscuring of roles. Infamous magicians, in both myth and history, have had a trickster or clown side to their character. Aleister Crowley, for example, is well-known for his love of pranks, practical jokes and alter egos, as was Alex Sanders, the infamous 'King of the Witches.' The Wise-Fool is a figure found in many cultures and systems: the Fool of the Tarot, the African Spider-God Anansi, and the Norse trickster, Loki. The magician, as the Fool, both mocks and threatens the establishment. Despite their poses and games, sacred fools often have a high status within their community.

To act the fool is to be deceptive. Once you have been established as a fool, there is a lot that you can get away with. This is a lesson that many magicians have appreciated. It is often better to be dismissed as a crank and laughed at, if being taken seriously means imprisonment and torture.

Zen masters in particular are famous for disguising their status, often responding to the questions of their disciples with humour or obscenities:

> *Q: Are all Magicians like you, such a mixture of the*
> *base and the divine?*
> *A: No, some are taller.*

Social Disguises

Don Juan, the (fictional?) Yaqui shaman made famous through
the writings of Carlos Castaneda, says that to become a brujo
(magician) one must first move away from all family and friends,
to a place where no one knows one's past self, where one can
cultivate the 'mask' of a brujo (i.e., the magical personality). The
cultivation of status and status disguise is an important consideration for magicians, especially for those who work in or with
groups. The higher the status people will accord you, the easier it
is to induce trance-states in others, or perform acts of healing or
similar magics. A group director who is playing a high status
role can enable other group members to let go during an inten-
sive ritual, since they are confident of the leader's ability not to
let things get too far out of hand. Note that playing high status in
a group is a role which can be adopted and then put aside when
the situation warrants it. The desire to have one's fellows accord
permanent high status to oneself has often led magicians into
claiming all kinds of exalted titles and grades, in a kind of one-
upmanship that is usually destructive for all parties concerned
and tedious to watch. We all play status games with each other
though, from time to time, and the following games can show up
the differing status roles we pursue.

Gurus and Disciples

For this exercise, one person takes on the role of a guru, and
other people become the guru's disciples, and beseech him to
answer questions on life, the universe and everything. The Guru
explains and the disciples hang breathlessly on every word. It's
not so much what is said that counts, but the way it is said.

Unfortunately there do seem to be a great many people who
are hunting for some kind of guru. In direct proportion, there are
those who would readily become gurus for the benefit of the rest
of us. Whilst some experienced magicians are involved in passing on information and helping others, there are also those who
are motivated entirely by financial gain, power over others,

sexual exploitation or just feeling important. For those who would pursue Gurus, discrimination before opening one's mind, wallet or legs is to be counselled. It would be prudent to, rather than accepting a teacher at face value, to ask why they are acting as teachers in the first place.

Often, all it takes is an impressive symbol system, either esoteric or quasi-scientific, to raise a person's status in the eyes of others. There are many cases of fringe medicines, which were successful, largely due to the clients' capacity to invest belief in them. When the various techniques were exposed as fraudulent, the rate of cures dropped dramatically. Much of magical healing involves tricking a person to heal himself through his unquestioning belief in the power of the magician.

Merry Pranksters

The Hidden Hand of Discordian activity can sometimes be inferred through peculiar signs and leaflets, strange messages or hoaxes which crop up from time to time. An example of Discordian-type street theatre is 'The Money Ritual.' The Money Ritual took place on the second of November 1985 in Leeds, England. Twenty people dressed as businesswomen and men enacted a piece of street theatre, illustrating the religious importance given to money in everyday life. They started by walking in single file behind their leader, who held high a large cardboard cutout of a pound sign, through a busy shopping centre. With hands clasped, prayer fashion, they chanted "Money, Moneya, Money, Moneya," and "Praise be to Money." They eventually stopped outside a bank, where they swore allegiance without conscience to the worship of money. They then continued through the city centre, where some people reacted by throwing money at them. At their final performance, the police moved in, and three members of the cast were arrested.

Advertising As Sorcery

Despite the increasing encroachment of the mass media upon our senses, there have been few attempts to examine the modern communications media from a magical perspective. Advertisements, the messages which slip through our visual field in the form of film and TV shorts, billboards, and in the countless magazines and newspapers, can be considered as a development of Sorcery Enchantment.

Advertisements have a Mythic dimension to them, as they display slices of a world which is larger than life and hyper-hyper-real, in fact. Advertising presents complete encapsulated mythologies, which concentrate imagery, symbolism and narrative in an economic, yet highly intense fashion, articulating and reflecting the dominant myths or latent imperatives relevant to that section of the population they are aimed at. Advertising is structured to cause an immediate impression. It is a form of persuasion which is subtle in the extreme, since it does not matter if the viewer perceives the mythic nature of the image, since the action of the presentation is stronger than any rational explanation.

Advertising is aimed almost directly at the unconscious strata of selfhood, and it may well contain elements such as humour or self-parody, to misdirect awareness away from its hidden messages. Many advertisements are structured according to three key factors: A *problem*, to which the advert offers a *promise*, which is made relevant to the target viewer by overt or covert reference to a *myth*. The mythic dimension makes an appeal to beliefs held by the viewer, who may be momentarily captured by the spell being woven, whereby particular aspects of the ego-complex (identity, attitudes, fantasies, worries) are reflected, reinforced and made flesh, momentarily, within the context of the image. This immediate appeal to components of the psyche is as much an unconscious process for the creator of the image as the viewer, as advertisers tend to discuss their creations in terms of appeal, although the specific narrative of an advertisement may be deliberately targeted at a specific population. The use, by advertisers, of media personalities, popular music from a variety of genres, and contemporary mythic images adds additional layers of inference to the power of the enchantment.

It is the everyday quality of advertisements which allows them their power for subtle influences. Modern advertising often recuperates images from religion, art, science and other genres of expression to express particular myths. The images may be laced, for extra effect, with a subtext which evokes, if only

fleetingly, a social taboo or source of anxiety within the chosen
population. The mythic elements also function in such a way as to reduce
levels of dissonance which arise within the viewer. Some advertisements can act to slightly raise levels of dissonance within a
viewer by hinting, obliquely, at the contradiction experienced
between the 'ideal imperative' of life as projected in the image,
and the real experience of the viewer. Hence the problem is
brought into focus, and the advert follows through with the
promise of the resolution of this dissonance, within the salient
mythical context, within which the viewer may, to varying
degrees, identify himself. In this form of sorcery, the aim is the
manipulation of desires and tastes, using images and sounds
which have become commodities in their own right.

Advertising pushes at the deep-seating cultural conditioning
that we are engaged in, over the issues of sex, money and power.
The most successful advertising enchantments are those which
influence the market in order to create a particular glamour of
taste and style.

Profaning the Sacred

Discordian activists have, on occasion, appropriated and sub-
verted the mythic nature of advertising for their own purposes.
The production of advertising material which, on the surface,
looks innocuous, but has a subversive message, can be used in a
similar way to the sorcerous projections of the mass media. Bill-
board advertisements have, from time to time, attracted some
ingeniously witty ripostes which actually contribute to the
memory of the advert. A well-known example is the car advert
which was captioned "If it were a lady it would get its bottom
pinched" which had the rejoinder added "If this lady was a car,
she'd run you down." Graffiti has shot from being regarded as a
nuisance to in some quarters, being regarded as an art form in its
own right. It also has a magical dimension, as a means of making
'hidden voices' heard; of reclaiming space and territory within
the urban environment, and may even become a form of magical
tapestry, denoting places of power, bursts of experience, and a
personal or collective tarot of colliding signs. A sign can have
many meanings, quite distinct from the intentions of those who

created it. An anecdote. I used to work at an occult publishing company in London. One morning, we found four weird symbols chalked on the pavement on the block where the shop was situated, forming a square. The priest from the church round the corner came round to complain that it was obviously one of our customers who had done it. I was sent out with a notepad to draw them, and theories of their origin and purpose began to abound. They were someone's attempt to magically attack the shop. They were symbols made by the local Tongs. They were Fascist symbols denoting the proximity of foreign businesses which would shortly be attacked by gangs of thugs. This theorising went on all day. Phone calls were made and faxes were sent, drawing in more ideas and feeding more fantasies. And in the end it emerged that a band had hired the church's cellar for a gig and the weird symbols were nothing more than markers for the band's fans showing them how to get to the gig. So, red faces all round, then. Symbols escape from their makers. Art crawls off the written page into the landscape. In Grant Morrison's *Invisibles* comic book series, the barbarous name 'Barbelith' appears as magical graffiti in his virtual Liverpool. Magicians in the real Liverpool, hip to the message of *Invisibles*, have started spraypainting Barbelith on walls. This may well lead to some confusion in those who are reading *Invisibles* as to the 'reality' of Barbelith—is it something Grant has made up or is it somehow real beyond the comic narrative? The power of entirely contrived magical fragments to take on a life and coherency of their own will be explored further, in *Liber Nasty*.

LIBER NASTY

In contrast to the playful anarchs of Discordia, I will now examine one of the so-called 'darker' aspects of modern occultism—the magic of the Cthulhu Mythos. This current has been of interest to Chaos Magicians, and Chaos Magic has been described from time to time as a form of Left-Hand Path magic, or even "the blackest form of dark power," so what better way to illustrate this than delving into the forbidden lore of things with tentacles...

Cthulhu Mythos Magic

For the last three decades or so, there has been a growing interest amongst contemporary magicians towards developing magical perspectives from non-historical sources or mythic worlds which are not rooted in a particular culture, but which have arisen from literature, science fiction, or modern, urban myths. A prime example of this kind of appropriation of belief-system is the Cthulhu Mythos created by the New England writer Howard Phillips Lovecraft and his associates in the 1930's, and embellished further by successive authors writing 'Lovecraftian' fiction.

Lovecraft's basic theme is that there is a group of alien entities called The Great Old Ones, who once ruled the Earth, but in the 'now' of his fiction, can only make themselves manifest through the rites of their followers and slave-races, or at critical periods "when the stars are right." Some of these entities hail from the distant stars, others, from other dimensions. Humanity, he hints in some tales, may well have been an experiment by one of these alien races, anticipating perhaps, the contemporary conspiracy theories of the "Greys." By carefully blending his fiction with real astronomical and historical facts, and creating a consistent narrative, Lovecraft made his tales atmospheric and believable. His narrators are ordinary people who consistently disbelieve in the build-up of supernatural events, until it is too late, and many of his stories end in gory death or a shocking revelation which changes the participants' lives forever. Other writers who contributed to magazines such as *Weird Tales* and who were associates of Lovecraft, used his fictional entities and added their own.

In the Cthulhu Mythos, humanity appears insignificant compared to the vast, cosmic beings from the void, whose very nature it is difficult to grasp. Even the briefest glimpse of them can shatter one's sanity. Despite the efforts of scientists to come to know the universe, contact with the greater reality of the Outer Ones brings home the truth that, as Lovecraft put it, "we live on a small island in a sea of chaos, and it was not meant that we should voyage far." Although Lovecraft is associated with horror fiction, his works contain more elements of science fiction, but the horror is there: the horror of man's insignificance revealed, and the horror of what is 'out there' beyond the boundaries of civilisation and rational science. Lovecraft's fiction is pervaded with cosmic agoraphobia: a subconscious feeling that behind the facade of Consensus Reality, there lurks deeper, darker, secrets; alien presence's which regard humanity in the same way that we might regard ants. Lovecraft also echoes the statement "Nothing is True" in his fiction, as the revelations experienced by his protagonists often render their former beliefs about the world to be invalid.

The return of the Old Ones involves, as Wilbur Whateley puts it in *The Dunwich Horror,* the "clearing off" of the Earth. That is, the clearing off of humanity, apart from a few worshippers and slaves. This apocalyptic reference can be asserted as metaphorical, or as referring to an actual physical catastrophe, Nuclear holocaust perhaps? Lovecraft possibly wished to emphasise that the Great Old Ones would give no more thought to wiping out humanity than we might give to wiping up water on a table. Exactly why the Old Ones wish to return to Earth is never clear, but we might assume that, for them, Earth is close to the bars and convenient for bus routes!

Lovecraft is careful to point out that most of the Old Ones are, in fact, mindless or 'idiot gods.' Only those who are already insane or degenerate could worship them sincerely. Only Nyarlathotep, the Crawling Chaos, is given a human semblance of intelligence. The Great Old Ones do not form a distinct pantheon, and in Lovecraft's original formulation, did not correspond to elemental stations or any notion of good versus evil. Such modifi-

cations of the Mythos came from August Derleth and later
writers. When it comes down to it, the Great Old Ones are huge,
horrible, and hungry. Little is known about them since to get a
good look at them is usually more than any human can stand, and
most encounters with them are inevitably terminal in Lovecraft's
fiction both for the protagonist and innocent bystanders (whom
the creatures often consume as *hors d'oeuvres* before making the
narrator the main course).

The Cthulhu Mythos contains all the key elements of a magical belief-system: information borne in dreams, a sacred topol-
ogy which includes both Astral Spaces, 'Dreamlands', and
sacred sites and locations. Though incomplete, there are relationships made between the various Elder Beings and a multitude of
slave-races which lurk beneath the sea and under the hills, and
which, occasionally, mingle their blood with humanity, producing vigorous and powerful mutant hybrids. Moreover, the
Cthulhu Mythos entities are beyond all existing frames of reference.

Though various magical writers have attempted to fit them
into existing magical models such as the Qabalah, they are, by
their very nature, 'undimensioned and unseen.' They can be
perceived only through dreams, pathworkings, subconscious
messages, or called briefly into manifestation through rituals
enacted at power spots, or sometimes, through a human vehicle.
In the Mythos, there exists a world-wide conspiracy of cults who
seek to worship and bind the Great Old Ones to their own ends.

Embedding the Cthulhu Mythos

The most common entry route into the Cthulhu Mythos is made
by reading the Mythos tales of Lovecraft and associates such as
Clark Ashton Smith. It is often reported by magicians who work
within this paradigm that the stories have a subtle emotional impact, which can often blossom into a creeping paranoia, or fear.

This often announces itself through dreams, which is appropriate, since Lovecraft's inspiration came largely through his
dream-experiences. Some magicians may feel prompted to make
images of their visions or feelings. Again, some of Lovecraft's
characters attempted to encapsulate their fleeting experiences
into sculpture, art, or prose. Such attempts at imaging are the

first results of the process of embedding the paradigm into one's awareness; the mythic breaking through the veils of conscious waking life, resulting in icons which may be usable as fetishes or talismans for later, willed exploration within the Mythos.

Dreamscaping

Dreamscaping is a technique which can be useful within a magical system such as the Cthulhu Mythos. A rigorous dream-diary is kept, and dreams which have consistent Mythos elements can become the basis of astral sequences of images, performed as a meditation. If these sequences are followed through as one drifts into sleep, one may find, in time, that Mythos Dreams become increasingly vivid, and the dream-experience can continue the consciously-created narrative. Eventually, one can search for specific clues and locations within the Personal Dream-time which is being woven. An example of a Cthulhu Mythos dreamscape sequence follows:

I stand upon a deserted tropical beach. It is night, and all is silence and stars, except for the muted creaking of the cicadas.

The stars are nameless and unknown; cynical even. Yet I recognise a subtle pattern in them; the foreshadowing of a vast glyph or sigil. The waves lap against the shore gently. Shimmering of blue and silver, flecked with gold. I know that this is a meeting, about to happen.

Gradually, I make out a shape bobbing seal-like amidst the foam. It comes towards me, an oil-black figure rising soundlessly from the waters. 'A Deep One,' as it moves closer. But not one of those that Lovecraft wrote of, this. A barely-formed messenger of shadow and abysses. It offers a goblet, and I drink a black, brackish fluid. Glutinous like treacle, but bitter. A moment of surging nausea, and I begin to retch black fluid upon the golden sand. I vomit and vomit and flow, until...

A moment of disorientation. I am sinking gently through a dark green mist. Below, I dimly perceive the outlines of masonry. Vast tumbled blocks of living stone. R'Lyeh.

I settle upon the foothills of rock. Glide easily across the great blocks. Pour myself through cracks and crazy angles. I divide myself into globules of consciousness, separated, yet united by the will to become. Exploring the pathways, oozing under doorways and re-uniting when the spaces allow. Flash of insight. A human form could not do this. This Shoggoth-body is ideal for traversing the tunnels and exploring the angles.

Fractal synthesesia; feeling bright, pulsing colours, flowing over crystal shards, sensing the tentacle-bearded faces which start from the pillars. A growing sense of being guided to a specific destination.

There. A crystalline space without entrance or exit. I have reached it by dripping through cracks and fractures between the growths. I focus on a spot on my surface, and concentrate. Pull it back to my centre, the place where the 'I' of mind floats. Draw inwards and pull and shape and vomit backwards. "Abaddon." And I am remade in human form.

Before me, there is a box-like structure. Not easy to identify. Something of which Escher may have seen in vision but never attempted to translate upon a draughts-man's table. A scrying glass, key, gateway, locus—all of these. Protected by a shimmering field of energy.

I reach for it with my left hand. It squirms at my touch and a shock of energy runs through my arm. Ah, outrage! Feeling of a vast eye opening. Webbed lids peeling slowly backwards. A curtain of darkness falls upon me like a hammer-blow. Sensation of being entombed under a mountain. Helpless. Then I am whirled away into the hinterlands of everyday dream.

This example attempts to carry over the emotional, or psychic, experience of working within this mythos. It should be noted that entry into this paradigm is a fairly slow process. Lovecraft's fiction gives the necessary clues to the appropriate techniques which the magician can employ to explore its possibilities.

Although Lovecraft wrote numerous horror stories, he had no belief or particular fascination with the actual occurrence of the fantastic. While he vehemently denied the existence of occult phenomena, his dreams gave him access to a wide variety of occult experiences and concepts, which he was unable to accept, and so branded the Great Old Ones as evil, and their cultist's practices as blasphemous. Magicians however, recognise the power of dream-borne images. The capacity to experience lucid dreams that are internally consistent and contiguous to each other is a primary element of shamanism, indeed in some cultures, potential shamans are recognised by the characteristics of their dreams. The dream as a psychic gateway for the vibrations of the Great Old Ones to enter human consciousness is a concept that recurs many times in Lovecraft's tales. His protagonists sometimes attend astral sabbats in which they are initiated into secret cults, are shown sanity-shaking mysteries, and receive the dubious benefits of the Elder Lore. Such experiences are fairly common amongst magicians working in any system, as both spontaneous events and the result of willed dreaming (using sigils for example) and experimentation with psychoactive agents.

Several of the Great Old Ones appear to those who seek the Elder Lore through dreams (or whose search into the unknown attunes them to the transmissions of the Old Ones), and the most prominent Old One is Cthulhu, a winged, cephalic star-being who lies 'in death's dream' inside a crypt within the elder city of R'Lyeh, beneath the Pacific Ocean. Lovecraft's story *The Call of Cthulhu* relates the events surrounding the brief appearance of R'Lyeh, which is heralded by a worldwide wave of insanity, as certain sensitive individuals pick up on the dream-transmissions of Great Cthulhu. In the Mythos, he is the lord of dreams, and acts as a kind of intermediary between human consciousness and the truly alien nature of the Old Ones such as Azathoth or Yog-Sothoth. His city, R'Lyeh, has recently been identified (by Dr. Michael Aquino) with Nan-Madol, a ruined stone city consisting of artificial islets on the Pacific island of Ponape. In the Mythos, R'Lyeh is constructed along the lines of a weird, non-Euclidean geometry, with strange angles and perspectives, in which the unwary can be swallowed up. The entire city is a series of gateways to other dimensions, and can be seen as a form of Kenneth Grant's Tunnels of Set. Weird angles and mathematics were also an interest of Austin Osman Spare, who perceived such things in dreams, but could not set them down on paper. R'Lyeh is a psychic gateway to the deeper strata of consciousness and dreams form the interface whereby there is two-way traffic of images from the waking awareness to the Deep Mind.

The Necronomicon

The central text associated with the Cthulhu Mythos is of course, the infamous *Necronomicon*, an ultimate grimoire of forbidden lore and blasphemous rites. The *Necronomicon* makes its first appearance in *The Nameless City* (1921) along with the now-famous couplet:

"That is not dead which can eternal lie
and with strange eons, even death may die."

In creating this mythic tome (which has in turn, acquired its own mythos) Lovecraft unwittingly created the enduring belief that his Cthulhu Mythos fiction was based on some arcane 'truth.' Having created this ur-text as a literary device, Lovecraft embellished the myth by writing a 'History' of the *Necronomicon*, and encouraged other writers to use it, and to add their own forbidden books to the mythos. Lovecraft received letters from fans asking him where the *Necronomicon* could be obtained, and since his death, the search has not abated—there are several books published which claim the 'title' of *Necronomicon*, and individuals still pop up from time to time claiming to have the 'true' text in their possession.

Lovecraft received the name "Necronomicon" in a dream (he describes this in a letter to Harry Fischer, February 1937). In attempting to translate it into English—as "An Image of the Law of the Dead" (NEKROS corpse NOMOS law EIKON image)—he was in effect, according to Lovecraft scholar Robert M. Price, doing something similar to that of the ancient oracles when they interpreted the glossolalic messages of the gods. Divine or oneiric revelations cannot be rendered directly into language and all one can hope to do is sketch the edges of the fading after-glow. A few years ago, for example, in a dream of a cyclopean monastery atop the Plateau of Leng, I was shown a series of tarot images of such intricate detail and vivid colour that, although it was (and remains) quite impossible for me to set them down, it is quite easy for me to call them to mind even as I write this article. The keeper of the images was quite willing to display them, but as he cynically commented at the time, knew that I would not be able to translate them from the dream-world to the physical world.

Both literary scholars and occultists have treated the name "Necronomicon" as a puzzle, attempting to discern a 'true meaning' in order that it might yield up its secrets, giving it a variety of translations, the "Book of Dead Names" is one popular version or they subject it to analysis using a variety of Gematrical methods. But the secret of the *Necronomicon* is elusive. Reading Lovecraft, we find that it becomes a hall of mirrors. When Lovecraft allows the reader to look over the shoulder of his protagonists who come across the dread tome, we find that the contents of the book are at best, cryptic. Phrases such as "nervously hinted" or "mercifully cloaked" are used to tantalize the reader into the necessary suspension of disbelief that all narrative rests upon. The awful truths in the *Necronomicon* are never disclosed but they are continually deferred through hints, allusions, and vague suggestions. Occasionally Lovecraft uses the *Necronomicon* to allude to still-darker tomes of arcane lore, such as the *Stanzas of Dyzan* or *The Book of Thoth*. (Not Crowley's work bearing that title!)

The promise of revealing whilst actually concealing or deferring information allows the reader to fill in the gaps as it were, and is a well-used literary device. Lovecraft himself may have been influenced by Robert W. Chamber's story-cycle, *The King in Yellow* which features a forbidden book which, much like the *Necronomicon*, the perusal of brings madness, terror, and spectral horror (Lovecraft 'reviews' *The King in Yellow* in his essay, "Supernatural Horror in Literature"). This device was much-used by the early chroniclers of Tantric practices. The Revd. William Ward, writing of famous tantric texts such as the *Yoni Tantra*, reverted to asterisks occasionally whilst describing "...things too abominable to enter the ears of man, and impossible to be revealed to a Christian public...."

The noted British occultist Kenneth Grant also employs this device in such a way that it becomes a magical technique. His 'Typhonian Trilogies' are not so much literal occult texts (he makes it very clear that they are not to be considered as practical books) as attempts to entice the reader away from reliance on text, towards the liminal source of magic; towards Gnosis, in the

sense of insight or direct 'knowing' (the word Gnosis is derived
from the Greek *gignösko*, which implies wisdom arising from
revelation, rather than mere knowledge).

In this sense, the 'secret' of the *Necronomicon* is that there is
no secret and like the inner temple at Jerusalem, it is empty. The
Necronomicon excites and entices by generating a sense of antic-
ipation, much like a door in a nightmare which is always slowly
opening, but never quite reveals what is on the other side. This
simultaneous concealment and revealment is itself paradigmatic
of both the Cthulhu Mythos, and magical processes in general.
The Mad Arab can only ever hint at meaning; Lovecraft's
doomed protagonists must, of necessity, draw a veil over their
shattering experiences. The horror must, to be effective, remain
unrevealed. William S. Burroughs puts it this way:

> "*As soon as you name something you remove its
> power... If you could look Death in the face he would
> lose his power to kill you. When you ask Death for his
> credentials, his passport is indefinite.*"
> — The Place of Dead Roads

It is for this reason that the published works which claim the
title of *Necronomicon* are ultimately disappointing. No literal
work can live up to the reader's imaginations of what might be
blasphemous horror. After all, some people found *Fanny Hill* to
be blasphemous. The only book bearing the title *Necronomicon*
that I have at all found unsettling is the artbook by H.R. Geiger.
The others, spell and ritual texts reminiscent of the medieval
grimoires, are not blasphemous in themselves. If one chooses to
work them, they may lead the magician towards shocking revelation, but this requires an individual leap into gnosis. Part of the
glamour attached to the *Necronomicon* is that one hopes to come
across it by chance in the depths of some dusty antiquarian book-
shop, rather than under the bright lights of a modern general
bookstore.

A useful magical perspective on the *Necronomicon* is to
regard it as an Astral Book. Astral Books can only be accessed
through dream or vision, and transmitted via automatic writing,
channelling or perhaps possession by a suitable entity or the
book itself! Astral Books are uniquely personal to those who

receive them—as messages springing forth, or perhaps hacked from the void by individual magicians. They may be of interest to others with similar interests and indeed, many such communications are interpreted by those who receive them as new 'truths' of which they are the prophets, and so feel impelled to spread the word, often through the medium of a vanity press! It is said that everyone has at least one book inside him, and I have occasionally used the following exercise to help others discover what the nature of this 'book' might be:

You are an author. In front of you is a large bookshelf. Study it until you find your book. What colour is the spine? What shape and colour is the lettering? What is written on the spine?

Take the book from the shelf. Weigh the book in your hand. How does it feel? Does it give off a smell? What does the paper feel like? What is the first thing you see on the front cover? Describe the front cover. What is written on it? Open the book and flick through the first pages. What does the text look like? Find the first page and begin to read...

I usually find that people can get as much as two to three pages into their book before the realization of what they are doing jerks them out of trance. It can be a useful start though. Other routes into this process include casting sigils to discover a book through dream, devising an astral journey to discover a book, or the similar technique of dreamscaping, which is described above. An astral book, however, may not take the form of linear text and sigils, diagrams, images and poetry—even adumbrations of strange entities—may be received by this process. The key is to resist the temptation to consciously interpret what flows forth and allow whatever arises to come out in whatever form *it* chooses. The artist-magician Austin Osman Spare was a master of this approach, often awakening from trance to find a finished picture before him.

Other Magical Elements in the Cthulhu Mythos

Scrying

Another key to unlocking the secrets of the Elder Lore is the technique of scrying—in a glass or crystal ball. Scrying glasses, mirrors and crystals which are attuned to transmit certain vibrations crop up in Cthulhu Mythos tales, often as a two-way process. The person who uses these devices glimpses other dimensions, but at the same time, the inhabitants of those dimensions become aware of the seer and eventually menace him. This phenomena is not unknown to magicians. The magical records of both Doctor John Dee and Aleister Crowley mention instances of spirits emerging from a scrying glass or mirror and manifesting. This echoes an old English folk myth that if you look in a mirror the Devil will come and catch you. Mirrors are weird things at the best of times. Gerald Durrell's short piece of horror fiction *The Entrance* is a fine example of the psychological horrors associated with mirrors. A basic approach to scrying is described in *Condensed Chaos*.

Shape-Shifting

The transformation or mutation from human to beast is a recurrent theme in Lovecraft's Cthulhu cycle of tales. It is often associated with the idea of degenerate country-folk or 'primitives' who have mated with one of the slave-races of the Great Old Ones, such as the Deep Ones. Occasionally, the protagonist himself (Lovecraft's protagonists are invariably male and women tend to be portrayed negatively as characters, when they appear at all) is, unbeknown to himself at the outset, a human-monstrous hybrid or has an ancestor who is an evil sorcerer, the genetic characteristics of which resurface as the tale progresses towards the inevitable climax where the protagonists accepts and embraces his genetic destiny. Another example of this theme is the artist Richard Upton Pickman who, in the story *Pickman's Model*, turns away from the human world in order to traffic with flesh-eating ghouls. He reappears in *The Dream-Quest of Unknown Kadath* as a ghoul himself! Again, this is a reminder of Lovecraft's message that direct contact (gnosis) of the forbidden lore irrevocably changes the individual. Once you have stepped (whether unwittingly or willingly) into the world of the Cthulhu Mythos, you will never be the same again.

Magical shape-shifting takes two basic forms. Firstly, there is the practice of Astral shape-shifting which basically consists of taking on zoomorphic forms in order to penetrate astral spaces. It is held that, in some magical systems, zoomorphic deities are best approached on the astral in bestial forms. The example of

Dreamscaping above incorporates astral shape-shifting. Taking on astral animal shapes may also be useful for working with so-called power animals. The other main approach is physical ritual whereby celebrant(s) take on the possession of animal or zoomorphic entities. This can involve the use of masks and the development of personal animal dance sequences and, sometimes, elaborate costumes. Entities discovered or encountered on the astral can be manifested through dance, costume and the crafting of masks. An example of this is the hive-entity Zannum, which was first encountered during a scripted guided journey into a bee-hive and later used in ritual work via the use of a mantra, dance, and a simple mask comprising of exaggerated compound eyes and waving antennae. It is common, during ritual shape-shifting, for celebrants to visualise and use kinaesthetic sensory techniques to invoke the astral form onto themselves. Shape-shifting into animal forms can result in altered sensory perception (cognisant with the animal used as a basis) and physiological oddities. Some magicians have reported, for example, that celebrants possessed by wolf-spirits give off a rank, animal smell.

Strange Angles

The imagery of labyrinths and mazes features strongly in Lovecraft's descriptions of places—from the twisted forests around Arkham to the winding, claustrophobic streets of the decaying slum areas his protagonists are forced to traverse. Again, this recalls the process of inward-turning which is the inner journey towards the unconscious or revelation which is a subtext in many of his tales. That one must lose oneself in order to find one's true self. This theme also appears in his description of R'Lyeh, Cthulhu's abode, in *The Call of Cthulhu*. It is further reinforced by Lovecraft's use of Non-Euclidean geometry and abstract mathematics. In *The Dreams in the Witch-House*. Lovecraft seems to suggest that the revelations of quantum physicists may lead towards the gnosis of the Great Old Ones. Bizarre imagery, somewhat reminiscent of Fractals, is also used in stories such as the *Call of Cthulhu*, *At the Mountains of Madness*, and *Through the Gate of the Silver Key*. In the latter, protagonist Randolph Carter is surrounded by *"...dim half-pictures with uncertain outlines amidst the seething Chaos...it was not chance which built these things in his consciousness, but rather some vast reality, ineffable and undimensional, which surrounded him and strove to translate itself into the only symbols he was capable of grasping."*

Frenzied Rites

In addition to the primarily solo techniques discussed so far, Lovecraft also alluded to frenzied rites by which groups of cultists summoned the beings from beyond the stars. These rites are reminiscent of Witchcraft, Shamanism, or Voodoo, or perhaps more accurately, rationalist perceptions of them. Such rites are related to physical power spots: typically stone circles, specially constructed buildings or strange landmarks. They often involve animal or human sacrifice, incestuous interbreeding, and in *The Dunwich Horror*, a *hieros gamos* between the entity known as Yog-Sothoth and a female cultist. Lovecraft continually alludes to the degenerate nature of Cthulhu cultists, probably reflecting his attitudes to race and intellectual attainment. But there is also an awareness of the degeneration of cult practices as the influence of the Old Ones dwindles in the world, due to the spread of materialism and the decay of rural communities. The entity Nyarlathotep occasionally appears as the mythical 'black man' or leader of the cultist's sabbat gathering—suggesting a human avatar as a base for cult worship, using the more physical routes into Gnosis such as dancing, flagellation, sex, chanting, drumming, hyperventilation and other ecstatic modes. Modern commentators on Cthulhu Mythos magic have mistakenly assumed that Terror is the main emotional gnosis, because this was the feeling often experienced by Lovecraft's protagonists (and indeed, Lovecraft himself). Although fear may initially be employed, it soon palls as an effective lever for gnosis, however.

What is important here is that within the Cthulhu Mythos, such rites demonstrate the interpenetration of magical realities: those of the beliefs of the celebrants, the sacred landscape, awareness of the terrors of Nature, and the dimensions from which the Great Old Ones can be called. Moreover, this perspective echoes the classical pagan viewpoint of the relationship between Nature, the gods, and humanity. For Lovecraft, the landscape itself is inimical to man. Man has no business there and if he does venture into the haunted forests and hills, he had better watch out. Lovecraft is well aware that the landscape is itself sentient and aware, that it has a soul, and moreover, that this soul can become somehow tainted. For the ancient Greeks, certain places were designated as belonging to the gods and, therefore, forbidden to mankind. Theopompus recounts the popular folk-belief concerning a sacred enclosure on Mount Lykaian:

> *"There is a precinct of Lykaian Zeus on the mountain, which no person is allowed to enter. If you disregard this law and go in it is absolutely certain that you will die within the year. And there was a further story they told, that things inside the precinct, man and beast alike, cast no shadow;..."*

Lovecraft used sound as a herald of the onset of dread in a landscape describing the piping of whippoorwills or the sounds of flutes or high-pitched piping, or the croaking of bull-frogs. These sounds imbue the dream-like quality of Lovecraft's landscapes with a dreadful foreboding. Again, this is reminiscent of Classical pagan beliefs. The Greeks were all too mindful of the power of a panic landscape; a place where strange things happen, irrespective of human will. In such places, humans are prey to powers greater than themselves and must respect a variety of ritual precautions. Such wild places are the domain of Pan. The association between such places and strange noises is also identified, as Apollodorus of Athens, writing in the 4th century BC points out:

> *"The mountains, the glens and all the grottoes of the mountains are liable to echo. There are all sorts of complicated noises in the mountains produced by dogs and wild and tame animals; their echoes become mixed together. So it often happens that people do not see the animals making the noises, but hear only the disembodied sound by itself, and so say that Pan is sounding the flute and syrinx in the cave with the nymphs."*

Barbarous Names

The Cthulhu Mythos also makes use of barbarous names from the titles of the Great Old Ones themselves, and the primal language used by cultists and slave-races (which some magicians have used as the basis for crafting Cthulhuoid languages). These tongue-twisting phrases are reminiscent both of the glossolalic speech so often encountered in possession-workings, and the barbarous speech found in the classical grimoires. Again, these serve to enhance the plausibility of the Cthulhu Mythos.

Given the above, then, it is unsurprising that contemporary occultists should be interested in the Cthulhu Mythos. Lovecraftian rituals have been served up by writers such as Anton LaVey, Michael Aquino, and Peter J. Carroll. Kenneth Grant, in his progression of 'Typhonian' works has made much use of Lovecraftian imagery in his interpretations of the work of Aleister Crowley and Austin Osman Spare. Michael Bertiaux, head of *La Coulvoire Noir,* the Voodoo-Gnostic order, has also incorporated elements of the Cthulhu Mythos into his work.

The attraction of the Cthulhu Mythos for magicians should now be obvious. While the magician may, initially, be attracted by the feeling of empowerment due to his moving into spaces where few others have dared to go, it is also important that the Great Old Ones are outside most human mythologies, reflecting the shadows of the Giants in Norse Myths, the pre-Olympian Titans in Greek Myths, and other groups of universe-builders who are thought to be too chaotic for the polite company of the gods of the ordered universe. The nature of the Great Old Ones as shadowy beings who can only be partially glimpsed is attractive and they cannot be assimilated and bound into orthodox systems of magic, and devising suitable approaches for working with them may well take the magician into areas of experimentation which he may not have been attracted to previously, such as exploring the dynamics of places of power, folklore, atavistic resurgence, or dream-working. The Cthulhu Mythos works because it contains gaps which the individual (reader or magician) can fill in by imagination. Rather than being a closed system, presented as a literal text to be followed, it invites personal exploration and elucidation via the individual's own liminal experience.

Beyond Good and Evil?

A strong undercurrent throughout Lovecraft's writing is a rejection of modernity. There is often a conflict of belief between civilised city-dwellers who are dismissive of superstition and folklore, and country-folk who are steeped in the wisdom of the Great old Ones, yet somehow degenerate and decayed. Lovecraft continually alludes to the degenerate nature of Cthulhu cultists which, as previously mentioned, probably reflected his attitudes to race and intellectual attainment. But there is also an awareness of the degeneration of cult practices as the influence of the Old Ones dwindles in the world, due to the spread of materialism and the decay of rural communities. Some commentators have accused Lovecraft of racist attitudes, but I feel it would be more accurate to say that in Lovecraft's fiction, no one individual or group can escape his sense of doom; scientists will at some point stumble upon the horrifying secrets of the universe, whilst country-folk, European Slavonics and South-sea islanders will degenerate into non-human mutants. Sorcerers who summon the Great Old Ones will at some point pay the price of insanity or death. Everybody gets it and the horrifying madness of "what is out there, waiting" is only a footstep away. Once you have passed into the realm of the Old Ones, there is no turning back.

There is no room for dualistic concepts of 'good' and 'evil' in Lovecraft's mythos. There are no forces of light who might be invoked to save us from the horror of the Old Ones. They may occasionally be outwitted, but this is more a matter of blind luck than any skill or ability of the part of humans. Even if one of Lovecraft's protagonists survive an encounter with the Great Old Ones, they are burdened forever with the knowledge of what lurks out there.

Some intellectuals, enthused by Lovecraft's visions, have attempted to place his mythos within a Nietzschean perspective, saying that the Great Old Ones represent the forces of Superman who stands beyond good and evil, aware only of primal desires and passions. Lovecraft makes it clear that the Great Old Ones are not merely a casting-off of traditional morality, that they have about as much interest in us as we do in cattle. Sooner or later, even the devout worshipper of Cthulhu will be eaten up.

Lovecraft's vision, his *futilitarianism,* is particularly appropriate to our current age, where postmodernist thinkers claim to
have destroyed the future and ransacked the past in an endless
search for kicks of one sort or another. Increasingly, we are
echoing Hassan I Sabbah's statement that "Nothing is True," or
perhaps more accurately, nothing can be trusted. Living as we
do, in a society which is rapidly mutating itself by means of
computers, camcorders and cable TV; in which men can walk on
the Moon, whilst others sell their children to the organ dealers;
where the mysteries of life are probed during DNA manipulation
and the realities of other people's death served up on prime-time
television, it is easy to be cynical, and difficult for any concept
of truth to remain inviolate and essential.

In a culture where the edges of present time are crumbling
into the future at a rate that is often difficult to comprehend, the
sense of connection to historical time is vague, to say the least.
The contradictions of post-Capitalism have fragmented consensus reality to a point where alienation and powerlessness are
endemic in our culture. Occultism offers an alternative: a sense
of connection, perhaps, to historical time when the world was
less complicated, where individuals were more in touch with
their environment, and, (allegedly) had more personal control
over their lives. The occult sub-genre holds up a mirror to Consensual reality. Occultists readily sneer at Slave-God religions
and then piss themselves in ecstasy buying a genuine set of
Aleister Crowley socks. There is much talk of the magician as a
dangerous rebel or anarch of the soul by people who go on to
legitimate their position by waving charters, certificates and
copyrighted logos. I mean, who really gives a fart, other than
those who will buy into anything which resembles even faintly
ancient wisdom. This is often the position taken by so-called
magicians who seek to elevate themselves (in the eyes of their
peers) by claiming to evoke demons, summon Satan, or command entities such as the Great Old Ones from other dimensions.
These are the cries of the powerless and fatuous attempting to
elevate themselves by claiming authority over forces which they
imagine can be controlled by such as they. There does seem to be
an attraction between would-be superman occultists and an
exhaustive range of dark gods, dead gods, deep-fried gods. It
seems to me that the would-be superman/satanist/mighty adept

magician (delete as appropriate) is, underneath all the justifications, out for legitimisation of himself as outsiders as it's easy to maintain such a view of yourself as the noble, doom-laden outsider, whilst at the same time being invisible and insignificant. Lovecraft's vision is that of the utter insignificance of humanity in the rolling darkness of the cosmos. I have usually found that those who profess to know this void, who call themselves Satanists, Supermen and Outsiders, are entangled in two virulent memes—BEING RIGHT and GETTING EVEN. Alas, apart from imagining themselves as the lords of De Sade's Castle of Silling, or dreaming of power without responsibility found in some paperback tome with a Latin name, these self-avowed creatures of darkness never quite seem to manage any actualisation of their 'will to power.' William S. Burroughs once commented that "anyone who can pick up a frying-pan owns death." All too often, it seems that many people are content with vicarious thrills, attempting to own death by surrounding themselves with the icons of their heroes. Isn't it a shame that most of those who cry that "Might is Right" will never get the chance to stamp on the weak—unless of course they cease to be 'outsiders' and join some institution which allows them to do so with impunity and government approval.

Mythos Madness

Within the occult milieu, there is a generally-held view that magical work with the Great Old Ones is considered inadvisable, due to various unspecified dangers. One explanation I have come across as to why this is so is that "...the Cthulhu Mythos entities do not respond to normal banishing rituals." In other words, they don't conform to normal expectations, so avoid them. Others say that the Cthulhu Mythos has a tendency to tip the unwary towards obsession or madness. To which I can only reply, "Yes, but so what?" Working with *any* magical system can lead you into madness, if you're up for it, as it were. The trick of course, is getting out of madness again, or at least learning to disguise it to everybody else. The fear of insanity when doing magic has to be confronted head-on. It will come whether you're messing with "things with tentacles" or the most basic book on new age witchcraft. Okay, Lovecraft's protagonists inevitably fear for their sanity, go stark staring bonkers or end up as a Cthulhu breakfast snack, but that doesn't mean that the intrepid magician *has* to as well. But if you want to stay the same, why are you doing magic in the first place? Consider instead that becoming 'obsessed' or dwelling on 'lurking things' might actually be *good* for you. In some ways, it is not dissimilar to childhood fantasies and fears about things under the bed. Whilst going into these states is undeniably weird, they are also intensely magical. I feel that part of the issue which makes these states problematic for some people is that as one tips into these weird states of mind, one begins to feel that one is losing control of what is happening. More accurately, one is losing the *illusion* that one is in control of what happens to one. It is the *fear* of what might happen, where one might go, that is often worse than the process itself. The fear holds us back from surrendering to the embrace of derangement. Occultists writing about Lovecraft sometimes say that he "drew back, on the brink of the abyss." And well he might, for it is difficult in the extreme to surrender oneself to an overwhelming sense of derangement. Yet at some point, one may find oneself driven to do exactly this.

Generally, my experience of personal identity work (Ego Magic) is that people (myself included!) only work on a particular issue (behaviour, attitude, etc.), if they recognise it as something which requires attention, and further, only if the drive to change outweighs the desire to stay the same. Sometimes we have to get into extreme situations before we realize how our behaviour contributes towards what happens to us. It can happen that, in working with extreme magical belief systems such as Cthulhu Mythos magic, our hidden demons take the opportunity to leap out, manifesting as dysfunctional behaviours. When this happens, we may (eventually) come to recognise them, acknowledge them as ours and do something about them. This is never easy, and often painful, but otherwise, such demons might remain hidden, gnawing away at us from within.

Further notes on the magical possibilities of the Cthulhu Mythos can be found in my short chapbook, *The Pseudonomicon* (Dagon Productions, 1997).

FURTHER READING

Adair, John, *Effective Leadership*, Pan Books, 1988

Angerford & Lea, *Thundersqueak*, TMTS, 1979

Artaud, Antonin, *The Theatre and Its Double*, John Calder, 1989

Bey, Hakim, T.A.Z., *Autonomedia*, 1991

Benson, Jarlath, *Working More Creatively with Groups*, Tavistock Publications, 1987

Burroughs, William S., *The Place of Dead Roads*, John Calder, 1984

Burroughs, William S., & Gysin, B., *The Third Mind*, John Calder, 1972

Carroll, Peter J., *Liber Null*, The Morton Press, 1978

Carroll, Peter J., *Liber Null & Psychonaut*, Samuel Weiser, 1987

Carroll, Peter J., *Liber Kaos*, Samuel Weiser, 1992

Crowley, Aleister, *Magick*, Samuel Weiser, 1994

Crowley, Aleister, *The Book of Lies*, Samuel Weiser, 1981

De Bono, Edward, *I am Right/You are Wrong*, Penguin, 1991

Dimock, Hedlock, Groups: *Leadership and Group Development*, University Associates, Inc. 1987

Dukes, Ramsay, *SSOTBME: An Essay on Magick*, TMTS, 1979

Finlay, Linda, *Groupwork in Occupational Therapy*, Stanley Thornes, 1993

Fries, Jan, *Visual Magick*, Mandrake of Oxford, 1992

Fries, Jan, *Seidways*, Mandrake of Oxford, 1996

Gleick, J., *Chaos*, Cardinal, 1987

Grant, Kenneth, *Nightside of Eden*, Muller, 1977

Harvey, D., The *Condition of Post-modernity*, Blackwell, 1989

Harvey, G., & Hardman, C., *Paganism Today*, Thorsons, 1995

Hine, Phil, *Condensed Chaos*, New Falcon Publications, 1995

Hine, Phil, *The Pseudonomicon*, Dagon Productions 1997

Hine, Phil, *Permutations*, an on-line collection of essays (Adobe PDF format), 1997

Hofstadter, Douglas R., *Metamagical Themas,* Penguin, 1985

Hyatt, Christopher S., (ed.) *Rebels & Devils,* New Falcon Publications, 1997

Johnstone, Keith, *IMPRO,* Methuen, 1991

Lee, Dave, *Chaotopia!: Magick & Ecstasy in the Pandaemon-Aeon,* Attractor, 1997

Mace, Stephen, *Addressing Power,* Privately Printed, 1996.

MacLellan, Gordon, *Touching Earth,* Capall Bann Publishing, 1996

Orpheus, Rodney, *Abrahadabra,* Looking Glass Publications, 1993

Pagels, Elaine, *The Origin of Satan,* Penguin, 1995

Rushkoff, Douglas, *Children of Chaos,* Flamingo 1997

Rushkoff, Douglas, *Cyberia: Life in the Trenches of Hyperspace,* Flamingo, 1994

Semple, Gavin, W., *ZOS-KIA,* Fulgur, 1995

Sennitt, Stephen, *Liber Koth,* Logos Press 1997

Shea, Gordon F., *Mentoring,* Kogan Page Ltd., 1992

Sherwin, Ray, *Theatre of Magic,* Sorcerer's Apprentice Press, 1985

Sherwin, Ray, *The Book of Results,* Revelations 23 Press, 1992

Starhawk, *Dreaming the Dark,* Beacon Press, 1982

Starhawk, *Truth or Dare,* HarperCollins, 1990

Wilson, Robert Anton & Shea, Robert, *Illuminatus!,* Sphere Books, 1982

Wilson, Steve, *Chaos Ritual,* Neptune Press, 1994

Zohar, Danah & Marshall, Ian, *The Quantum Society,* Flamingo, 1994

Comics

The Invisibles, Grant Morrison, D.C. Comics

Those Annoying Post Brothers, Matt Howarth, Ripoff Press

World-wide web

Chaos Matrix: www.sonic.net/fenwick

Phil Hine's Fifth Aeon Egregore: www.phhine.ndirect.co.uk